Sunset
Arizona
TRAVEL GUIDE

By the Editors
of Sunset Books
and
Sunset Magazine

Lane Publishing Co.
Menlo Park, California

Research & Text:
Barbara J. Braasch

Coordinating Editor:
Suzanne N. Mathison

Design:
Cynthia Hanson

Maps:
John Parsons, Eureka Cartography

Illustrations:
Martha Dern

Calligraphy:
Donna Prime

Our thanks...

The editors of Sunset Books are deeply appreciative of the help we received from many people and organizations throughout the state of Arizona. Special thanks go to Stephen Tripp, Arizona Office of Tourism; Lloyd Axelrod, Phoenix & Valley of the Sun Convention & Visitors Bureau; Patti Spaulding, Metropolitan Tucson Convention & Visitors Bureau; Imogene Braziel; Anne Giles and Rusty Gant, Rancho de los Caballeros; Sam Lowe, The Phoenix Gazette; Vince Chelena; Virginia Graham; and Margery Craig.

For their way with words, we thank copy editors Fran Feldman and Phyllis Elving.

Hours, admission fees, prices, telephone numbers, and highway designations in this book are accurate as of the time this edition went to press.

Cover:
Hovering over the desert floor, the setting sun casts a golden glow over the starkly beautiful terrain. Photographed by Willard Clay.

Photographers

Arizona Office of Tourism: 63 right. **Craig Aurness:** 114 bottom. **Sue Bennett:** 63 left. **Alan Benoit:** 6 bottom left, 114 top, 119 right. **John Blaustein:** 14 bottom. **Larry Brazil:** 47 top, 95 bottom. **Jerome Burnett:** 42. **Glenn Christiansen:** 3, 34. **Willard Clay:** 27, 47 bottom, 55 bottom, 95 top. **Ron Cohen:** 22 bottom. **Ed Cooper:** 19, 58, 79. **Betty Crowell:** 111. **John Elk III:** 106 top. **Tim Fuller:** 39 bottom. **Dave G. Houser:** 66 bottom. **Philip Hyde:** 22 top. **Dorothy Krell:** 90, 103 top. **Russ Lamb:** 39 top. **Luther Linkhart:** 98 bottom. **Marie Mainz:** 71 top. **David Muench:** 50, 87 bottom, 106 bottom, 122. **Josef Muench:** 11, 127 left, 127 center. **Don Normark:** 66 top, 74, 98 top, 103 bottom. **Charles O'Rear:** 119 left. **Betty Randall:** 127 right. **John Running:** 6 bottom right, 30 bottom, 87 top. **Chad Slattery:** 30 top. **James Tallon:** 6 top, 55 top left, 55 top right, 71 bottom. **Darwin Van Campen:** 82. **Rolf Zillmer:** 14 top.

Contents

Hopi kachina dolls

SPECIAL FEATURES

An Overview

Winter or summer, Arizona offers something to tempt the tourist. If you want to eat well, sleep late, and simply sit in the sun, your choice of lodging and dining ranges from the very simple to the luxurious. More active visitors find ample opportunities for horseback riding, fishing, boating, hiking, desert picnicking — and even skiing.

Amateur geologists can spend many field days poking around the countryside. Plant lovers can investigate the saguaro, cholla, prickly pear, yucca, and other varieties of desert vegetation. History buffs will find innumerable monuments and archeological ruins to explore, many telling the story of an Indian population that thrived hundreds of years before Columbus was born.

Land of surprises

Though Arizona is one of the nation's fastest growing states (Phoenix and Tucson have doubled and redoubled their population in the last 35 years), it's still a land of "wide open spaces"—and likely to remain so for a long time to come.

Arizona's far-flung reaches come in a variety that surprises many visitors. The state is not all desert. At Flagstaff, more than a mile high, snowstorms sometimes blanket the city as late as May, and in the White Mountains a popular winter sport is ice-fishing. The number of lakes, too, is a surprise; one result is that Arizona has more boats per capita than almost any other state in the Union.

Everyone has heard of the Grand Canyon; few people know that the country's largest Ponderosa pine forest lies near this great gorge. Not long ago Arizona was a part of the Old West. Today you can still watch a blazing "gun battle" or an Indian ceremonial dance.

You might expect steaks that dangle over the edge of your plate and some of the country's finest Mexican food. But don't overlook the Indian taco or the urban areas' fine cuisine.

What's the temperature?

Arizona can be classified in five climate zones based on elevation. The low-lying Sonoran Desert stretches across southwestern Arizona and up along the Colorado River, with an enclave in the southwestern corner (Yuma, Parker, Lake Havasu City, Phoenix and vicinity, Gila Bend, Ajo, Sells). Normal summer temperatures here range from 72° to over 100°, topping 110° in some places. Winter temperatures run from 39° to 67° and rarely drop below freezing.

The high desert foothills (Tucson, Nogales, Benson, Tombstone, Douglas, Winslow, Wickenburg, Prescott) are cooler, generally from 63° to 94° in summer and 31° to 59° in winter. The warm highlands (around Payson, the Tonto Basin, the Apache reservations, and scattered areas of the southeast) range from 61° to 92° in summer and 27° to 57° in winter.

The cool highlands, mountains above 6,500 feet (Williams, Flagstaff, the Mogollon Rim, the White Mountains and the Chuska Mountains east of Canyon de Chelly) usually offer refreshing summer temperatures of 44° to 78°; deep snow often covers them in winter, with temperatures of 14° to 44°.

The high plateau of the northeast (Navajo and Hopi reservations and the strip north of the Mogollon Rim) normally ranges from 60° to 94° in summer and 27° to 55° in winter, with light snow that often melts between snowfalls.

Late autumn, winter, and spring bring most visitors to the desert; summer makes the mountains popular. Throughout the state, summer thunderstorms and brief, heavy rains occur in July and August. They're heaviest in the upper elevations. This is also the season of flash floods in the desert.

Detailed maps can be found on the pages indicated below.

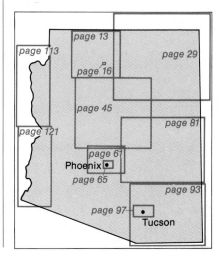

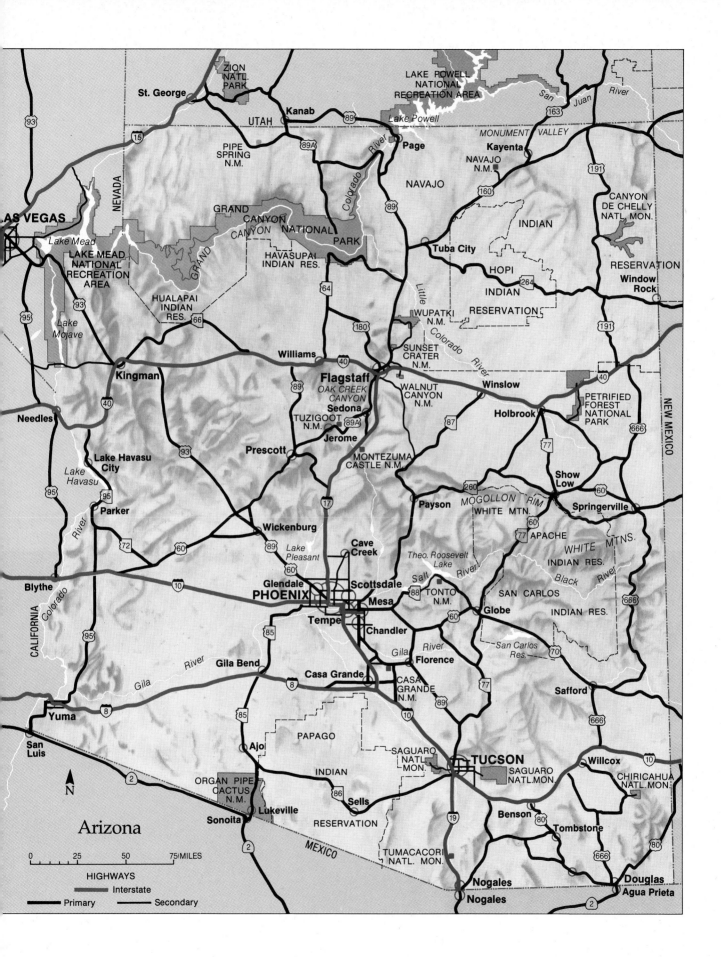

Arizona

0   25   50   75 MILES

HIGHWAYS
Interstate
Primary   Secondary

Floating horde of inner-tubers, many towing coolers, bobs off in the annual spring race on the Colorado River at Parker.

Horseman stands atop a well-matched pair for the dramatic Roman-riding exhibition at the Prescott Rodeo. Other equestrian events in this mountain town take place during the popular Frontier Days in July.

Traditionally costumed Hopi maiden portrays a tribal kachina spirit during the Rainbow Dance. Some mesa-top villages welcome visitors to ceremonial festivities.

6 AN OVERVIEW

Calendar of events

A swirl of velvet skirt, the sound of mariachis, and the stomping of boots —Arizona's lively celebrations combine rich Indian traditions, Spanish lifestyles, and touches of the Old West. More recent residents have contributed gem shows, football games, sailboat races, and concerts.

Arizona visitors will find something on the agenda every weekend. The following list includes only a sampling of the entertainment available. Other events are mentioned throughout the book. For a complete listing of activities, write to the Arizona Office of Tourism, 1480 E. Bethany Home Road, Phoenix, AZ 85014. For more information about a specific event, contact the Chamber of Commerce of the city listed. In the Phoenix area, you can call the Visitors Hotline at (602) 840-4636 for a two-minute recorded message about current activities.

January

Fiesta Bowl Classic, Tempe. One of the nation's top bowl games, viewed by more than 75,000 football fans.

Sled Dog Races, Greer. High up in the White Mountains, you can watch dogs mush across the snow.

Lost Dutchman Days, Apache Junction. A parade, a rodeo, concerts, and a carnival take their theme from the Lost Dutchman Mine in the nearby Superstition Mountains.

February

Quartzsite Rock and Gem Show, Quartzsite. The single largest tourist attraction in the area for rockhounding enthusiasts.

All-Arabian Horse Show, Scottsdale. Show and auction, with open house at many nearby private farms.

La Fiesta de los Vaqueros, Tucson. Four-day rodeo called by the city "the world's largest non-mechanized parade."

Parada del Sol Rodeo and Parade, Scottsdale. Includes a street dance, rodeo, and the longest horse-drawn parade in the world.

Gold Rush Days, Wickenburg. Parades, dances, rodeos, gold panning, gem show, arts and crafts exhibits, carnival, melodrama, and other festivities.

O'Odham Tash Indian Pow Wow, Casa Grande. Highlights include ceremonial dances, rodeos, and an all-Indian basketball tournament.

March

Rodeo of Rodeos, Phoenix. One of the state's largest and most spectacular arena attractions.

April

Tucson Festival, Tucson. Indian, Spanish, Mexican, and American traditions blend in two weeks of dances, crafts shows, musical entertainment, and other festivities.

Copper Dust Stampede Days, Globe. Folksy rodeo celebration includes parade, barbecue, and dance.

May

Colorado River Cruise, Blythe, CA. A flotilla of canoes cruises down the Colorado from Blythe to Martinez Lake and back in this two-day event.

June

Flagstaff Festival of the Arts, Flagstaff. A six-week celebration of the arts features artists and musicians from all over the country.

July

Frontier Days, Prescott. Arizona's territorial capital comes alive with rodeo, parade, and contests around the plaza.

Canoe and Rowboat Race, Show Low. High-water adventure in the White Mountains.

August

World's Oldest Continuous RCA Rodeo, Payson. Festivities along the Tonto Rim's cowboy haven.

Smoki Ceremonial and Snake Dance, Prescott. "Indian" dances by businessmen's group in traditional costume.

September

Annual Mountain Men's Rodeo and Parade, Williams. Features the famous Bill Williams Mountain Men.

Navajo Nation Fair and Rodeo, Window Rock. Traditional Navajo tribal fair presents the world's largest Indian rodeo and native dances, foods, and exhibits.

Arizona Old-Time Fiddler's Contest, Payson. Popular two-day event decides the state championship.

October

Annual Helldorado Days, Tombstone. Old-time event gives Tombstone the look of the Old West; gunfights, parades, and contests.

London Bridge Days, Lake Havasu City. Weekend of festivities centers on the city's bridge.

Papago All-Indian Powwow and Fair, Sells. Crafts, a parade, dances, and ethnic food highlight the fair.

November

Four Corners States Bluegrass Music Finals, Wickenburg. Three days of regional competition.

December

Fiesta Bowl Parade, Phoenix. One of the 10 largest parades in the country, with floats, horses, and bands.

All-Indian Rodeo, Parker. Indians compete in traditional events.

Tumacacori Fiesta, San Jose de Tumacacori. Indian dances, foods, and crafts.

The Essentials

Friendly Arizona welcomes visitors. You'll have no problem finding information about the state's attractions, recreational facilities, and accommodations. Throughout the chapters of this book we've included addresses for visitors bureaus major cities and in towns. For general information, write to the Arizona Office of Tourism, 1480 E. Bethany Home Road, Phoenix, AZ 85014. You'll also find state Tourist Information Centers along major highways.

Getting around

Phoenix is Arizona's main gateway. Major airlines serve the city's Sky Harbor Airport from all parts of the country; from there, commuter airlines reach all parts of the state. In addition, some airlines offer direct service from outside the state to Tucson and the Grand Canyon.

Scheduled transportation is also provided by Amtrak and by Greyhound and Trailways bus lines.

A number of tour operators put together special-interest vacation packages, including guided camping trips, ghost town excursions, Indian reservation tours, and shopping expeditions. Most tours depart from the Phoenix and Tucson areas. We've included the names of local operators in certain regions.

It's easy to get around the state on your own. Arizona's highway system includes two east-west and one north-south interstate highways. Connecting roads penetrate all sections of Arizona. For tips on desert driving, see the next page.

Lodging choices

Arizona visitors should experience no difficulty in finding suitable accommodations along major highways. These principal routes are dotted with hotels, motels, resorts, bed and breakfast inns, and trailer parks, particularly in and around larger cities and towns.

Reservations are essential during busy seasons in popular tourist areas such as Grand Canyon National Park, and they're advisable as a general rule anywhere.

The Phoenix & Valley of the Sun Convention & Visitors Bureau operates a Valley Reservation System for more than 100 hotels, motels, and resorts in the Phoenix-Scottsdale area, plus the Grand Canyon National Park Lodges. It also handles reservations for rental cars, apartments and condominiums, bus and air tours, and mule rides into the Grand Canyon. From out of state, visitors can call (800) 528-6149, toll free. Within the state, phone (800) 221-5596.

Some of Arizona's resorts operate on a seasonal basis. Most motels and hotels operate year-round, offering greatly discounted off-season rates.

Guest ranches

Arizona's specialty is the desert guest ranch, once known as the "dude" ranch (see page 73). Emphasis is on comfort — and sometimes luxury. Horses, swimming pools, and tennis courts are common; even a golf course is included at Rancho de los Caballeros.

Appealing primarily to winter visitors, such ranches are clustered around Wickenburg, Phoenix, and Tucson. Near Sedona in the Verde Valley country, and scattered elsewhere at higher elevations around the state, you'll find ranches open for summer-season guests.

Camping facilities

Campgrounds usually are equipped with fireplaces, picnic tables, garbage pits, and sanitary facilities. Not all have water. Throughout this book we've given addresses for various Forest Service and state and national park campgrounds. For further information, contact the Arizona Office of Tourism.

Desert camping. The best months for desert camping are from November to April. You'll find spring months (late February to early April) the most popular because that's the time the desert comes alive with colorful blossoms. January and February nights are cold, but the days are usually clear and warm. Spring and autumn days range from warm to hot; the nights may be cool.

The main problems involved in desert camping revolve around the desert's unpredictability — strong and sudden winds, wide fluctuations in temperature, and limited sources of food, water, and fuel.

If you're unfamiliar with camping in the desert, the following suggestions might be helpful. Don't set up your camp in dry washes; in summer and early fall these washes are avenues for flash floods. For most desert campers, a tent is not enough. You'll need some type of windbreak to protect sitting and cooking areas.

With few exceptions, you'll need your own water and fuel supply. Winds can make cooking over a campfire impossible; for this reason, most desert campers use a gasoline stove. Fresh food doesn't keep well in the desert, so you'll have to depend for the most part on canned and dried items.

These rules of hiking are extremely important in the desert: before you wander off, tell someone where you're heading and when you expect to return; look for landmarks along the way to aid you in retracing the trail; don't hike alone. Sunburn lotion, a large canteen, and a first-aid kit are essentials.

Visiting Indian reservations

Visitors are welcome on the Indian reservations, but they should bear in mind at all times that they are guests on the Indian's land and should act accordingly.

Indians may be willing to pose for photographs, but they may consider this a service to the visitor and expect to be paid for it. Ask permission before taking a photograph of an Indian or his family. No cameras are permitted on the Hopi Indian Reservation.

Because most Indian ceremonies are of a religious nature, photographing them is generally prohibited. An admission fee may be charged. Some Indian ceremonial dances are never performed in public; some are performed before only a limited number of spectators.

Hunting & fishing

Deer are found in most of the forested areas of Arizona. In addition, some parts of the state contain elk, antelope, black bears, javelinas (peccaries), wild turkeys, bighorn sheep, and sizable populations of wildcats, coyotes, and mountain lions.

The national forests in Arizona provide many popular fishing lakes and about 500 miles of trout streams. The Colorado River offers several hundred miles of fishing water, yielding largemouth black bass, crappie, trout, and channel catfish. Lake Havasu, Lake Mead, and Lake Powell are the most popular and heavily fished waters along the river. The waters below Hoover Dam and Davis Dam are popular for rainbow trout fishing.

A valid Arizona fishing license is required for all fishing. Persons fishing from a boat on waters that border another state may have a valid license from either state and a special use stamp from the other.

You'll find details on hunting and fishing in each section of this book. For more information, write to the Arizona Game & Fish Department, 2222 W. Greenway Road, Phoenix, AZ 85023.

A skiing survey

Arizona has some excellent ski areas. Fairfield Snow Bowl, on the slopes of San Francisco Peaks 14 miles northwest of Flagstaff, is one of the best-developed areas in the state. Other skiing destinations include Mt. Lemmon, 40 miles northeast of Tucson; Bill Williams Mountain, 4 miles south of Williams; and Sunrise, in the White Mountains on the Fort Apache Indian Reservation. You'll also find excellent cross-country trails at Mt. Lemmon and around the Grand Canyon (see page 44).

Desert driving tips

Though the climate where you're traveling will affect driving conditions, you should be aware of the following items wherever you are.

Gasoline. Throughout Arizona, outside of metropolitan areas, service stations may be many miles apart, even on major roads. Fill up your tank when you start out and when you can along your route.

Water. The above also applies to water. Check your radiator and carry extra water if you're crossing the desert (even on a freeway) or venturing off main roads.

Dirt and gravel roads. Much of Arizona is still served by unpaved roads, many suitable only for four-wheel-drive vehicles. In the mountains and highlands, many side roads are closed by winter snows; during spring thaws and after summer thunderstorms, they're often too muddy for travel. It's best to plan trips to the high country for summer or early fall. In wet weather, be prepared with chains. If you're exploring back roads at any time, it's a good idea to carry a tow rope, shovel, tire pump, air pressure gauge, reliable flashlight, and some sacks for traction in slush or sand.

Livestock. When driving through open range, watch out for cattle and sheep. Slow down when you approach a rise or a blind curve.

Flash floods. Along roads that dip into washes, signs may warn that you're in a flash flood area. The summer thunderstorms that quickly dump inches of rain on mountains and hills can fill those dry washes with rushing, silt-laden water— bank to bank. Be aware of the possibility of flash floods if you're driving during the summer storm season.

Breakdowns. If your car breaks down and leaves you stranded, especially on a desert road, stay with your car and wait for help.

If you're on a very remote road and must walk for help, wait until dark and insist that your family stay with the car. Take some water with you, leaving the rest for the people staying behind. Go back the same way you came and don't try any short cuts.

A little knowledge of the Grand Canyon prompts a craving for more; a great knowledge of it prompts a greater craving. When you look into its depths, you're looking back some 20 million centuries. Nowhere else on earth can you do so. Nowhere else is geologic history, beginning with the oldest exposed rock on earth, so clear and orderly.

From either the north or the south, you approach the canyon through rather flat country of familiar-looking fields and forests. Occasionally, the land is broken by picturesque gullies. Suddenly, at the edge of the Grand Canyon of the Colorado, you're confronted with one of the most sublime spectacles of this planet.

Yet as you stand on the brink for the first time, your impulse may be to turn away, not for any fear of height nor for the juxtaposition of incredible wilderness in an otherwise subdued landscape, but rather for disbelief, even saturation, with the astonishing size of it all.

The canyon saga

"Ours has been the first, and will doubtless be the last, party of whites to visit this profitless locality," reported Lt. J. C. Ives as he explored the Grand Canyon region in 1857. There is perhaps more poetry than prophecy in this statement — and in his later remark: "It seems intended by nature that the Colorado River, along the greater portion of its lonely and majestic way, shall be forever unvisited and undisturbed."

Since Ives's time, the Grand Canyon has been the home of ranchers, miners, prospectors, horse thieves, hermits, and bootleggers. Around the turn of the century, its vastness was laced with an ambitious network of trails. Hotels, tourist camps, orchards, and gardens were situated at various levels all the way down to the river, and cable cars transported visitors from one side of the canyon to the other.

But the canyon triumphed. The resorts petered out, cable cars rusted in their moorings, and neglected trails disappeared. Today, you look out over a canyon where maintained trails are few and the only habitations are the hidden ancestral home of the Havasupai Indians (see page 20) and a few tiny green oases like Phantom Ranch.

A national park

For 277 river miles, the Colorado River slices through Grand Canyon National Park, dividing the park so that the tourist areas on the North Rim and the South Rim, though only 10 miles apart as the crow flies, are nevertheless separated by a 214-mile drive.

When visitors speak of the park, they are usually referring to the South Rim and its year-round tourist facilities, concentrated in bustling Grand Canyon Village. The higher North Rim, directly across the canyon, is blanketed by heavy snows in winter. Accommodations there, though comfortable and attractive, are fewer, and facilities are somewhat scaled down in comparison with those at the South Rim. The North Rim is a favorite of those who prefer less elbow rubbing and less commotion — and those who have seen the impressive views of the canyon from the South Rim.

Viewing the canyon is easy. You can fly over or through it, whirl in a helicopter along its steep walls, hike or ride a mule into its depths, challenge the river by boat, or simply peer over the side from one of the many lookouts along the canyon rim.

For a brochure on these and other choices, write to Grand Canyon National Park, Grand Canyon, AZ 86023.

Sunset paints the Grand Canyon walls. Stark silhouettes of canyon formations stretch out as far as the eye can see. This vast, unforgettable view is Arizona's premier attraction.

Grand Canyon

The Essentials

The busy South Rim or the more remote North Rim, grand lodge or primitive campground, ranger-guided walks or strenuous backpacking expeditions, viewing the canyon depths from the back of a mule or from the seat of a swooping helicopter — these are only some of the decisions you have to make when planning a visit to the Grand Canyon.

Getting to the canyon

Except when winter closes the road to the North Rim, it's easy to reach both sides of the canyon from major highways. Information on traveling to the South Rim by car from Flagstaff and Williams is on page 16; routes to the North Rim are detailed on page 21.

Bus and train. Major bus lines serve both Flagstaff and Williams with connections on commuter buses to Grand Canyon Village on the South Rim. You can also detrain at Flagstaff (Amtrak) and catch a bus to the village.

Plane. Commuter airlines fly daily to Grand Canyon Airport (South Rim) with connections through Phoenix and Las Vegas, Nevada. Buses transport passengers from the airport to the village. Grand Canyon Airlines also provides scheduled service between the North and South rims. Charter planes fly to the North Rim from several cities.

Getting around Grand Canyon Village

Grand Canyon National Park Lodges, the South Rim concessionaire, operates a free courtesy shuttle on a 30-minute schedule from mid-October to March. From April to mid-October, minibuses swing through the village every 15 minutes, and from mid-May through September, the minibuses also operate along the scenic West Rim Drive (the route is closed to private transportation during this period).

Taxis are also available.

Auto rentals. You can arrange for a chauffeur-driven van at the Transportation Desk in Bright Angel Lodge and Yavapai Lodge. Cars can be rented at Grand Canyon Airport.

Getting around the North Rim

On the north side of the canyon, your touring choices are limited to car, feet, or horse or mule. You might find a tour bus available; check at the Grand Canyon Lodge.

Staying at the canyon

No matter when you visit the canyon, advance reservations are suggested, especially during the very busy season between Easter and Labor Day. Make reservations for mule rides and river trips as far in advance as possible. In the winter, visitor facilities are limited to the South Rim.

Can you make an impromptu visit without reservations? Yes, if you're prepared to stay outside the park and drive from as far away as Flagstaff, Williams, Cameron, Jacob Lake, or even St. George.

Grand Canyon Village. Grand Canyon National Park Lodges operates all accommodations on the South Rim except the National Park Service campgrounds. For reservations, write to Box 699, Grand Canyon, AZ 86023, or telephone (602) 638-2401.

El Tovar Hotel, built in 1905 of native stone and rough-hewn logs, is the patriarch of the South Rim and one of the most famous hostelries in the nation. Located on the canyon rim, this historic three-story hotel offers fine accommodations in a rustic atmosphere. Each room has a bath, phone, and television. Rates are comparable to those of metropolitan hotels; room service is available only in this hotel. It's open all year.

Bright Angel Lodge, another long-time favorite, offers both lodge rooms and rimside cabins. It's open year-round.

Thunderbird and Kachina Lodges, located on the rim between El Tovar Hotel and Bright Angel Lodge, are modern facilities featuring deluxe, up-to-date rooms. They're open all year.

Yavapai Lodge, back from the rim in the woods near the visitor center, is a modern lodge-motel open from March through December. The large cafeteria here serves three meals a day.

The Trailer Village has 84 sites, all with cold water, electricity, and sewage hookups. It's open year-round but there's a 7-day limit from May 1 through October 21. Trailer spaces must be reserved; there is a fee.

The Motor Lodge, open all year, offers motel rooms and cabins and the lowest rates. The cafeteria serves three meals a day.

Mushwhip, the park's newest facility, is an architecturally pleasing 12-building complex with spacious, well-appointed rooms, all equipped with baths, phones, and televisions. It's open all year.

Outside the village. Just south of the park entrance on State 64 is the Moqui Lodge and restaurant. At Tusayan, just south of Moqui, you'll find several additional motels. The old hotel at Cameron, on the bank of the Little Colorado, offers comfortable accommodations just an hour's drive from Grand Canyon Village. You'll find plenty of large motels in Flagstaff and Williams.

At the North Rim. Lodging and meals at the North Rim are available at Grand Canyon Lodge and outside the park (see page 21). The lodge offers visitors a choice of accommodations — motel rooms, cottages, and rustic cabins.

Camping. The National Park Service operates two campgrounds on the South Rim — one in Grand Canyon Village and a smaller one at Desert View. The Mather Campground, in the forested village south of the visitor cen-

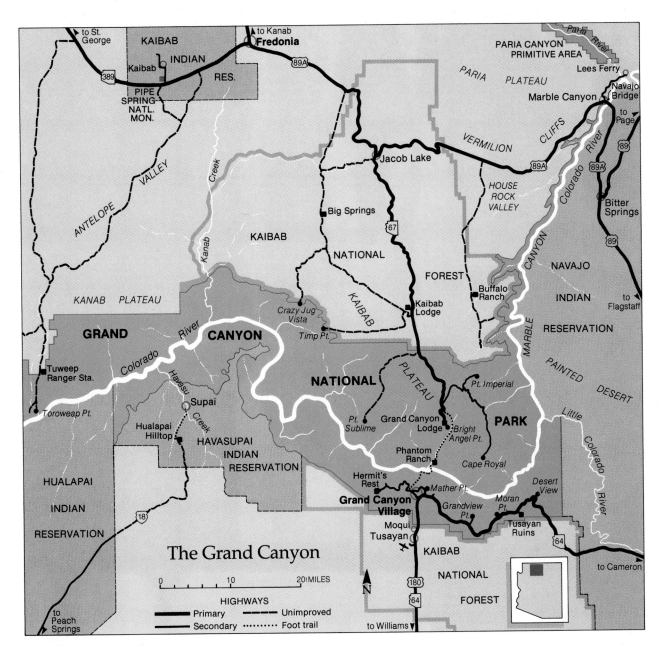

The Grand Canyon

HIGHWAYS
—— Primary   --- Unimproved
—— Secondary ···· Foot trail

ter, has 319 campsites and piped water. It's open all year. At the nearby Camper Service Building are showers and a laundromat. The big general store sells groceries and supplies.

The campground in Desert View (at the eastern end of the park) has 51 campsites, piped drinking water, but no trailer hookups. There's a small fee. Admission is on a first-come, first-served basis, with a 7-day limit. It's open from about mid-May to October, depending on the weather.

Just south of Tusayan, the Forest Service Ten-X Campground has 70 campsites with trailer parking. Facilities include toilets but no trailer hookups. Bring your own drinking water. Open April to November, the campground limits stays to 14 days. There's also a privately operated campground near Tusayan.

North Rim camping information can be found on page 21.

Dining at the canyon

Diverse is the best way to describe the Grand Canyon's eating facilities, which range from snack bars to formal restaurants. These South Rim spots run the gamut from moderate to expensive: Arizona Room (steaks and barbecue dinners), Bright Angel Coffee Shop (open all day year-round), El Tovar Dining Room (lounge adjoins), Moqui Lodge (open from March through December), Motor Lodge Cafeteria (open from Memorial Day through Labor Day), Yavapai and Bright Angel fountains (open from spring through early autumn), Yavapai Lodge Cafeteria and fast food counter.

North Rim restaurants and refreshments are located at Grand Canyon Lodge on Bright Angel Point and outside the park.

Descending zigzag trails is one way to get a closer look at the canyon. From the South Rim, you can take a 1-day ride to Plateau Point or a 2-day trip to Phantom Ranch. From the North Rim, mule rides take you to Roaring Springs (9 miles round trip).

Whitewater soaks—but doesn't spill— Colorado River dory riders. From late spring through early autumn, river runners offer exciting rides ranging from 1 day to 3 weeks.

What to do

The many activities available at the Grand Canyon allow you to enjoy your canyon experience in whatever way you prefer. You can be as active or as indolent as you like.

Flying into the canyon. Flying tours of the canyon are available from Grand Canyon Airport at Tusayan and from Williams, Page, Phoenix/Scottsdale, and Las Vegas. Helicopter tours leave from Tusayan. You can get information at transportation desks, the visitor center, or the airports mentioned.

Bus tours. A 2-hour tour of the West Rim leaves El Tovar Hotel and Bright Angel Lodge, stopping at Trail View (overlooking Bright Angel Trail into the canyon), Hopi and Pima points, and Hermits Rest.

A 3½-hour East Rim tour from these hotels travels eastward to Desert View, with stops at Lipan Point, Moran Point, and the Yavapai Museum.

At sunset, a 1½-hour tour wends through Grand Canyon Village with stops at the Yavapai Museum and at Yaki Point to view the sunset.

Horseback riding. Several guided excursions are available through Apache Stables, located at Moqui Lodge, from Memorial Day through Labor Day.

Nature hikes. Both long and short hikes on self-guiding nature trails, paths, and undeveloped trails are available between the Yavapai Museum and Hermits Rest, a distance of 9 miles. Other hikes begin at many of the canyon overlooks.

National Park Service rangers offer guided nature walks and hikes on a regularly scheduled basis throughout the year. Contact the park visitor center for times.

Backpacking expeditions led by experienced guides can be arranged with advance notice through Grand Canyon Trail Guides. You can rent the equipment you'll need.

River runs. For information on boating on the Colorado River — from 1-day raft trips to 21-day oar-powered dory runs — see page 25.

Into the canyon — by mule

Every day, weather permitting, all year long, the famous mule trains plod in and out of the canyon depths from the South Rim. To ride the mule train you must be in good physical condition, not pregnant, at least 4′7″ tall, under 200 pounds fully dressed and equipped, and fluent in English. There are no exceptions. Riders are required to sign a liability release.

This is not a trip for people who fear heights or riding. At many points sheer rock walls drop hundreds of feet from the trail's edge. It's not unusual for acrophobia victims to ask to dismount at the first stopping point and hike back up to the rim. By then, it's too late for a refund.

Choice of trips

The 1-day, 12-mile round trip on the Bright Angel Trail takes you down to the Tonto Plateau overlooking the Inner Gorge, about two-thirds of the total descent. You'll ride as long as 2½ hours at a stretch without dismounting on the 7-hour trip. The fee includes mule, guide, and box lunch.

The 2-day trip (16 miles round trip) to Phantom Ranch descends the Bright Angel Trail as far as Indian Gardens, then follows Garden Creek, Pipe Creek, and the River Trail to Phantom Ranch. It returns up the steeper South Kaibab Trail. Overnight accommodations are at Phantom Ranch, the rustic resort on Bright Angel Creek.

From December 1 through February, a 3-day, 2-night trip to Phantom Ranch is offered. The extra time in the canyon permits hiking, swimming, wading, and photography.

Phantom Ranch trip rates include mule, guide, box lunch on the trail, cabin (single occupancy), dinner, and breakfast. Up to four riders can share a cabin and split the cost.

For reservations

You can get complete information by writing to Grand Canyon National Park Lodges, Box 699, Grand Canyon, AZ 86023, or by phoning (602) 638-2401; or check with the lodges' transportation desks.

These rides are extremely popular: reserve as early as possible—at least 6 months ahead for summer mule trips. You may include a deposit, but acceptance isn't final until you appear, obviously tall enough, in good health, under the weight limit, and speaking English.

The South Rim

The South Rim of the Grand Canyon is enjoyable year-round, though there are seasonal changes at its 7,000-foot elevation. Each season brings a new setting to this magnificent stage.

From June to September, daytime temperatures climb into the 80s or 90s with cool 40° readings at night. Especially brilliant at sunrise and sunset, the warm sun highlights the rusty hues of the upper canyon walls. These colors contrast sharply with the dark shadows that reach deep down to the canyon floor. Sudden thunderstorms and turbulent skies often surprise visitors in July and August, and set a different mood — one that's a favorite of many photographers.

Autumn, with its clear days, is brief; the first snow falls in October or November. From the first snowfall into April, nights may be frosty, but daytime temperatures are in the 40s or 50s.

Getting there

If you're approaching from the west on Interstate 40, turn north on State 64 at Williams. The drive to the park is a pleasant 60 miles through rolling hills covered at lower elevations with bunch grass, junipers, and desert shrubs, then with Ponderosa pine forests near Tusayan, a growing community just south of the park boundary.

From Flagstaff, you can reach the canyon from two directions. U.S. 180 angles northwest out of the city on the west side of the San Francisco Peaks, meeting State 64 about 30 miles south of Grand Canyon Village.

A second route takes you north from Flagstaff on U.S. 89 almost to Cameron on the Navajo Reservation. There you turn west on State 64 and enter the park near the easternmost development at Desert View.

If you prefer to fly to the South Rim, regularly scheduled airlines to Grand Canyon National Park Airport depart from Las Vegas and Phoenix/Scottsdale, with bus service to Grand Canyon Village. A regional airline serves Flagstaff.

Transcontinental bus lines stop at Flagstaff and Williams, and local bus lines connect both towns to the village.

Amtrak goes to Flagstaff; from there you can catch a bus.

Where to stay

Park lodging facilities offer a total of 904 rooms, but during the busy season from Easter to after Labor Day, the South Rim has many more visitors than those facilities will accommodate. During this period, you must have reservations to stay inside the park. Visitors without such reservations can stay at a motel or lodge at Tusayan, Flagstaff, Williams, or Cameron.

You can camp at one of two campgrounds in the park, or at two campgrounds near Tusayan. From November to April, there's plenty of room, but reserve for holidays. Trailer space in the park must also be reserved.

For additional information on accommodations at the South Rim, see page 12.

Getting around

Grand Canyon Village stretches about 1½ miles through the forest of the South Rim; facilities are clustered at each end of the dumbbell-shaped development. Connecting them is a ¾-mile paved road through the forest — traffic can be heavy — and a nature trail along the rim, part of a 3½-mile rim trail.

On foot. You can visit everything in the village on foot without exertion. Outside the village, distances are great. The West Rim Drive to the viewpoint at Hermits Rest is 8 miles, and the East Rim Drive out to spectacular Desert View is 27 miles.

By bus. From mid-May through September, shuttle buses provide transportation around the village, as far east as the Yavapai Museum, and along the West Rim Drive. During that period, private autos are not allowed on the West Rim Drive.

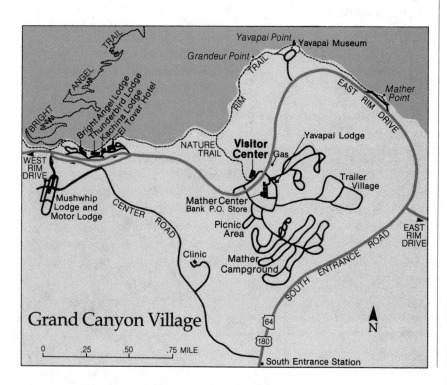

Grand Canyon Village

What's grand about Grand Canyon?

As you stand at the edge of Grand Canyon and gaze down the neatly stratified rocks into the depths of the canyon, you're looking back some 20 million centuries. When you descend into the canyon, you not only pass through many of the major climate zones found in North America but also see a bewildering variety of plants and animals that, outside this canyon, would require an entire continent to find a suitable environment.

The birth of a chasm

The erosive forces that created this enormous cleft in the earth's crust are the same as those that carve a roadside gully. In the beginning, a quiet river flowed through a gently sloping plain. As pressures from within the earth slowly tilted the surface, the river began to run faster, cutting a deeper track. The deepening channel caused land on both sides to erode, creating a V-shaped canyon.

Today, Grand Canyon is 277 miles long, 4 to 10 miles wide, and 5,000 to 6,000 feet deep.

A chronicle of time

The canyon exposes a wealth of earth history; the story is written in neatly deposited layers used by geologists as a primer.

Among the rock of the inner gorge is the oldest man has seen exposed on this planet. At the base of the great abyss, the hard, black, 2-billion-year-old Vishnu Schist rises out of the Colorado River to form the canyon's first stratum. Between that schist and the buff gray Kaibab limestone lining the rim nearly 6,000 feet above are three of the earth's five identified geological periods and five of the earth's seven major life zones.

Walking a continent

In a hike to the bottom of the canyon and back up again, you experience a variation in climate and in plant and animal life ranging from that of Mexico's Sonora Desert to Canada's Hudson Bay, from the blazing heat, yucca, and spiny lizards of the low-desert bottom to the subarctic blue spruce that thrive at the top of the canyon.

Viewing the canyon

Many splendid viewpoints perch along the South Rim. Each has its own characteristics, no one overlook giving you a complete view. Then, too, the canyon scene changes constantly as the sun crosses the sky, shadows move down into the depths, and haze softens the light.

Mather Point. As the main road into Grand Canyon Village from the south entrance (U.S. 180) swings west toward the village, it approaches the rim of the canyon at Mather Point. Most visitors get their first glimpse of the canyon here. For different outlooks, try the East Rim Drive, a continuation of State 64, ¾ of a mile south of Mather Point.

Along the East Rim Drive. Scattered between Mather Point and Desert View are five major vista points, as well as several "wall stops" where the road approaches the rim.

Yaki Point, about a mile from the village on the road east, juts out into the canyon and offers views over a 200° arc. Three miles east of Yaki Point is a trail down the hill to Duck-on-the-Rock, a curious, much-photographed formation with views northeastward.

Grandview Point, 5 miles east of Yaki Point, affords another view northeastward and a look at a good stretch of the river itself.

Moran Point, 6 miles east of Grandview, offers broad views westward and is a late-afternoon favorite. From here, you can see the white water of Hance Rapids in the river below.

Another 5 miles east is Lipan Point, considered by many the most beautiful South Rim overlook. Because this and the next two points are in the bend of the river, you can look back up its length.

Navajo Point, a mile east and close to Desert View, offers another vista.

Desert View. If you approach the Grand Canyon from the east on State 64 (from Cameron), your first view into the canyon will be at Desert View. For many visitors, this is a favorite spot. From here you look both ways from the apex of a right-angle bend in the canyon—north to the notch where the Little Colorado enters and west toward the South Rim promontories. Here, too, is a 70-foot watchtower, built of native stone on a steel frame. The glass-enclosed observatory top is the highest point on the South Rim.

Along the Rim Trail. A more or less continuous trail runs along the rim from Mather Point to Hermits Rest. Paved from Yavapai Point to Maricopa Point and level in most sections, it provides a sharp contrast to Inner Canyon trails. Though you'll find specific overlook points, the trail offers grand views along its entire length. At the eastern end, Yavapai Point provides broad views both upstream and downstream. In the Yavapai Museum, exhibits describe various geologic formations in the canyon. Just west is Grandeur Point, with a slightly more westerly view.

On the West Rim Trail, you can walk to Maricopa Point for more views across the canyon and toward the east. Here the trail ends; to reach Hermits Rest 8 miles beyond, you can hike, bike, or ride the shuttle bus along the West Rim Drive.

Nature trail. A part of the Rim Trail—including the section between the Yavapai Museum and the visitor center—is also a nature trail. A guidebook describing plant life, evidences of the canyon's geologic history, and aspects of its ecology is available at the center or at the trail heads.

The West Rim Drive. West of Maricopa Point, the Powell Memorial commemorates the explorer Major John Wesley Powell, who led the first boat party down the river and made the first geological survey of the canyon. Just west of it is Hopi Point and the best views from the West Rim Drive. From Mojave Point, less than a mile away, you also have fine sunset views. From Pima Point, 3½ miles farther, you may hear the roar of the rapids visible below.

The drive is closed to private autos from mid-May through September. Shuttle buses leave every 15 minutes from the West Rim Interchange (just west of Bright Angel Lodge) and stop at each viewpoint. The round trip takes about 1½ hours, but most visitors stop to walk around the vista points and catch a later bus. You can take a good look from all points in half a day.

Hermits Rest. At the end of the drive is Hermits Rest, a little building erected in 1914 around a huge stone fireplace, at the head of the Hermit Trail. You'll find rest rooms here.

Other points of interest

To understand the geology, ecology, and human history of the Grand Canyon, be sure to take advantage of the fine exhibits and educational programs offered by the National Park Service, particularly at the visitor center, the Yavapai Museum, and the Tusayan Ruins and Museum. Certain commercial establishments also add to the enjoyment of this unique area.

Visitor center. First-time park visitors may want to make the visitor center, located 3 miles north of the south entrance, their first stop. Open daily from 8 A.M. to 5 P.M., the center provides information on hiking and camping, issues overnight backpacking permits, and sells books, pamphlets, and maps. A 12-minute narrated slide program shown on the hour and half-hour focuses on the canyon's history, life zones, and habitation by man. On display in the courtyard is a collection of early river-running boats.

Yavapai Museum. From the glass-enclosed viewing room in the small stone museum at Yavapai Point, you'll enjoy panoramic vistas extending to the suspension bridge that crosses the river on the trail to Phantom Ranch. Museum exhibits include rock formations, a fascinating geologic time clock, and information on how the canyon was formed. Both children and adults will appreciate the 3-minute cartoon video of the canyon.

Several times daily, park rangers present special programs, including a ½-mile hike to Grandeur Point. Check the park newspaper, *The Grand Canyon Guide*, for schedules or inquire at the museum or visitor center. The museum is open from 8 A.M. to 5 P.M. daily, until sunset during the summer.

Tusayan Ruins and Museum. Just south of the East Rim Drive about 4 miles east of Moran Point are the ruins of a small, 800-year-old Indian village. A cluster of low stone walls among the trees outlines the Pueblo-type houses and a kiva. The small museum offers descriptions of prehistoric and contemporary North American culture and displays objects recovered during the 1930 excavation. Guided archeology walks take place daily at 10:30 A.M. and 1:30 P.M.

Grand Canyon Theatre. South of the park in Tusayan, the Grand Canyon IMAX Theatre's huge screen and fine sound system combine to capture the canyon's history and beauty on film. Performances are on the hour from 10 A.M. to 9 P.M. daily.

Into the depths

You really can't feel the impact of the Grand Canyon until you've seen it from the bottom, where the awesome 1-mile depth suddenly becomes a reality. In contrast to the cool Transition life zone of predominantly Ponderosa and piñon pine and Utah juniper forest on the South Rim, the canyon floor brings visitors to the Lower Sonoran life zone: a desert of cactus and yucca populated by lizards, rattlesnakes, and other desert animals. Summer temperatures here can top 120°.

From the South Rim you can ride a mule all the way to the bottom or hike in and stay overnight at Phantom Ranch or at the campgrounds. Overnight camping requires a permit.

Hiking in. You can make short day hikes to points on the Bright Angel or Kaibab trails, or hike all the way down to overnight accommodations at Phantom Ranch; or you can camp at free campgrounds on the main trails.

Rangers rate the 16-mile round trip to the river as "an exhausting hike," even for experienced trekkers. It's not recommended as a 1-day hike. The National Park Service suggests that hikers carry one gallon of water per person per day.

If fatigue stops you or you have an accident on the trail, rescue by mule is expensive. There are emergency telephones on both the Bright Angel and Kaibab trails.

Accommodations for hikers. You'll need reservations to stay overnight at Phantom Ranch, which offers both rooms and a dormitory.

Campgrounds are available free of charge near Phantom Ranch, at Indian Gardens on the Bright Angel Trail, and at Cottonwood on the North Kaibab Trail to the North Rim. However, camping spaces must be reserved, and all campers must have permit tags.

For information or reservations, write Backcountry Reservations Office, Box 129, Grand Canyon National Park, AZ 86023.

Mather Point and other South Rim over-

looks provide panoramic views across the

canyon and sweeping vistas up and down

the Colorado River, which flows 277 miles

through the park.

Clear, turquoise blue Havasu Creek gushes out of the ground to give water to the tiny, remote Havasupai Indian Reservation, a 518-acre, idyllic canyon oasis that's home for the tribe's 300 members.

Visitors can see their village and explore the narrow canyon and leaping waterfalls below it. Overnight accommodations include the Indians' motel-like lodges and a nearby Indian campground.

But to get there, you'll either have to hike or ride a horse 8 miles from the end of the road, which is 62 miles by paved and seasonal dirt roads from the nearest point on State 66, or arrange an expensive helicopter flight.

Getting there

To drive to the parking area above the canyon, turn north onto Indian Route 18 about 7 miles east of Peach Springs (on State 66). Paved for about 40 miles, the road leads to Fraziers Well and Hualapai Hilltop. Check road conditions first at Peach Springs.

There's ample parking space at Hualapai Hilltop. If you've made advance arrangements, you arrive in time to meet the pack train the Indians have brought up from the village (one horse for you, one for your gear). Riders can carry a camera, sandwich, and canteen, but that's all.

The hot, dusty trail drops 2,000 feet in 6 miles to the creek—a good picnic spot. The village is 2 miles farther. In summer, the temperature here may top 110°.

The village

In the village the trail widens to become the main street. At its center stand two guest lodges, a snack bar, a post office (the last one served by pack train), and a tourist office at which visitors register and pay a small trail fee. Small homes, including a few prefabs flown in by helicopter, are scattered among the cottonwoods and willows.

Some villagers still sell the tightly coiled baskets that were once used for carrying food and water.

The falls

Major attractions are the travertine pools and three beautiful waterfalls in the canyon below the village. The farthest—3 miles downstream—is Mooney Falls, which at 196 feet is higher than Niagara Falls.

Navajo Falls. The first of the three, Navajo Falls lies below the village just off a well-defined trail. Though not as spectacular in its leap as the other two drops, this cascade emits a mighty roar. Below the falls, several bathtub-shaped travertine pools provide pleasant splashing.

Havasu Falls. About a mile down the trail is Havasu Falls. Though hiking here isn't difficult, it's usually possible to rent a horse in the village to reach this point. You'll enjoy swimming or wading in the pools below the wide, showy falls.

Mooney Falls. It's a 1-mile trek on foot from Havasu Falls to Mooney Falls. Once you clamber down the cliff, you can swim in a pool below the falls and marvel at the rock-frosting of minerals deposited by the blue green water.

Below Mooney Falls, the trail dwindles and almost disappears down the Colorado River.

By following the creek downstream (wading across it on occa-sion), you'll reach the river in a few miles.

Staying overnight

The Indians maintain lodges and private rooms for visitors; there's a small charge. You can cook in a community kitchen (groceries are available at the store) or you can eat in the village snack bar.

The Indian campground 2½ miles below the village provides water, picnic tables, grates, and pit toilets for campers. There's also a small campground at Navajo Falls, 1½ miles below the village. Bring your own fuel or buy some at the store. A fee is charged for camping, and reservations are required.

Make reservations for saddle and pack horses and for accommodations by writing to Havasupai Tourist Enterprise, Supai, AZ 86435, or telephone (602) 448-2121. Campers can reserve sites by phone or by writing to "Campground Reservations" at the same address. Reserve or confirm reservations over the phone from Hualapai Hilltop before you head down the trail.

The North Rim

The North Rim is at its colorful best in late September and early October. Groves of golden aspen, absent from the pine and juniper woods of the South Rim, sparkle against the shadowy blue curtain of tall spruce and fir that make up much of the forest cover of the Kaibab Plateau.

Snow falls early and deep on the North Rim, which is a thousand feet or so higher in elevation than the South Rim. Roads and concessions are closed during the winter. The actual closing date of the North Rim entrance road depends on the snowfall. Indian summer may last into November; or the road may be closed temporarily by a mid-October storm, only to dry off and remain not only passable but also warmly inviting until late November.

Getting there

The usual approach to the North Rim from Arizona is north from Flagstaff on U.S. 89 to Bitter Springs, then north and west on U.S. 89A to the turnoff of State 67 at Jacob Lake. From the north, the nearest major highways are Interstate 15 near St. George and U.S. 89 from Salt Lake City.

From Jacob Lake, it's 30 miles to the park entrance (there are no gas stations between Jacob Lake and Kaibab Lodge, just outside the park) and another 13 miles to the rim. The road up the Kaibab Plateau climbs gradually to over 8,800 feet before descending to the rim.

Where to stay

Compared to the South Rim, accommodations are few on the North Rim. From mid-May to October, Grand Canyon Lodge offers rustic cabin, cottage, and motel accommodations. For reservations, contact TWA Services, Inc., Box TWA, Cedar City, UT 84720.

Outside the park, motel rooms are available at Kaibab Lodge, 5 miles north of the North Rim entrance station, and at Jacob Lake, 30 miles north of the entrance station. Other lodging can be found at Fredonia, Marble Canyon, Page, and at Kanab, Utah.

A close-in, privately owned campground with improved sites is located in a quiet, wooded spot sprinkled with aspen leaves only a short distance from a store and other camper services. The longest you can stay is 7 days. Trailer utility hookups are not available at this location.

Groves of golden aspen sparkle against the shadowy blue curtain of tall spruce and fir that make up much of the forest cover of the Kaibab Plateau.

Camping is not allowed elsewhere on the North Rim, but there's a small Forest Service improved campground at De Motte on State 67, just north of the park boundary, and campgrounds at Jacob Lake.

Another view

The higher, more imposing North Rim provides a totally different view of the canyon. Nature's intricate engineering of this enormous channel is much more apparent here — deep side canyons, freestanding islands of rocks reaching up from the canyon floor, and narrow promontories that intrude into the canyon.

During much of the year, as the sun inclines toward the south, the opposite South Rim reflects a more somber mood as its walls are darkened by long shadows.

Four major viewpoints dot the North Rim.

Bright Angel Point. The tip of this promontory is a ¼-mile walk from the road where you'll get your first look into the canyon. Below it, on the east, lies the trail down to Phantom Ranch and the river. Bright Angel Point is also the site of Grand Canyon Lodge, center for accommodations at the North Rim.

Cape Royal. Jutting out into the big bend of the canyon, Cape Royal is the southernmost point on the North Rim. From here, and from Angel's Window (a gaping hole punctured through a narrow promontory by the relentless forces of nature) less than a mile north, you can look across the north-south gorge to the Painted Desert.

The cape is 26 miles from Grand Canyon Lodge on a paved road.

Point Imperial. At 8,800 feet, this high point is the northernmost roadside viewpoint; it overlooks the beginning of the Grand Canyon where the Colorado River emerges from narrow Marble Gorge. It's located 3 miles off the Cape Royal road on an eastward turnoff about 8 miles from Grand Canyon Lodge.

During your stay, enjoy the luxury of taking a whole day to drive 58 miles — the combined round-trip distance to Point Imperial and Cape Royal. Take lunch and water along.

Point Sublime. From this point, you get the westernmost view of either side, and you'll see the narrowest opening between the two rims. To reach Point Sublime, go back north on the highway almost to the park entrance. A primitive road turns off and heads 17 miles through pine and aspen groves to the point. The road's not always open, so inquire at the ranger station or at the information desk in the lodge.

The North Rim supports great forests of aspen, royal oak, and conifers. At 8,000 feet, autumn color arrives earlier here than on the opposite rim, which is 1,000 feet lower.

Canyon depths offer explorers challenges, surprises, such as this hidden waterfall, and impressive scenery. To reach the bottom, you hike down, ride a mule, or take a boat trip through quiet water and pounding rapids.

Getting around

If you're not driving a car, you can still see the highlights of the North Rim on foot or on horseback.

Hikes. Along the rim between the lodge and North Rim Campground lies the gentle, 1½-mile Transept Canyon Trail. The Uncle Jim Trail starts at the Kaibab Trail parking lot, a little north of the campground, and takes you 3 miles through the trees to an overlook above the trail and the main canyon.

On the Widforss Trail (10 miles round trip), you'll hike through forested land to a canyon overlook from the next promontory west of Bright Angel Point. Ken Patrick Trail winds for 12 miles through forest and along the rim from Point Imperial to the North Kaibab trailhead.

Trail riding. You can take a guided 3-hour horseback trip to Uncle Jim's Point. Sure-footed mules also go down the North Kaibab Trail.

Nature walks and programs. During the summer, naturalists conduct a wide variety of nature walks and other special programs. Check *The Grand Canyon Guide* for schedules.

The park naturalist at Cape Royal presents geological programs daily. There are also campfire programs nightly next to North Rim Campground and illustrated presentations at Grand Canyon Lodge.

Into the canyon

From the North Rim you can descend into the canyon on a mule or on foot. The trip is tougher than from the South Rim, since you start from almost 1,000 feet higher up.

By mule. You can make a 9-mile, daylong mule trek to Roaring Springs and back, or take a shorter, 3½-mile ride down and back. You must reserve ahead for either trip. Write to Grand Canyon Scenic Rides, Kanab, UT 84741.

Hiking in. If you're in very good shape, you can hike down to the canyon floor on the North Kaibab Trail. It's 14 miles one way, and the National Park Service recommends that you break it up with an overnight rest at Cottonwood or Bright Angel campgrounds. The climb back up is even more rugged; you ascend 5,800 feet in that 14 miles. Ask for hiking information at the ranger station's Backcountry Reservations Office. A permit is required for an overnight stay.

Tuweep area

Confirmed backcountry probers are discovering the breathtaking vistas of the Tuweep area, its spacious campground, and its spectacular lava flows.

When you reach the majestic overlook at Toroweap Point, you'll be rewarded with one of Grand Canyon's most magnificent views. Until 1975, this part of the western section of the Grand Canyon was called Grand Canyon National Monument to distinguish it from the national park area to the east.

To reach this region, turn south from State 389 on the Kaibab Indian Reservation, west of Fredonia, near Pipe Spring National Monument (see page 25). The unpaved roads, unsuitable for passenger cars in wet weather, are almost a guarantee of solitude. It's 65 miles on graded road from the Pipe Spring turnoff to the Tuweep Ranger Station and another 5 miles on unimproved road to Toroweap Point. From the overlook here there's a sheer drop of 3,000 feet to the river.

Though you'll pass a few ranches along the way, don't count on finding gasoline, even in an emergency. Fill your tank just before you go and carry an extra supply of gas in a safe jerry can. Have water with you, too.

Toroweap Overlook. The approach to Toroweap Point is through a wide break in the plateau called Toroweap Valley. At the end of the valley, ahead of you and right on the lip of the gorge, is a unique landmark in a land of flat-topped mesas and abrupt rimrocks—a smoothly rounded, sagebrush-dotted pile of volcanic cinders called Vulcans Throne.

Gazing upstream from the overlook, you see the geometrically shaped, sedimentary ledges and cliffs and talus slopes of the Grand Canyon. Downstream, for mile after mile, thick lava flows form steep, dark deltas over ridges and gullies or hang like frozen black waterfalls on the cliffs.

> *When you reach the majestic overlook at Toroweap Point, you'll be rewarded with one of Grand Canyon's most magnificent views.*

Far below you, the floods of the river have undercut, exposed, and polished a glittering black embroidery of columnar basalt bending every which way. Directly across the chasm, Prospect Wash has sliced its deep canyon right through a cinder cone.

Camping. If you've brought water, you can camp in the shelter of piñon pines and low rock outcrops; a limited number of undesignated, primitive campsites with tables are available. If it's too windy (or the spaces are all taken), you can go back a mile, turn off the main road at the rustic rest rooms, and go on a few yards to another campground in the lee of a sandstone overhang.

North of the Grand Canyon in Arizona's northwestern corner is the Arizona Strip, a stretch of land about 50 by 140 miles. Separated from the rest of the state by the Colorado River, the area was settled by early Mormons who moved down from Utah. Because of the great barrier formed by the Grand Canyon, the strip is historically and culturally linked more closely to Utah than to Arizona.

Much of the region is grassland or sparsely forested with piñon, juniper, cottonwood, and willow; in the Mount Trumbull area (southwest of Fredonia), more than 4,000 acres of Ponderosa pines dominate the landscape.

From the north, roads lead into this corner of Arizona from St. George and Kanab, Utah. From the east and south, you can reach the area on U.S. 89A by way of Marble Canyon (Navajo Bridge) and Jacob Lake. You'll find lodges, motels, and hotels at St. George, Kanab, and Fredonia, and an inn at Jacob Lake.

Marble Canyon

Sheer drama awaits the traveler approaching the Arizona Strip from the east. Looking breathtakingly fragile, the slender, shining steel arch and deck of Navajo Bridge span 616 feet across the gorge, 467 feet above the Colorado. Redwall limestone cliffs, some rising 800 feet, make this stretch of water a favorite of river-running photographers.

The only way to fully appreciate the awesome beauty of this colorful canyon is in a boat or raft. River trips begin at Lees Ferry, 4 miles north of the bridge, where the Paria River meets the Colorado. Here you'll find a ranger station, launch ramp, and campground. It's a favorite fishing spot and the terminus of 1-day raft trips from Glen Canyon Dam.

You'll find stores, lodging (Marble Canyon Lodge, Vermilion Cliffs Lodge, and Cliff Dwellers Lodge), and service stations along U.S. 89A just southwest of Lees Ferry.

Paria Canyon

Lees Ferry marks the southern end of the Paria Canyon Primitive Area, a narrow, sinuous chasm slicing 40 miles northwest from the Colorado River. It's for hikers only, and once you enter the narrow canyon vault with its vertical walls soaring to 1,200 feet, you go all the way and exit at the far end, or turn around and go back; there are no side routes out. It's a 5-day trek from end to end. Of course, you can take a short day-hike as far as you want. Be prepared to wade at many points.

Permits are required. You can obtain them (currently at no cost) from the U.S. Bureau of Land Management, Box 459, Kanab, UT 84741, or from the ranger (from April to October) at the White House entrance on U.S. 89.

The Arizona Strip is historically and culturally linked more closely to Utah than to Arizona.

Start your hike at the White House trailhead, 1.8 miles downstream from where U.S. 89 crosses the Paria River in Utah. Before you enter the narrows, inquire at the ranger station to be sure water conditions are safe. Flash floods make the area hazardous, especially during the summer months.

For a detailed brochure on Paria Canyon, write to the Bureau of Land Management at the above address.

House Rock Valley Buffalo Range

As you travel west from Navajo Bridge toward the Kaibab Plateau, you'll come to a sign pointing south into the House Rock Valley Buffalo Range. Here, between the Kaibab high country and the desert rim of the Grand Canyon, bison roam free.

To visit the range, take the easy 21-mile drive south on a good dirt road to Buffalo Ranch, refuge headquarters. The supervisor will answer your questions and tell you where you might be able to see buffalo in some of the nearby draws.

Onto the Kaibab Plateau

Ordinarily, travelers overlook the two-thirds of the Kaibab Plateau that is national forest land in favor of the one-third that is in Grand Canyon National Park. Actually, the national forest is a wonderful region in which to camp in solitude and study wildlife—and it contains roads to more points on the Grand Canyon's North Rim than you find inside the park.

Two overlooks reward motorists with serene, enticing views of the Grand Canyon. One drive leads to Crazy Jug Point—take forest roads 292 and 292A from Big Springs or De Motte Campground and through Big Saddle Hunting Camp (all are maintained roads). The prettiest approach to Timp Point, the second viewpoint, is through Quaking Aspen Canyon—the last part of the route is "primitive" but not difficult.

You'll come upon marshes and mud on the plateau, but no perennial streams and little surface water of any kind — just a few springs piped into stock tanks, and some small ponds and shallow sink holes called "lakes." Carry your own supply of water.

Jacob Lake and Kaibab Lodge are the only places where you can buy gas (outside the national park), so don't let your tank run low on a backcountry trip. Always expect to get stuck in the mud and equip yourself accordingly.

Among the Ponderosa pines you may catch a glimpse of the spectacular white-tailed Kaibab squirrel, a species found nowhere in the world except on the Kaibab Plateau. This is also the summer range of the Kaibab deer herd; you'll frequently see deer from the highway.

Though you can camp almost anywhere you like on the Kaibab, the only "improvements" you're likely to encounter — aside from the Jacob Lake campground, the De Motte Campground, and a primitive campground at Indian Hollow — are crude hitching rails and shaky tables left by other campers.

For more information on the area and on camping conditions, contact the Kaibab National Forest, North Kaibab Ranger District, Box 248, Fredonia, AZ 86022.

Pipe Spring National Monument

Located on the Kaibab Indian Reservation near the Utah border, the monument is a favorite picnic oasis for motorists traveling between Zion National Park and the Grand Canyon. The 40-acre tract preserves an old Mormon fort originally built to guard Pipe Spring, the only source of water for many miles.

You can browse through the fort, then retreat to the shady picnic grounds for lunch. In addition to the historic fort and three other buildings, you'll discover many pioneer tools and furnishings. A member of the National Park Service is on hand daily to guide visitors through the buildings and tell the fort's history.

Running the Colorado

"We are swept broadside down, and are prevented, by the rebounding waters, from striking against the wall . . . We toss about . . . in these billows, and are carried past the danger."

This is how John Wesley Powell, a one-armed ex-artillery major, described the first known boat ride down the turbulent, often violent, Colorado River in 1869. In that year the major took a small party in four boats down the length of the Green and the Colorado rivers. Two of the boats and three men were lost.

Much has changed since that early river run. Today's boats are much better designed to take the pounding rapids, and the river's raging water is somewhat more tranquil now. But running the Colorado is still one of the best—and most exciting—ways to study the river and the canyons.

Colorado River tours

Tours down the Colorado are many and varied. You can join a large group and run the river in big nylon and neoprene pontoon-type rafts, or you can choose a tour that uses smaller, more maneuverable wooden dories.

The rafts and boats are powered either by motors or by oars. An oar-powered craft is likely to give you a ride closer to what Major Powell and his party experienced. Almost all the craft used are compartmentalized, making them virtually unsinkable.

Safety is a primary consideration on the tours. The guides are all veteran river runners, skilled in maneuvering through the rapids and well informed about the sights. Meals, usually cooked by the guides, are included.

Generally, basic equipment is provided: a life jacket and a waterproof bag to hold your sleeping bag and clothing. Tour operators will supply you with equipment lists.

Itineraries for the tours are carefully planned to include hiking and exploring the river banks and canyons along the way. Most tours allow you to run all the rapids, though you may prefer to pass on a few and walk along the bank. Though it's a rare occurrence, boats can be upset in the rapids.

For reservations

To get your preferred time and type of tour, make reservations for the 1 to 21-day trips as early as possible (up to a year ahead for the longer runs).

Write to National Park Service, P.O. Box 129, Grand Canyon National Park, Grand Canyon, AZ 86023, for tour listings and information.

For additional information on dory trips, write to Grand Canyon Dories, Box 3029, Stanford, CA 94305.

Contact John Wesley Powell Memorial Museum, Box 547, Page, AZ 86040 to learn about 1-day float trips—5 hours of smooth-water drifting from Page to Lees Ferry.

The dot in the distance grows larger. Finally you see it is an old man, standing beside the road. When you pull up and open the car door, he gets in without hesitation or comment, sits solemnly and silently as you drive perhaps 5 miles, perhaps 20, then signals you to stop.

At the roadside he nods his thanks and heads off down the arid slope. There is no more evidence of human habitation here than at the point where you picked him up. You watch for a moment, then drive on. Obviously, he knows where he is and where he's going.

Sometimes when you drive the vast expanse of his reservation, you need such a reminder as this old Navajo to reaffirm that the land is populated. Despite the fact that a tribe that numbered 15,000 a century ago now totals more than 150,000, and despite new highways that have brought a surge of tourists, you gaze much of the time over seemingly unoccupied land.

Paying a visit

There are at least three good reasons to visit the Navajo-Hopi country: to absorb its dramatic, sculptured sandstone scenery; to inspect its archeological relics, evidence of an advanced civilization of a thousand years ago; and to learn a little about its present occupants, whose distinctive cultures still survive long after those of many North American tribes have all but disappeared.

Travelers with such interests have been wandering through this country for decades, but until recently they formed only a small fraternity. These early visitors shared a willingness to accept mild discomforts and possible hazards of traveling long distances, far from any town, on often-unimproved roads.

Now, pavement penetrates much of the reservation, opening this remote and beautiful land to a new group of travelers as appreciative — if not as adventurous — as the prepavement pioneers. Today's visitors still feel the same sense of discovery as the earlier explorers.

The Navajo Indian Reservation, the nation's largest (more than 25,000 square miles), spills across state boundaries in northeastern Arizona, southeastern Utah, and northwestern New Mexico. The Hopi Indian Reservation and surrounding former Hopi-Navajo joint holdings (a portion of the old Moqui reservation, reapportioned as a result of litigation) are an "island" within the Navajo lands.

Part of the vast Shonto Plateau, this is high country, ascending from 3,500 feet to over 10,000 feet at Navajo Mountain. Hopi villages cling to the slopes of Black Mesa, a tableland that rises over 6,200 feet above sea level.

When to go

If you visit the region in spring, you'll gamble on the weather as you do on any spring trip into high country. March and early April often bring howling winds and dust storms. You're likely to find the land at its very best from mid-April through May — a time when grass covers valley floors, wildflowers carpet the hills, and spindle-legged lambs cavort in flocks.

Summer heat descends around mid-June and is punctuated at fairly regular intervals by short, violent, traffic-stopping thunderstorms that continue through early September. Late September and October again bring ideal travel weather—warm, clear, sunshiny days and chill nights. By November, winter—and with it snow and cold—begins to close in.

A land of stark beauty, Monument Valley contains striking spires and carved buttes, all part of the vast Navajo Indian Reservation. Investigate the renowned region on your own or join a guided tour to penetrate beyond marked roads.

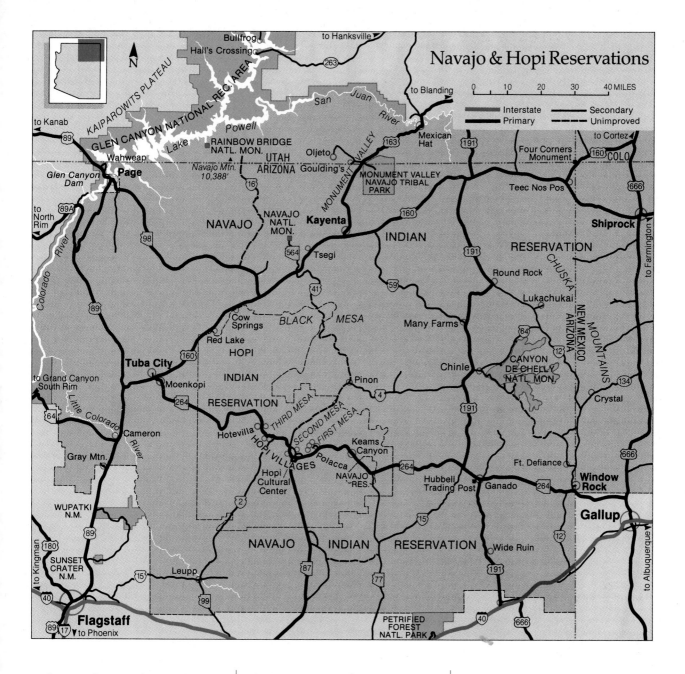

make a quick swing through the Hopi villages, and take a day trip to Lake Powell. Other towns along Interstate 40 between Flagstaff and Gallup, New Mexico, offer limited accommodations. Motels in the western tip of Colorado and in southeastern Utah provide access to the northeastern corner.

At Glen Canyon National Recreation Area, most visitors gravitate to Wahweap, but accommodations are also available at other marinas (see page 41) and at Page.

In this chapter we mention lodging and camping facilities at Canyon de Chelly, Monument Valley, and on the Hopi Reservation. In addition, you'll find limited rooms on the reservation at the following places: Window Rock, Keams Canyon, Kayenta, Tuba City, and Gray Mountain.

Because of the limited number of accommodations, it's wise to make reservations ahead of time, particularly during the major tourist seasons.

Food & entertainment

Like accommodations, restaurants in this area aren't plentiful and, with few exceptions, couldn't be considered gourmet dining. Most of what's available is listed with the major attractions. Larger towns on the reservations usually have one or more cafes serving standard fare. No alcoholic beverages are permitted on the reservations.

Be sure to try some of the specialties of the region: Navajo taco, fry bread, and the various Hopi dishes made from cornmeal.

Entertainment is limited to sightseeing, shopping for native arts and crafts, and hopefully encountering a ceremonial dance or tribal fair.

Swinging through the steps of the Squaw Dance—a version of "ladies' choice"—Navajos display traditional dress and some of their lovely turquoise and silver jewelry.

Using her surroundings for inspiration, a Navajo weaver creates one of the tribe's best-known products. Though rugs are as individual as fingerprints, connoisseurs can pinpoint the general area of origin by pattern and choice of colors.

The Navajo Nation

As you travel the reservation, you'll see evidence of the social and economic revolution that has been underway among the Navajos in recent years.

After the Navajos signed a treaty in 1868 and returned home from four years of exile at Fort Sumner, New Mexico, their livelihood depended principally on sheep raising. But growth of the tribe and its herds increased the demands on the overgrazed rangelands. The Great Depression brought further changes. By the end of World War II, a study of the reservation resources warned that not more than half the tribe—even if its size remained the same—could be supported by the arid land.

Fortunately, new sources of income were emerging. Uranium, oil, coal, and gas discoveries brought lease-bonus and royalty payments, and Congress voted long-range rehabilitation funds.

The Navajo Tribal Council, the tribe's governing body, began developing policies for economic diversification; it invested in job-creating tribal enterprises — irrigation projects, coal mining, forest products, arts and crafts outlets, and tourist facilities — and encouraged private corporations to establish plants on reservation land. These efforts, together with support from the Bureau of Indian Affairs, have resulted in a slow but steady broadening of the tribe's economic base.

The promotion of tourism proceeds at a lively pace; in addition to working with outside tour operators, the tribe may soon offer its own tour packages.

Dineh—"The People"

Navajos have traditionally been seminomadic, following their flocks, living in simple hogans of logs and earth in winter and in simpler shade ramadas in summer. Seldom do you see more than two or three hogans together; the only towns on the Navajo reservation have grown up around governmental or industrial centers.

But Navajo housing patterns are slowly changing. Traditional hogans are being replaced by modern houses and mobile homes (though the doors still face east toward the rising sun); sometimes you see the old and new houses side by side. Planned communities are spreading out around commercial developments, and settlements are gradually taking on the appearance of any southwestern crossroads cluster.

The pickup truck (jokingly referred to by the Indians as the "Navajo convertible") has replaced the horse as the principal mode of transportation in most areas.

Modern dress has replaced traditional attire for most young Navajos. Only in the more remote areas will you see the jewel-like velvet shirts worn by men and long, flowing skirts favored by many women. But however they dress, the tribe's members still display the fine turquoise and silver jewelry for which they are famous.

Window Rock

The seat of tribal affairs, Window Rock gives dynamic evidence of the tribe's entrance into the economic mainstream. The once-sleepy town near the intersection of Navajo Route 12 and State 264, just west of the New Mexico border, has turned into a busy intersection where long lines of pickup trucks wait patiently through two or three cycles of traffic signals to turn into the spacious parking lot of the metropolitan-style shopping center.

At the intersection you'll find the Navajo Arts and Crafts Guild and the excellent Navajo Tribal Museum. By all means browse awhile in the guild's display room. Even if you aren't planning to buy, you'll enjoy looking over the displays and comparing quality and prices. Much of the Navajos' best work is here: weaving, silver, leather, painting, and carving. The museum (open weekdays) offers a look at their history and culture.

Nearby is a zoological and botanical park. West of the intersection on State 264 are the rodeo and fairgrounds.

The road north leads to tribal headquarters. Tribal affairs are run from here by the tribe's elected governing body, the Navajo Tribal Council. Buildings blend with the massive red sandstone shapes around them; the large, round window in the rock—for which the town was named—overlooks the complex.

Of particular interest is the Navajo Tribal Council Building, shaped like a hogan and containing murals that depict the tribe's history.

Navajos have traditionally been seminomadic, following their flocks, living in simple hogans of logs and earth in winter and in simpler shade ramadas in summer. Seldom do you see more than two or three hogans together.

The Navajo Tribal Fair—a lively celebration combining arts and crafts exhibits, agricultural displays, a rodeo, tribal ceremonials, and a carnival — takes place at Window Rock on the second weekend in September.

If you're looking for a place to stay on this side of the reservation, the tribe owns a small motor inn in town. The rooms are clean and comfortable. You'll find a pool and restaurant on the premises and several cafes across the street.

Hubbell Trading Post

In 1876, Don Lorenzo Hubbell founded his trading post at Ganado (where State 264 and U.S. 191 cross) and it's still doing business in the old reservation tradition. Here the Navajos visit with friends and trade their wool, rugs, jewelry (and paychecks) for groceries and supplies.

More than just a trader, Hubbell was the Navajos' friend, settling family quarrels, explaining government policy, and helping the sick. When he died in 1930, he was buried next to his wife, two sons, a daughter, and his long-time Indian friend Many Horses on a small hill overlooking the trading post.

Now a national historic site, the trading post is operated by an independent proprietor. Don't overlook the rug room; it's crammed with one of the area's best selections.

At the small museum in the complex, you can watch local Navajo women working on traditional looms. Rangers also conduct guided tours of Hubbell's home, which contains a fine collection of paintings and artifacts.

The trading post is open daily except major winter holidays.

Neighboring Ganado was named for one of the chiefs who signed the 1868 treaty between the Navajos and the U.S. Government. It's the site of a Presbyterian mission, hospitals, and parochial schools.

Canyon de Chelly

Nestled in a magnificent canyon setting, prehistoric dwellings resembling toy villages draw visitors to Canyon de Chelly National Monument.

The Navajos call it *Tsegi*, "rock canyon." For more than 300 years, its fortresslike walls provided a sanctuary against enemy forces that, at times, threatened to subdue or destroy the Navajo people.

Today, the stubbornly preserved tribal heritage of the Navajos is giving way to the complexities of modern life, but Canyon de Chelly (*de shay*) still offers sanctuary to those who prefer the old ways. Each spring they return to plant their crops, tend their orchards, and graze their sheep in the quiet manner of their forefathers.

Monument Valley is a land of fantastic buttes and spires of colorful rock rising from the 5,000-foot desert floor.

Unlike the Grand Canyon, this beautifully proportioned canyon complex is a size to which humans can relate. On its 100-plus-mile course, the canyon plunges from a depth of 30 feet to a depth of over 1,000 feet and contains over 100 prehistoric sites, most dating from the 11th and 13th centuries.

Getting there and around. The entrance to the canyon is on Navajo Route 64 just past the town of Chinle, a few miles east of U.S. 191. Scenic drives along both canyon rims allow access to spectacular overlooks, but, with one exception, visitors are not allowed within the canyon unless accompanied by an authorized guide. The exception is the mile-long hike from the canyon rim down to White House Ruin (see right).

From around Memorial Day through Labor Day, park rangers conduct daily hikes into the canyon from monument headquarters and present programs at the evening campfire in the public campground; informal interpretive programs take place at most of the overlooks. Inquire at the visitor center for the day's programs. The headquarters museum offers unusually good exhibits on the history of the canyon and its inhabitants.

Full or half-day tours of Canyon de Chelly and Canyon del Muerto begin at the lodge near the mouth of the canyon. Nearby, a concessionaire offers day-long horseback trips to White House Ruin.

The Anasazi Ruins. Concern for the preservation of the unique cliff dwellings of the Anasazi — "the ancient ones" who built their multistoried apartment houses in open caves on the canyon floor and along its walls — prompted a joint arrangement between the Federal Government and the Navajo Tribe in 1931. The agreement, which established the 130 square miles of the Canyon de Chelly-Canyon del Muerto complex as a national monument, stipulates that the administration of the area will not interfere with the rights or privacy of the Navajo people who still live here.

White House Ruin, the one most frequently seen by visitors, is typical of the centuries-old cliff villages hidden in canyon caves throughout Arizona's red rock country. It's named for a long, white plastered wall.

Antelope House, in tributary Canyon del Muerto 7 miles above its junction with Canyon de Chelly, is named for the large red and white antelopes painted on the cliffs above it.

Mummy Cave Ruins, about 8 miles farther up Canyon del Muerto, once contained 90 rooms and 3 ceremonial kivas.

Where to stay. Accommodations, meals, and canyon tours are available at Justin's Thunderbird Lodge near the mouth of Canyon de Chelly. For information and reservations, write to the lodge at Box 548, Chinle, AZ 86503. Accommodations are also available at nearby Chinle.

The 92-unit Cottonwood Campground is located in a grove of tall trees at the mouth of the canyon.

For more information on visitor services, write to Canyon de Chelly National Monument, P.O. Box 588, Chinle, AZ 86503.

The Four Corners

Some 63 miles north of Canyon de Chelly, U.S. 191 meets U.S. 160 after passing through Many Farms, site of the Navajo Community College. A short drive east on U.S. 160 takes you through Teec Nos Pos, where a well-known trading post displays the intricate Teec Nos Pos rugs. Just beyond is the turnoff for Four Corners, where Arizona, New Mexico, Colorado, and Utah meet. A tile-inlaid concrete slab marks the only spot in the United States where that many state boundaries converge.

U.S. 160 continues northeast toward Mesa Verde National Park in Colorado.

At Teec Nos Pos, New Mexico Highway 504 continues eastward to Shiprock, the gigantic rock sculpture that was a landmark to pioneers. At Shiprock, the state highway intersects with U.S. 666, the north-south route.

Monument Valley

The most famous section of the entire reservation, Monument Valley is a land of fantastic buttes and spires of colorful rock rising from the 5,000-foot desert floor. It's also a good place to catch glimpses of the traditional Navajo way of life. You'll see sheepherders tending flocks and weavers designing rugs.

Now a Navajo Tribal Park, the valley lies astride the Arizona-Utah border on U.S. 163, which heads north from U.S. 160 at Kayenta.

Just a few miles north of Kayenta, the valley's huge red rock pillars loom into view. The impressive landscape may look familiar — this remote area has been the setting of many western movies.

On your left stand Half Dome and Owl Rock promontories, located on the eastern edge of broad Tyende Mesa. On your right rise isolated Burnt Foot Butte, then El Capitan. About 24 miles north of Kayenta, you pass through Mystery Valley with Wetherill

---

Navajo rug geography

A Navajo weaver carries the entire pattern for a rug in her head as she works, and no design is ever repeated exactly. Still, some general pattern types prevail, and a connoisseur can tell where most rugs come from.

Black, white, and brown are natural wool colors. Aniline dyes account for the brilliant reds, blues, and other bright colors in some rugs. Painstakingly brewed vegetable dyes, a more recent development, produce wonderfully soft colors; dealers often have charts showing the plants that produce these dyes.

These are some of the centers of Navajo weaving and the most typical styles associated with them:

Tuba City area is known for "storm pattern" rugs, designed with a center box shape connected by lightning symbols to smaller squares in the corners. Black, white, gray, and red are the most common colors, but you can find other colors.

Teec Nos Pos, near the Four Corners, is the center for the outline rug—geometric shapes in the design are outlined in another color. Often, many bright aniline-dye colors are woven into a single rug.

Shiprock and Lukachukai regions produce most of the *yei* blankets. The design consists of narrow, elongated figures representing supernatural beings. The rugs themselves don't have any religious significance, however. Yei blankets most often have a white background and are popular as wall hangings.

Crystal, north of Window Rock, uses vegetable dyes in brown, yellow, rust, green, and black tones. Bands of color, sometimes in wavy lines, make up the simple design.

Wide Ruin-Pine Springs, near the reservation's southeastern corner, produces some outstanding examples of vegetable-dye rugs in soft

shades, along with some designs in bolder colors.

Ganado area is best known for its rugs of red, black, gray, and white geometric designs. The dark red used in these rugs has become known as "Ganado red." Today, vegetable dyes are also used here.

Chinle, located near Canyon De Chelly, is noted for borderless striped rugs. Squash blossom designs, see illustration, are often encased in broad bands of solid vegetable-dyed colors. Aniline dyes are sometimes sparingly used.

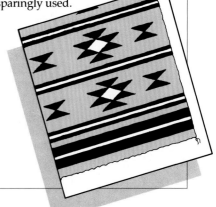

"Apartment for rent, needs some repair" might read a sign on Navajo National Monument's ancient Betatakin ruin. For a closer appraisal of the property, you join a ranger-led hike down the steep canyon wall into the sheltering cavern.

Mesa on your right and cross the Arizona-Utah border.

A half-mile north of the state line is a crossroads. To the left lie Goulding's Trading Post and Lodge and Oljeto, site of another trading post and a good airstrip. To the right the road takes you to the Monument Valley Visitor Center. From the glass-walled observatory you catch excellent views of some of the better-known rock formations — the Mittens and Merrick Butte.

In the visitor center are a geological museum and a crafts room displaying — and selling — local art. This is also the place to buy your guide to Monument Valley attractions. Nearby are a picnic area and a public campground.

If you have time, you can enter the park (the Navajos charge a small fee) and take a 14-mile drive on marked roads to view the more famous landmarks: the tall, slender Three Sisters spires and the Totem Pole and Yiei Bichai group. A 15-minute round-trip walk from North Window rewards you with panoramic views.

For more valley information, write to Park Headquarters, Box 93, Monument Valley, UT 84536.

Tours. To explore the valley more thoroughly, you can arrange for a guided tour in a four-wheel-drive vehicle; their operators are permitted to go beyond the marked roads.

The following companies offer tours: Goulding's Trading Post and Tours, P.O. Box 1, Monument Valley, UT 84536; Crawley's Navajo Nation Tours, P.O. Box 187, Kayenta, AZ 86033; and Crawley's Canyon Country Scenic Tours, P.O. Box 426, Mexican Hat, UT 84531. Navajo Scenic Tours at Window Rock also offers day-long tours.

Where to stay. Goulding's Lodge has long been a favorite; for many years it was the only place to stay. Now you'll find modern motels at Kayenta and Mexican Hat. Reservations are advised. Goulding's also operates a campground near the lodge.

You can also reach Monument Valley from U.S. 160 from Cortez, Colorado, and from U.S. 163 from Monticello, Utah. There are accommodations in both areas.

Navajo National Monument

Another group of prehistoric cliff dwellings — Betatakin, Keet Seel, and Inscription House — is preserved in Navajo National Monument, about 20 miles west of Kayenta. You can see Betatakin from monument headquarters, but it's a grueling half-day hike to visit it (guided groups only). You'll spend a day on a primitive trail, on foot or on horseback, to reach Keet Seel, the largest cliff dwelling in Arizona. Inscription House, 25 miles to the northwest, is closed indefinitely.

To reach the monument (7,268 feet in elevation), you follow State 564 from its junction with U.S. 160. The road climbs through juniper and piñon forests to the visitor center and Betatakin.

At the visitor center you'll find a well-stocked crafts store and a Navajo hogan exhibit. A small campground is nearby.

Betatakin. For a good view of Betatakin, take the easy walk (a mile round trip) from monument headquarters around the head of the box canyon and look across from the opposite rim.

The ancient apartment house rests inside a great cave in the canyon wall far below the headquarters building. To see it at close range, you must join a scheduled hiking group guided by a ranger. It's a 3-hour round trip and a very tough climb back up. Don't try it if you're in poor shape.

Keet Seel. The largest cliff dwelling in Arizona, this 160-room village, located 8 miles north of Betatakin, is accessible by trail. From Memorial Day through mid-September, weather permitting, it's open to 10 visitors a day. You must register a day ahead at monument headquarters. At that time you can arrange to hire horses from the Nava-

jos. If you're hiking, be prepared to splash across a stream several times.

To register in advance, to reserve horses, or to ask questions, write to Navajo National Monument, Tonalea, AZ 86044, or phone (602) 672-2366.

Around Tuba City

Capital of western Navajoland, Tuba City lies just north of the junction of U.S. 160 and State 264. In the town, you'll find trading posts, a motel, and several restaurants (don't miss tasting the Navajo version of a taco — on fry bread). The large white building is the Community Center, used for everything involving a crowd: committee meetings, medical clinics, movies, and dances. The town hosts the annual Western Navajo Fair during the third weekend in October.

> *Another group of prehistoric cliff dwellings — Betatakin, Keet Seel, and Inscription House — is preserved in Navajo National Monument, about 20 miles west of Kayenta.*

Dinosaur tracks. Some 180 million years ago, this part of Arizona was an oozy mud flat where dinosaurs roamed. They left their footprints in the mud, which eventually hardened into rock. About 5 miles west of Tuba City on U.S. 160 is the clearly marked turnoff to the tracks. Visitors can picnic under shade trees near a small reservoir about 3 miles south on the same gravel road.

Trading posts. Along U.S. 160 and 89 from Tsegi to Gray Mountain, you'll pass a number of trading posts. Two of the most traditional are at Red Lake and Cow Springs. You'll often find rugs and crafts for sale; the Red Lake area is the birthplace of the "storm pattern" rug design (see page 33).

Little Colorado Gorge

West of the Cameron intersection, State 64 climbs through barren, rolling hills toward the pine-forested highlands of Grand Canyon's South Rim.

Paralleling the highway on the north are the cliffs marking the gorge of the Little Colorado River. The land rises— and the gorge deepens — as the river moves to its confluence with the main stream in the Grand Canyon.

About 32 miles west of Cameron, the highway and the gorge converge at a spectacular overlook. Though the gorge here is not as deep as the Grand Canyon, it is much narrower, so it gives the impression of greater depth. From a railed walk along the top of a sheer cliff, you peer straight down to the muddy river below.

In good weather, Navajo women display beadwork and other jewelry for sale at the edge of the parking area.

Shopping for Indian art

Travelers to the Southwest have long been fascinated by the skill of Indian artists and craftspeople. Fine Indian work is still being produced today, despite the quantity of mass-produced imitations on the market.

Learning how to recognize quality Indian art is your best defense against imitations. Museum displays can help train your eye and aid you in shopping wisely; museum gift shops are excellent sources of authentic items. Indian art shows and displays at state, county, and tribal fairs across the Southwest offer both good shopping and the opportunity to meet Indian artists. Other reliable places to shop are tribal-sponsored stores, artists' studios, and reputable galleries and shops.

Rugs. The Navajos, well known for their beautiful handwoven rugs, learned weaving from the Pueblos, who weave only specialized pieces today. Use of native dyes and natural colors and fine, tightly woven handspun yarn gives these rugs the beauty and durability for which they're valued, but the long process required to achieve these qualities limits the quantity of good rugs on the market.

When you're shopping for a rug, check that the corners don't curl,

that there are no wrinkles, and that edges are straight. Pry apart the fibers to check the warp—it should be wool, not cotton.

Pottery. Hopis and many Pueblo groups dominate pottery making, which is done by the ancient coil method rather than on a potter's wheel. In contrast to weaving, the ceramic arts are flourishing all across the Southwest.

Prices reflect the size and quality of the object and the reputation of the artist. Rub your finger across the design on a pot; the paint shouldn't rub off.

Baskets. The time-consuming art of basket-weaving is concentrated among the Hopis and the Papagos; Hopi baskets are more scarce and more expensive. Quality of design and fineness of stitch determine price, and pieces that at first glance look similar actually may vary quite a bit. Inspect a basket for firmness and evenness of weave before buying— hasty, open-stitch work will dry and loosen.

Jewelry. The silver and turquoise jewelry of the Zunis, Navajos, and Hopis is very popular, and some Indian silversmiths have expanded

their craft to include such objects as hollowware, flatware, and small silver sculptures. Silver is the dominant element in the often massive Navajo jewelry; Zuni work emphasizes the stones and often includes shells, jet, and coral. Finely drawn overlay characterizes Hopi silvercraft.

Reading the art. Designs on pottery, rugs, jewelry, and other objects are often purported to symbolize words or ideas. Listen to these stories with some skepticism—most designs serve the same function as those used in abstract art.

The brightly colored kachina dolls, though, do represent spirits (see page 40). Though the Navajos are producing some kachinas, this is traditionally a Hopi art form.

The Hopi Reservation

Surrounded on all sides by the vast Navajo lands is the Hopi Reservation. The enclave lies astride State 264, about midway between U.S. 89 on the west and U.S. 191 on the east.

Villages cling to the southern heights of three mesas, which the Hopis matter-of-factly call (east to west) First Mesa, Second Mesa, and Third Mesa. Actually, they're not individual mesas but three fingers of the giant Black Mesa reaching southwest from its long ridge.

The Hopi Agency is at Keams Canyon at the eastern end of the reservation on State 264, about 10 miles northwest of the intersection with State 77. At Keams Canyon Arts and Crafts, you'll find a fine selection of Hopi (and other tribes') artwork.

For more information, contact Hopi Tribal Headquarters, P.O. Box 123, New Oraibi, AZ 86039, or phone (602) 734-2441.

The Hopis

Related culturally to the Pueblo people of northern New Mexico, the Hopis, unlike the Navajos, live in fixed locations. They have dwelt in their mesa-top villages for centuries: Oraibi has been inhabited since about A.D. 1150, probably longer than any other community in the United States.

Villages, therefore, are the focal points of Hopi affairs; again unlike the Navajos, the Hopis have not developed a strong central tribal government, though they do have a tribal council.

The Hopi reservation is completely surrounded by lands once designated by the government as joint holdings with the Navajos. But in 1977, the government identified the exact areas belonging to each group; relocation of people in both tribes is presently underway.

From the time of their participation in the Pueblo Revolt of 1680, during which the Spanish were ejected from Indian lands, the Hopi people have remained culturally independent.

Later Spanish conquests did not include the Hopis, and most of the tribe today continues to resist the influence of modern civilization.

Religious ceremonies. Religion plays a predominant role in their culture. Nowhere is this more evident than in their many colorful ceremonies, the most famous of which is the Snake Dance (climaxing many days of ceremonies in late August); during this ritual dancers carry live snakes in their mouths. The ceremonies are held in a different village each year; religious leaders of some villages bar non-Indian visitors during important ceremonies, including the Snake Dance. Presently, Shungopovi's Snake Dances are still open to the public.

From late December through the July "home dances," many other ceremonies take place at which the participants impersonate the various *kachinas*, the spiritual beings from the Hopi underground heaven (see page 40). Many of these are on weekends, but dates and locations are not publicized, and seeing them is usually a matter of luck. If you happen to be on the reservation, inquire about them at a shop or at your motel.

Protocol. Once you arrive at a village where the ceremony is being held, the Hopis will accept you graciously as long as you observe the following ground rules: dress properly (no shorts), be unobtrusive, and in no way interrupt or interfere with what's happening. Cameras, recording equipment, and even sketch pads are strictly forbidden. If you have a camera, lock it up out of sight in your car before entering the village. No alcohol may be brought onto any reservation.

The colorfully costumed dancers, moving solemnly in a line to the muffled drumbeat, transform the monochromatic villages. Sometimes, antics of mudheads or other clowns draw laughter from the understanding crowd. Children often receive gifts from these playful characters.

Hopi villages

All the Hopi villages are situated on or just off State 264 and, with the exception of one, are on or beneath the fingers of Black Mesa.

The mesa-top villages — dry, sun-baked, and often treeless—may seem desolate; when there's not a dance, very little attracts visitors to them. If you do stop, you'll usually be treated politely, and somebody will approach and ask if you need help with something (it may be the village policeman, though this will not be evident by his appearance). The villages are not public places, and visitors are few except for those on guided tours.

On the banks of washes and in the flats below the mesas, the Hopis cultivate their crops: many varieties of corn, squash, melons, and beans. Peach orchards produce small fruit that is dried in the sun.

Traveling west to east across Hopiland, you'll pass by 12 Hopi villages.

Moenkopi. One of the largest of the Hopi communities, Moenkopi dates from the late 1800s. Because it's situated near Tuba City, along State 160, the village is one of the least traditional.

On the east side of the village, you'll see the typical stone and plaster Hopi architecture. The fields around Moenkopi have been farmed for hundreds of years.

Third Mesa. The road climbs gradually up to Third Mesa, about 45 miles from Moenkopi. Side roads lead to Bacabi and Hotevilla, both founded in this century. Traditional Hotevilla still follows ancient Hopi ways. Women in both villages weave wicker baskets.

On this mesa finger lies Old Oraibi (closed to non-Indians). Continuously occupied since around A.D. 1150, it's considered the oldest settlement in the United States. Once the largest of the Hopi villages, its population dwindled over the years and many of the buildings were abandoned, but rebuilding is underway and the village is once more returning to life.

Just past the entrance to Old Oraibi is the Monongya Studio of Hopi Art (open to the public).

New Oraibi (also called Kykotsmovi) is a modern settlement at the base of Third Mesa. Here you'll find the tribal office, trading post, several gas stations, and a food store.

Looking back to the west as you enter town, you'll catch glimpses of Old Oraibi perched above terraced fields. Before starting up towards Second Mesa, you'll pass the Hopicrafts workshop and crafts store. Much of the silver overlay jewelry is produced here.

Second Mesa. Though it's only 5 miles from Third Mesa, Second Mesa appears very remote. The thin, finger-like mesa projection gives the feeling of being on an island above a sea of desert.

Three venerable villages occupy this land: Shungopovi (formerly the village of Maseeba, founded at the foot of the mesa in the 1100s), Shipaulovi, and Mishongnovi. Shungopovi, regarded as the religious heart of the Hopi world, is the site for many dances and the center for all the traditional Hopi crafts. Beside the highway on Second Mesa stands the Hopi Cultural Center (see right).

First Mesa. It's a descent of about 8 miles from Second Mesa to the modern village of Polacca, today a center for Hopi potters. Its convenient location attracts many residents from the mesa-top villages of Sichomovi, Hano (not really a Hopi village), and Walpi. To see these ancient settlements, you take a side road up the slope from Polacca. Sichomovi is the last village to which you can drive; to reach Walpi, you have to walk a few yards up to the top of the mesa.

In the late 17th century, a group of Tano Indians from New Mexico fled here to escape the Spaniards, and the Hopi allowed them to remain in what is now Hano. Walpi, on the point of the mesa, is considered the most picturesque of the Hopi villages. Its unpainted buildings, made from the same rock as the mesa, seem to grow out of the ground.

Hopi Cultural Center

Beside the highway on Second Mesa is the Hopi Cultural Center, a complex that includes a motel, museum, restaurant, campground, and several shops. The handsome center's austere style harmonizes with the angular landscape and native structures.

The motel's comfortable rooms (few with TV and none with telephones— but nobody has complained) make a pleasant base for exploring the villages. Reservations are advised. In the restaurant you'll discover Hopi dishes as well as the regular fare.

The museum contains excellent displays of Hopi historical relics, crafts, and old photographs. As in the villages, no cameras are permitted.

The Hopi Arts & Crafts Silvercraft Cooperative Guild, where you can see and buy excellent silverwork, weaving, pottery, basketry, kachina dolls, and paintings, is across the campground, directly west of the center. You may see Hopi silversmiths creating their distinctive jewelry in a studio adjacent to the showroom.

Indian silver styles

The Zunis of New Mexico and the Navajos and Hopis of Arizona have each developed their own distinctive styles of silver jewelry.

Zuni. The technique most characteristic of Zuni jewelry is *inlay* or *mosaic*, in which pieces of blue turquoise, black jet, red coral, and white mother of pearl are carefully fitted together and glued onto a solid base.

This style led to the development of *channel* work: a raised silver grid design separates individual stones, and the entire surface is smoothed.

Probably the oldest form used by the Zunis is the setting of single stones into individual bases, which led to *cluster* settings of small stones and then the finely cut stones of *needlepoint*. The most recent Zuni development is *nugget* jewelry: naturally shaped stones are polished and set in a contoured silver base.

Navajo. Navajo silversmiths make both *hammered* and *sandcast* jewelry. In the first method, silver is hammered into a thin layer to be cut and then filed or stamped with a design. For sandcasting, a design is carved into a piece of soft rock, which is then filled with melted silver. The hardened piece of silver, distinguished by a ridge formed by the groove of the mold, is then filed and polished.

Hopi. The most popular Hopi silverwork technique is *overlay*. A design is cut out of a sheet of silver, and the sheet is soldered onto a second sheet of silver. The cut-out area is then blackened.

Another heirloom-in-the-making rests in the hands of a skilled Hopi basket-weaver. Scarce coiled baskets command high prices for their fine workmanship and quality of design.

Churning along Lake Powell's shoreline, replica paddle-wheeler carries passengers from the marina to Glen Canyon Dam on a tour of Waheap Bay.

Brightly painted kachina dolls delight visitors to craft shops and museums throughout the Southwest. To the Hopis, these colorful dolls represent ancestral deities who dwell in the San Francisco Peaks near Flagstaff and return each year to the mesas, bringing rain.

The dolls are prized by collectors beyond Hopi villages as some of the most meaningful and colorful examples of Indian art.

The kachina cult

Though the kachina cult—the belief in kachina spirits, the ceremonial function of masked kachina impersonators, and the carving of kachina dolls—is shared by the Zuni Indians of New Mexico and by some of the pueblos along the Rio Grande, its most widespread acceptance is among the Hopis. Each Hopi individual is involved in the cult in some way, and the Hopis are the group that developed the carving of kachina dolls into a popular and profitable art form.

Hopi children are initiated into the ritual of the kachina cult between the ages of 6 and 10. During ceremonial dances in the village plaza, they receive dolls to help them identify the distinctive mask and costume of each of the kachina spirits. These dolls are traditionally displayed on the rafters and walls of their homes.

The pantheon of kachina spirits includes some 250 to 300 deities, ranging from a gift-bearing Santa Claus type to a ferocious black ogre who disciplines disobedient children. Others may represent an animal, a plant or flower, a heavenly body (sun, moon, or stars), or a legendary figure from Hopi history.

Many kachinas are identified only by their particular ceremonial roles (runners, clowns, or escorts) or by some idiosyncrasy in costume or behavior. There is no fixed number of accepted kachinas; new ones are introduced almost every year during kachina ceremonies but return the next year only if they develop a popular following or bring about some beneficial effect.

Ceremonial calendar

The Hopi kachina ceremonial calendar begins on December 21 with the arrival of a single kachina from his underworld home and ends when all the kachinas depart from the village in late July. As many as 200 spirit impersonators take part in one of the largest dances in February.

Visitors are often welcome at one of the weekend kachina dances or at other ceremonies, such as the famous Snake Dance in August. For information on dates and location, check with the Hopi Cultural Center Motel on Second Mesa when you're in the area, or with the Museum of Northern Arizona in Flagstaff in advance of a trip. No cameras are allowed and accommodations on the mesas are limited.

Shopping for dolls

Authentic Hopi-made kachina dolls are carved from the roots of cottonwood trees, then carefully painted and clothed. The price of a kachina doll depends almost entirely on the quality of the workmanship. A well-executed doll around 8 inches tall sells for about $100; elaborate detail work in the carving or costume design can push the price up to $200; certain kachina dolls sell for much more.

Several Hopi entrepreneurs manufacture a line of "tourist-trade" kachinas that are popular items in roadside curio shops. These simulated kachina dolls (not true representations of a particular kachina spirit) usually can be recognized by the simplicity of the lathe-turned body and by a tepee-shaped notch representing the feet at the front of the solid base. Genuine, hand-carved kachinas have individually carved feet.

Even the simulated kachinas have their imitators, made from balsa, pine, fir, and sometimes old broomsticks. Some imitations bear the label "Indian made" but are manufactured by non-Pueblo Indians who probably have never seen a real Hopi kachina. Others come from as far away as Japan and may be made from ceramic, plastic, or plaster.

Your best assurance of authenticity is to buy directly from Hopi craft outlets on the reservation, from reputable Indian art dealers, or from museum shops.

The Heard Museum in Phoenix and the Museum of Northern Arizona display a wide selection of kachina dolls.

Lake Powell

Sparkling blue water, magnificent red sandstone formations, fine fishing, and varied opportunities for boating attract visitors to Lake Powell, a 186-mile-long body of water created by the Glen Canyon Dam.

The tremendous lake and the now-broadened Colorado and San Juan rivers extend into the southeastern corner of Utah. The Navajo Reservation reaches across the Arizona-Utah border to the southern boundary of the Glen Canyon National Recreation Area.

Area headquarters are at Page, Arizona, a town that was born of the construction boom and has remained as a tourist center. At the John Wesley Powell Museum (6 Lake Powell Boulevard), you'll find old photographs of the canyon and the then-wild Colorado River down which this colorful, one-armed river runner ventured in the 1860s. Here, too, is an early version of the boats still used to run the river, as well as a replica of Powell's boat.

Glen Canyon Dam

Spanning the Colorado River on a steel arch below the dam, U.S. 89 overlooks the dam and the broad expanse of the lake. Completed in 1964, the dam rises 710 feet above bedrock, 583 feet above the original river channel, and is 1,560 feet across at the crest. You get a good view from the walkway on the bridge.

On the canyon rim at the west end of the dam, the Carl Hayden Visitor Center offers displays and information about the dam and lake. Free self-guided tours of the dam start here.

Marina line-up

Four marinas around the lake offer accommodations and boat rentals. A fifth — a floating marina called Dangling Rope — is accessible by water only and has no accommodations. All five marinas have a first-aid station, weather reports, a boat fuel and repair area, and stores.

Wahweap, 4½ miles north of the dam on the west side, is the lake's principal recreational facility. From here, you'll get your first good look at the lake's far-reaching arms. Wahweap has a large marina, a trailer and camper village with utility hookups, a lodge, motel, and a 118-unit campground (bring your own firewood or fuel). Contact Del E. Webb Recreational Properties, Box 29040, Phoenix, AZ 85038.

In Wahweap are the district ranger's office and the headquarters for the concessionaire who operates the marinas, tours, and boat rentals, including houseboats.

Hall's Crossing has a large fleet of houseboats and smaller craft for rent. Write to Hall's Crossing, Blanding, UT 84511. You'll also find housekeeping trailers and a 32-unit campground.

Bullfrog (Hanksville, UT 84734) rents houseboats and other craft and has a 48-unit motel and restaurant, housekeeping trailers, and a small campground.

Hite rents some houseboats and smaller boats. The address is Box 1, Route 1, Hanksville, UT 84734. Accommodations are limited to a few housekeeping trailers and primitive camping sites along the shore.

Camping sites

At the three largest marinas (Wahweap, Hall's Crossing, and Bullfrog), the National Park Service also maintains campgrounds with barbecue grills, picnic tables, and rest rooms; no showers or hookups are available.

Many boaters pack camping gear into their craft and camp at secluded beaches. Shoreline camping is permitted everywhere on the lake except at Rainbow Bridge, but you must be a mile or more from developed areas.

Boating

If your time is short, or you don't want to pilot a boat, take one of the many guided boat tours originating in Wahweap and Bullfrog.

If time permits only one half-day tour, the 100-mile round-trip cruise to Rainbow Bridge gives you the best sense of the lake's size and beauty.

The 95-foot *Canyon King*, a festive paddle-wheel riverboat, makes 1-hour Wahweap Bay tours, 2-hour sunset cruises, and slightly longer sunset cruises with a champagne buffet.

Boat owners will find free launch ramps at all marinas. Marina staff will instruct you in the operation of your rental boat, and you'll get a copy of boating regulations for the lake. An invaluable reference is *Stan Jones' Lake Powell Boating and Exploring Map*, which shows the main channel buoys, numbered according to miles from the dam. You'll find copies for sale at marinas.

When to go

Autumn, probably Lake Powell's loveliest season, finds daytime temperatures in the high 70s and surface water comfortable enough (about 70°) to swim or water-ski.

The cool weather brings some of the best times to hike side canyons and to fish for striped and largemouth bass, channel catfish, and crappie. At all marinas you can buy fishing licenses and charter fishing boats.

Located at an elevation of 3,700 feet, Lake Powell generally enjoys mild winters, though cold spells aren't unusual from December through February. Wind can be a problem in the spring; summer is hot and more crowded than at other times of the year.

For information

Because Lake Powell has become a very popular tourist attraction, reservations are advised. For accommodations at the various marinas, see above. For information about the area and park service facilities, write to the Superintendent, Glen Canyon National Recreation Area, Box 1507, Page, AZ 86040.

Central Arizona

Multispired Cathedral Rock stands like a sentinel over Oak Creek. A symphony of color year-round, the area blazes in autumn, attracting visitors from all over the state.

*N*o visitor can claim to know Arizona without having visited the historic and varied country in the center of the state.

In this land you pass from cactus desert to high, barren mesa, up to irregular stands of juniper, and then to splendid forests of Ponderosa pine. This is where Arizona changes its face, with lowland desert rising to meet the 200-mile-long escarpment of the Mogollon Rim. Here, Sonora shrubbery gives way to junipers on rolling hills and thick pine forest near and around the top of the rim.

Cutting through this transition zone are wild and beautiful gorges carved by silt-loaded rivers, as well as lofty buttes and pinnacles of colorful sandstone exposed by erosion. Other natural attractions you'll discover include forests of petrified wood, a waterfall higher than Niagara, cinder cones, and several miniature versions of the Grand Canyon.

Throughout the area are the relics of the prehistoric cliff-dwelling and pueblo-building Indians, the prospectors and miners who searched for copper and gold, and the soldiers, pioneers, and cattle kings who settled and subdued the Wild West.

Getting around the interior

With Flagstaff as the unofficial capital of the northern boundary of Central Arizona, we include attractions as far east as the New Mexico line and as far west as the Lower Colorado River area. To the south, the region is bounded by the ever-growing satellite cities north of Phoenix.

It's easy to cover the state's central section. Two major freeways — Interstate 40 (formerly Route 66) and Interstate 17 — provide easy access to the region's main highways and byways.

Interstate 40, one of the most traveled east-west highways in the nation, cuts a 400-mile-long swath through the state between Gallup, New Mexico, and Needles, California. Interstate 17, the major highway between Flagstaff and Phoenix, bisects the center of the state; turnoffs from the freeway lead to Prescott, the Verde Valley, and Sedona and Oak Creek Canyon.

Other year-round highways provide access to northern and western ski areas and to sunny guest ranches in the Wickenburg area.

An inviting introduction

Central Arizona is a land to savor slowly. Consider making a base in each of its divergent regions so you can explore nearby attractions at your leisure. Towns vary in size and in the type of visitor facilities available, but there's usually no lack of accommodations, restaurants, grocery stores, and service stations.

As with any region in Arizona, reservations are suggested for the busy seasons, which differ depending on the destination. If you're heading to ski country in the winter, to a guest ranch in the spring, to an Indian crafts show in summer, or to Oak Creek Canyon for autumn color, it's wise to make reservations ahead.

The Essentials

The convergence of two major interstates (17 and 40) in the northern reaches of Central Arizona makes access to many of the area's attractions quite easy. Other major highways — U.S. 89, 89A, and 93 on the west and States 87 and 77 to the east—also angle through the center of the state.

Flagstaff, at the hub of the major highways, makes a good base for daylong trips to such areas as Sedona and Oak Creek Canyon, Verde Valley, Walnut Canyon, Meteor Crater, and even as far east as the Painted Desert and Petrified Forest. Also, it's only a little over an hour's drive to the Grand Canyon.

Though many of the other destinations discussed here are separated by only a few miles or a few hours of driving time, there's so much to do in each area that we suggest you set up additional bases so you have sufficient time to explore each one.

Getting around

No matter where you stay, you'll need a car to thoroughly cover this region. Rental cars are available in many of the larger cities.

Guided tours from Flagstaff include a good deal of the area on 3 or 4-day itineraries. Also available are jeep trips from Sedona into the surrounding red rock country and bus trips from Prescott to neighboring ranches. Check local chambers of commerce for additional information.

Where to stay

Accommodations range from small motels to resort settings in major tourist areas. You'll even find a small bed and breakfast in Jerome.

Forest Service campgrounds are scattered throughout the region. In fact, camping is the best way to see the vast Mogollon Rim country.

Flagstaff. Little America, a surprisingly luxurious hotel-motel complex on large, tree-shaded grounds, is among the many stopping spots in Flagstaff. Amenities include a pool, two restaurants, and a fine gift shop.

Along Interstate 40. You'll find a choice of conveniently located motels in larger towns along this highway: Kingman (the Quality Inn has a pool, sauna, jacuzzi, and fitness center), Williams, Winslow, and Holbrook. Most motels have restaurants on the property or nearby.

Sedona and Oak Creek Canyon. This popular area fills up quickly, so make reservations well in advance. Among your choices are lodges along the creek, such as Garland's; resort motor

To Grand Canyon for skiing

For cross-country skiing enthusiasts, the extra layer of drama provided by snow makes the Grand Canyon an irresistible touring destination. From Flagstaff, you could scoot over for a skiing adventure when a good snow hits the South Rim.

Flagstaff is Arizona's most accessible center for skiing. In addition to Fairfield Snow Bowl (see page 48), the state's oldest and second largest ski area, neighboring national forest lands offer millions of acres for cross-country skiing, including a few signed trails.

South Rim

There's only one problem with South Rim skiing. It gets only about 60 inches of snow a year, and you usually have to show up within 24 hours of a storm to ski before the snow melts. Bring your own skis.

The best trails are Kaibab National Forest roads about 12 miles southeast of Grand Canyon Village on State 64, near Grand View Point.

North Rim

On the North Rim (1,200 feet higher), snow is abundant but hard to reach. The road is kept open only to Jacob Lake, at the junction of U.S. 89 and State 67, 43 miles from the rim. Jacob Lake Inn (open in winter) is the ski-touring hub.

Skiers with a week to spare and snow-camping savvy can ski to the North Rim, hike down the North Kaibab Trail (it can be icy), and continue up to the South Rim via the Bright Angel Trail.

For the required free camping permit, write to Backcountry Reservations, Grand Canyon National Park, Box 129, Grand Canyon, AZ 86023.

To keep advised of snow conditions, call the park at (602) 638-7888, daily from 8 A.M. to 5 P.M. For recorded road and weather information any time, call (602) 638-2245.

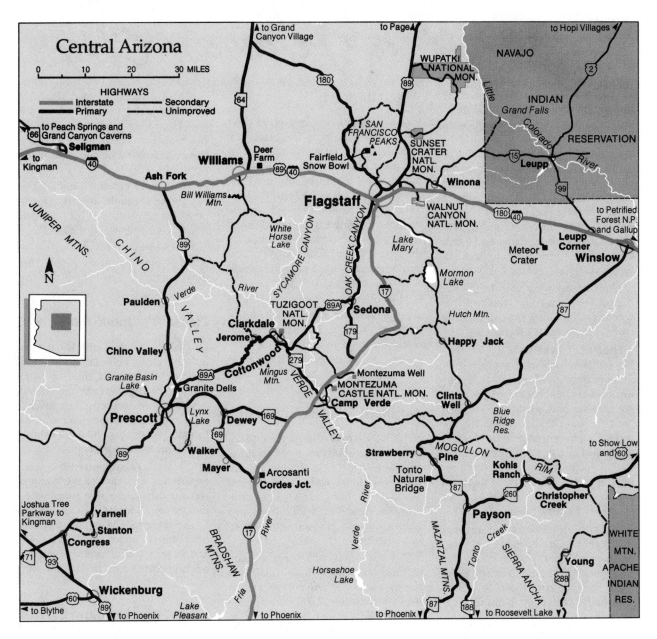

Central Arizona

0   10   20   30 MILES

HIGHWAYS
Interstate — Secondary
Primary — Unimproved

to Peach Springs and Grand Canyon Caverns
66
to Kingman
40   Seligman
Ash Fork
Williams
Deer Farm
64
89   40
Fairfield Snow Bowl
to Grand Canyon Village
180
to Page
SAN FRANCISCO PEAKS
SUNSET CRATER NATL. MON.
89
WUPATKI NATIONAL MON.
to Hopi Villages
NAVAJO
INDIAN
Grand Falls
2
RESERVATION
15   Leupp
Winona
Flagstaff
WALNUT CANYON NATL. MON.
180   40
99
to Petrified Forest N.P. and Gallup
Meteor Crater
Leupp Corner
Winslow
87
Lake Mary
Mormon Lake
Hutch Mtn.
Happy Jack
Clints Well
Blue Ridge Res.
to Show Low and 60

JUNIPER MTNS.
CHINO
Paulden
Verde River
White Horse Lake
SYCAMORE CANYON
OAK CREEK CANYON
17
89A
TUZIGOOT NATL. MON.
Sedona
179
Bill Williams Mtn.

N

Chino Valley
Clarkdale
Jerome
Cottonwood
Mingus Mtn.
279
VERDE VALLEY
Montezuma Well
MONTEZUMA CASTLE NATL. MON.
Camp Verde
Granite Basin Lake
89A
Granite Dells
Prescott
Lynx Lake
Dewey
169
69
Walker
Mayer
Arcosanti
Cordes Jct.
17
Verde River
MOGOLLON RIM
Strawberry
Pine
Tonto Natural Bridge
87
Kohls Ranch
260
Christopher Creek
Payson
Joshua Tree Parkway to Kingman
Yarnell
Stanton
Congress
71   93
89
60
Wickenburg
to Blythe
89   to Phoenix
BRADSHAW MTNS.
Fria River
Lake Pleasant
to Phoenix
Horseshoe Lake
Verde River
to Phoenix
MAZATZAL MTNS.
Tonto Creek
SIERRA ANCHA
Young
288
188
to Roosevelt Lake
87
WHITE MTN. APACHE INDIAN RES.

inns, such as the large Poco Diablo, with golf, tennis, racquetball, and swimming facilities; hotels; and motels in and around town.

Prescott. Motels along U.S. 89 include the Prescottonian, Colony Inn, and Sierra. Cottages are available at Loba Lodge outside town.

Wickenburg. You'll find several motels in the downtown area, including the Rancho Grande. Just outside of town are a number of guest ranches, generally open from October through May; most include meals in the price. Horseback riding may cost extra.

Food & entertainment

You'll find plenty of reasonably priced meals in restaurants throughout Central Arizona.

Flagstaff boasts several spots to dine, among them The Gables Restaurant, Granny's Closet, The Steak House, and the dining room at Little America (dancing).

If you're in Sedona, make reservations at Fournos, a tiny restaurant west of town on U.S. 89A. It's open Thursday through Saturday for lunch and dinner. Other good restaurants in the Sedona area include L'Auberge de Sedona and Orchard Inn & Grill.

In Jerome, don't miss the little lunch spot downstairs on Jerome Street; bread, rolls, and pastry are baked on the premises. You'll also find several restaurants on the main street.

Two of the guest ranches around Wickenburg, Los Caballeros and Wickenburg Inn, open their dining rooms to visitors on a space-available basis; you'll need to make reservations in advance.

Some of the region's special events are discussed in this chapter; for information on other events, contact local chambers of commerce. Generally, Flagstaff and Sedona provide the most active nightlife.

Flagstaff, a Gateway City

Located at the junction of Interstates 17 and 40, Flagstaff is the hub of northern Arizona. From here you can be in Indian country in less than an hour, reach the Colorado River in 2 hours, or get to the Painted Desert and Petrified Forest in just over an hour. Flagstaff is also less than 2 hours from some of Arizona's most popular tourist attractions—Grand Canyon, Wupatki, Sunset Crater, Walnut Canyon, Meteor Crater, Oak Creek Canyon, and San Francisco Peaks.

Many tourists stop here to enjoy the city's close-in attractions and to use it as a base for exploring the surrounding country in short loop trips.

Situated at an altitude of 7,000 feet, Flagstaff may have snow any time from October through May and surely during January, February, and March. Average annual snowfall is 73 inches, but because of the low humidity, the snow cover melts rapidly and snow removal after a storm is prompt. However, if you're driving to Flagstaff during the winter, call the highway patrol first to check on road conditions. It's a good idea to carry chains.

Summers are moderate (for Arizona) at this altitude. Temperatures in June, the warmest month, may reach the low 90s. During July and August, afternoon showers cool the pine forests surrounding the more-than-mile-high city.

This is the time of the Summer Festival, a 6-week series of cultural activities that includes concerts by the Flagstaff Symphony Orchestra and guest musicians, and plays performed by the Northern Arizona University drama department and guest actors. Among other attractions are children's performances, film classics, and art exhibits at the Coconino Center for the Arts.

Before you start your explorations of Flagstaff and its environs, stop at the Chamber of Commerce, 101 W. Santa Fe Avenue, for maps, guidebooks, and specific directions for the drive-yourself tours described on the back of city street maps.

About the town

Flagstaff's name and one of its chief livelihoods came from the pines surrounding the city. Pioneers who arrived here in 1876 stripped the branches off a tall tree and used the tree as a flagpole on the Fourth of July. Though the pioneers moved on, the flagpole remained. Other settlers arrived, attracted to the area nestled on the alpine slopes of Mt. Elden and the San Francisco Peaks; a sawmill and railroad soon followed.

The old downtown area still stretches along the tracks of the Atchison, Topeka, and Santa Fe Railroad; you can enjoy a snack at the turn-of-the-century Weatherford Hotel on Leroux Street.

Northern Arizona University

In 1893, the Arizona Territorial Legislature awarded Flagstaff a reformatory. Failing to appreciate this honor, the townspeople instead turned the red sandstone building into a teachers' college, forerunner of Northern Arizona University, one of the state's three public universities.

Two campuses with varying architectural styles (Old Main on North Campus is the "reformatory that never was") serve some 12,000 students and 600 professors, about a third of Flagstaff's population.

Lowell Observatory

Observatory domes aren't framed in wood these days, but they were when Lowell Observatory was built back in 1894. Nearly hidden in a pine forest on a 7,250-foot hilltop at the outskirts of town, the observatory appears rather unimposing from a distance. But its domed buildings house seven separate telescopes and an impressive collection of data on our solar system. Important work here includes the discovery of Pluto in 1930 and early evidence in support of an expanding universe.

A visitor center is open weekdays from 10 A.M. to noon and 1:30 to 4:30 P.M. Hour-long guided tours at 1:30 P.M. include a slide lecture and visit to the 24-inch refractor telescope dating from 1897.

Friday-night viewing tours are held from June through August. They're popular; get tickets well in advance from the Chamber of Commerce.

The observatory is at the end of W. Santa Fe Avenue, about a mile from downtown.

Flagstaff's "moon lab"

On Cedar Avenue atop McMillan Mesa is the headquarters building of the U.S. Geological Survey's Center of Astrogeology. Though no tours are offered, exhibits in the reception area describe the geologic mapping of the moon, the formation of craters, and the training of astronauts in lunar geology.

Studies here supported the space exploration program of the National Aeronautics and Space Administration. Nearby Sunset Crater and Meteor Crater (see pages 48 and 49) served as field laboratories for astronaut training and for testing lunar exploration methods and equipment.

Scenic road to Grand Canyon

U.S. 180 between Flagstaff and the South Rim of the Grand Canyon is a scenic, 81-mile drive that's pleasant at any time of year. In spring, the highway is lined with the bright reds, blues, and yellows of high-country wildflowers. During summer, the dark green of pines and junipers stands out vividly against the red volcanic earth, and billowing thunderheads pile high in the afternoon sky. Autumn brings the golden hues of aspen to the roadside; often, before all the brilliant leaves have fallen to the ground, heavy snows sweep down from the lofty San Francisco Peaks to cloak the land in white. Snowplows keep the road open to traffic.

Winter snowfall brings lines of skiers eager to try the runs at Fairfield Snow Bowl near Flagstaff. Chairlifts serve both gentle beginner slopes and 11,600-foot Mt. Agassiz.

Outlined in snow, lofty San Francisco Peaks, Arizona's highest, tower above Sinagua Indian ruins at Wupatki National Monument.

...Flagstaff, a Gateway City

Pioneers' Historical Museum. Located 2 miles from downtown Flagstaff on U.S. 180, this museum is housed in an old tufa rock building that's historically interesting for itself (originally it was a county hospital), as well as for the objects it contains. Antique pictures, furniture, and personal belongings of early pioneers fill two floors.

Behind the main building is an old barn with a fire engine, logging equipment, and vintage tools. A period cabin also stands on the grounds.

Two art centers. To the rear of the historical museum property is the Art Barn, a privately owned gallery that shows the work of local artists. The Art Barn is open daily year-round from 10 A.M. to 5 P.M.

Next door rises the modernistic Coconino Center for the Arts, a county-owned multi-use facility for art shows, lectures, concerts, and other performing arts events.

Museum of Northern Arizona. Flagstaff's Museum of Northern Arizona is one of the most authoritative sources on the geology, biology, and anthropology of Arizona and on Indian arts and crafts. Surrounded by a pine forest, the handsome, tile-roofed stone buildings sit back from U.S. 180 behind a timber arch on pillars of native stone. It's located a mile north of the Pioneers' Historical Museum, on the opposite side of the road.

In the museum's six galleries you'll see a variety of unusual and informative exhibits on the art, archaeology, ethnology, and natural history of the Colorado Plateau.

One award-winning anthropology exhibit, "Native Peoples of the Colorado Plateau," presents an intriguing interpretation of the prehistoric, historic, and contemporary cultures of this region. Extensive displays that include ancient tools, ceramics, Hopi pottery, kachina dolls, Navajo rugs, jewelry, and Pai basketry document 11,000 years of human occupation in the area.

Visitors can buy authentic Indian crafts in the museum shop; here you'll find one of the state's best collections of contemporary southwestern jewelry, baskets, rugs, kachina dolls, Hopi pottery, paintings, and sculpture.

In addition to permanent exhibits, the museum holds several special exhibits each year that interpret and display the works of artists and craftspeople. Two of the most popular are the Hopi and Navajo shows each July.

The museum is open from 9 A.M. to 5 P.M. daily except major holidays.

Fairfield Snow Bowl. Perched on the northwestern slopes of the rugged, volcanic San Francisco Peaks, Snow Bowl is the oldest and best-known ski area in Arizona, with about 750 acres for skiing.

Two double chairs reach both gentle beginner runs and 11,600-foot Mt. Agassiz. The mountain peaks, considered by the Indians to be the sacred home of the gods, are often capped with clouds, but on clear days, views from the top are awesome—vast snow-dusted volcanic lands visible to the Grand Canyon and beyond.

Snow Bowl is open daily during the season, usually from late November through late March.

A swing off U.S. 89

Two diverse and fascinating national monuments — Sunset Crater and Wupatki National Monument — are reached by a scenic loop off U.S. 89, northeast of Flagstaff. For the first few miles the spectacular San Francisco Peaks on the west loom above green meadows framed by dark pine forests. The turnoff eastward to Sunset Crater is about 15 miles north of Flagstaff.

Sunset Crater. The great cinder cone of the extinct volcano, named for the red and yellow hues of the rim, dominates the landscape. During a 4 to 6-month-long eruption in the winter of 1064–65 (according to tree-ring studies), it

threw out a billion tons of lava and ash over 800 square miles, totally destroying the pit houses of the Indians who lived in the area. But the volcanic ash, mulching and enriching the soil, created fertile land for planting crops that later drew Indians of four different cultures to the area.

At the visitor center (open year-round except Christmas and New Year's) 2 miles east of U.S. 89, graphic exhibits trace the history of the entire region, and seismographs record tremors all over the world. Across the road is a 44-unit, improved Forest Service campground, open from April 1 to November 15.

Wupatki National Monument. Lying about 18 miles north on the same paved road is Wupatki National Monument, which encompasses more than 800 ruins of Indian villages. The largest structure — Wupatki (Hopi for "tall house")—was more than three stories high and contained more than 100 rooms during the 12th century.

The visitor center displays the historical artifacts of the Indians who moved here to take advantage of the fertile fields resulting from the Sunset eruption. The tribes exchanged agricultural techniques, tools, and art forms. Nearby is the smaller Lomaki ruin, and 9 miles north is the Citadel, another large structure still unexcavated. Booklets about the self-guiding trails identify the ruins.

The forest lakes

To the south of Flagstaff, a chain of forest-rimmed lakes offers a variety of fishing and other recreational activities, as well as an inside look at the nearly 2 million acres of Coconino National Forest. All the lakes lie at around 7,000 feet in elevation. The fishing is best from May through September.

To reach the lakes, turn southeast from U.S. 89A onto Lake Mary Road, 3 miles south of Flagstaff.

Off Interstate 40

Many of Central Arizona's scenic attractions lie east and west of Flagstaff off Interstate 40. To the east, en route to the New Mexico border, are the tremendous Meteor Crater, the Petrified Forest and its long vistas of the Painted Desert, and turnoffs to the Mogollon Rim, White Mountains, and Navajo and Hopi reservations.

West of Flagstaff, Interstate 40 takes a similar path to that of former "Route 66" until just past Seligman. From there, the old highway swings northwest past Grand Canyon Caverns and the Hualapai Indian Reservation before turning southwest toward Kingman. Interstate 40 follows a more direct course to Kingman.

East of Flagstaff

East from Flagstaff, the highway cuts through forested land for several miles before reaching a high grassland mesa intermittently mantled with greasewood, sage, juniper, and piñon. You'll see rainbow-striped crags, cross gorges carved into the plateau by seasonal rivers, and travel through rolling range country.

Both Winslow and Holbrook have good accommodations. Campers can head south into Apache-Sitgreaves National Forest. Check at the Winslow and Holbrook chambers of commerce for more information about camping.

Walnut Canyon National Monument. The remains of more than 300 small Sinagua Indian cliff dwellings dating from the 12th century are preserved here. The Sinaguas first occupied the canyon about A.D. 1000. They applied masonry skills learned from other Pueblo Indian groups to wall up weathered limestone shelves in the canyon sides, creating a series of joined rooms. Overhanging rock protected the homes from weather, as well as from enemy attack.

To reach the monument from Flagstaff, drive east about 7 miles on Interstate 40 to the entrance road. The monument encompasses the 400-foot-deep, horseshoe-shaped canyon of now-dry Walnut Creek; a ¼-mile hiking trail takes visitors past the ruins on the sides of a steep, rocky peninsula.

From the monument's visitor center at the canyon rim, the trail drops a steep 185 feet to level out at the neck of the peninsula. From here it's an easy loop walk past about 25 cliffside rooms. You can see about a hundred more rooms notched in the opposite canyon walls. The round trip takes about 40 minutes.

Walnut Canyon is open daily; you pay a small admission fee. Picnic tables are located near the visitor center. A short rim trail leads to the canyon edge.

The Grand Falls. When the spring runoff from the Mogollon Plateau snowpack keeps streams flowing full, a detour off Interstate 40 will bring you to one of the most surprising sights in the high desert — the roaring, plunging, 185-foot Grand Falls of the Little Colorado River.

Meteor Crater has excited the interest of scientists and travelers from all over the world.

The falls are seasonal and sometimes in dry years never reach impressive size. Normally, though, they run during the winter and the spring thaw, dry up in May, then flow again during the summer rains in July and August. It's a good idea to inquire at Flagstaff or Winslow about the level of the Little Colorado before you make the trip.

To reach the falls, turn off Interstate 40 either at Winona, 17 miles east of Flagstaff, or at the Leupp junction, 10 miles west of Winslow. For either route, inquire at the turnoff for exact directions. The Winona route is the shortest from the highway (about 20 miles); the last 8 miles are unpaved.

Meteor Crater. Almost a mile across, 3 miles around the top, and 570 feet deep, Meteor Crater has excited the interest of scientists and travelers from all over the world.

Scientists generally agree that the crater was formed about 50,000 years ago when a 60,000-ton meteoric mass of iron and nickel struck the earth. It disintegrated on impact and splashed nearly half a billion tons of rock over the surrounding surface.

The rim of the crater rises 150 feet or more above the plain and is visible for miles as a white scar against the desert. American astronauts came here to study crater geology and to rehearse "moon-walk" sampling procedures.

Energetic visitors can take the steep, rocky trail down into the crater, where they can examine old mining equipment. When the weather is hot, it's best to forego this hike — there's no breeze at the bottom of the crater, and it catches the full heat of the sun.

A longer hike, but a much easier one, is the trail around the rim. It affords many excellent views and passes an abandoned camp where glass sand was once mined from underlying sandstone.

Excellent exhibits in the modern, air-conditioned museum on the north rim explain the formation of the crater; large fragments on display attract many visitors. Recorded narrations both in the museum and at adjacent overlooks answer many questions.

The crater and museum, the snack bar, and the gift shop, which sells good Indian jewelry, are open daily.

To reach the crater, drive east from Flagstaff on Interstate 40 about 37 miles; a paved road heads south 5 miles to the crater site.

Navajo and Hopi lands. The Navajo and Hopi Indian reservations (see pages 26–41) are only a few miles north

These trees in Petrified Forest National Park fell 200 million years ago. Frozen in time, they're preserved by silica and beautifully dyed by iron oxide and magnesium.

as you drive Interstate 40 between Winslow and Gallup; Navajo lands flank the highway on both sides as you approach the New Mexico border.

Routes providing access to the reservations head north from or near Winona, Leupp Corner, Winslow, Holbrook, Chambers, Houck, and Lupton. Most of these roads are paved.

Petrified Forest National Park. What is probably the world's largest and most colorful collection of petrified wood is on view in Petrified Forest National Park. Other attractions include cross-sections of ancient mineralized trees infused with agate, jasper, and other semiprecious stones, ruins of Indian villages, petroglyphs, and overlooks of the Painted Desert.

The park is arranged in two sections to the north and south of Interstate 40, connected by a narrow corridor. Twenty-seven miles of paved road run through the park between Interstate 40 and U.S. 180. At each end are a visitor center and a restaurant; there's a gas station at the north entrance. At either end you can pick up a guidebook and map. At the Painted Desert Visitor Center (north end), a 17-minute film shows how wood becomes petrified.

Open year-round during daylight hours, the park charges a small admission fee. Visitors are asked to help preserve the park for future generations by not disturbing any natural features, especially petrified wood.

The Painted Desert stretches across the northern section of the national park, entered off Interstate 40 about 25 miles northeast of Holbrook. From here, north of the highway, a winding road following the rim of the Painted Desert allows for both close-up examination of the multicolored layers of sand and distant views toward the northwest. Pause for a picnic by the side of the road for a long look at the sunset. The Painted Desert Inn Museum at Kachina Point (open in summer) contains cultural history exhibits.

Conditions on the Painted Desert are excellent for cross-country hikes, especially in autumn. Rangers at the visitor centers can provide suggestions and issue overnight permits.

To the south, about 11 miles from the north entrance in the narrow corridor separating the two sections, lie the Puerco Indian Ruins. Low stone walls outline the prehistoric Indian pueblo village. A few rooms are excavated and partially restored. Nearby is Newspaper Rock, covered with scratched petroglyphs—a message center of the ancients. You climb down 120 steps to reach the huge sandstone block.

Farther south are the Tepees, small conical peaks shaped by erosion, and Blue Mesa, where erosion has left petrified logs on pinnacles of sandstone.

Another 2 miles brings you to Agate Bridge, a log more than 100 feet long with a 40-foot wash beneath it, and the Jasper Forest overlook, from which you'll see masses of mineralized logs littering the valley floor. Beyond are Crystal Forest and The Flattops area.

The main petrified wood exhibits are near the southern visitor center in the Rainbow Forest area. Here are the Giant Logs, a museum whose displays explain how the fallen trees became preserved as stone, and a picnic area. The southern entrance is off U.S. 180 about 18 miles southeast of Holbrook.

Flagstaff to Kingman

The countryside changes dramatically as you head west. Pine-studded forests give way to upland desert as the elevation drops some 3,600 feet.

Both Interstate 40 and State 66 are busy routes offering several places to turn off for gas or a bite to eat. It's 143 miles from Flagstaff to Kingman on the interstate; detouring on the more scenic State 66 adds another 20 miles.

Grand Canyon Deer Farm. About 25 miles west of Flagstaff is Grand Canyon Deer Farm, a good place to stop if you're traveling with children. Walk among several types of deer, touch them, and let them eat from your hand. If you're there in June and July, you'll be in time for the fawns.

In addition to deer, you'll encounter pygmy goats, llamas, miniature donkeys, peacocks, and other animals.

The deer farm is open daily from May to September; it's closed on Monday and Tuesday in early spring and autumn, and closes for the winter on Thanksgiving. There's a moderate admission fee.

Williams, a mountain town. Located at the road junction offering the shortest route from Interstate 40 to Grand Canyon Village, Williams is a popular stopover for tourists headed for the canyon. This friendly town caters to the needs of travelers and offers dining and accommodations. A few miles from town you'll find Forest Service campgrounds at Cataract, Kaibab, and Dogtown lakes.

Probably the world's largest and most colorful collection of petrified wood is on view.

For some of the best views of the countryside, drive to the summit of Bill Williams Mountain, 4 miles south of Williams.

The winters, though moderate, bring enough snow to turn the mountain into a winter sports area suitable for both beginning and intermediate skiers. A 1,500-foot Poma lift (450-foot vertical rise) and a 700-foot rope tow operate on weekends and holidays. Skiers will find a lodge, ski rentals, and a snack bar.

White Horse Lake. Eighteen miles southeast of Williams, White Horse

Lake is tucked away in the Ponderosa pine country of Kaibab National Forest. Each spring the Arizona Game and Fish Department stocks the lake with several thousand legal-size rainbow trout. The Forest Service maintains campsites with tables, fireplaces, and some trailer spaces (stays are limited to 14 days). At lakeside are housekeeping cabins, a small store selling groceries and fishing tackle, and rowboats and paddleboats for rent.

To reach White Horse Lake from Williams, follow the paved Perkinsville Road (Fourth Street) south for 8 miles to a marked intersection; turn left and continue another 10 miles to the lake.

Sycamore Canyon. Seventeen miles long and as deep as 2,000 feet, this rugged gorge roughly parallels Oak Creek Canyon, which it resembles topographically. But the resemblance ends there, for Sycamore Canyon is the heart of a 47,762-acre wilderness area reserved for hikers and horseback riders.

To reach an overlook on the rim, follow a very rough dirt road, normally passable in a passenger car in dry weather, from the White Horse Lake road; the marked turnoff is 16 miles from Williams, 2 miles short of the lake. From the rim you'll see the sycamore-shaded creek channel bordered by a maze of eroded red sandstone, white limestone, and dark brown lava.

For information on hiking trails, ask at the ranger stations at Williams or Sedona, or write to the Supervisors of Coconino National Forest, 114 N. San Francisco Street, Flagstaff, AZ 86001; the Kaibab National Forest, 800 S. 6th Street, Williams, AZ 86046; or the Prescott National Forest, 344 South Cortez, Prescott, AZ 86301. All three national forests border the area.

Grand Canyon Caverns. Twelve miles east of Peach Springs on State 66, Grand Canyon Caverns offers a cool stopping place for summertime travelers.

On the 45-minute tour you'll see caves in the early stages of stalactite-stalagmite formation, even though they've been developing for more than 300 million years. The water that created them drained away long ago as the Colorado River cut below their level deeper into nearby Grand Canyon.

The caverns are open daily (closed Christmas Day), and 45-minute tours are conducted throughout the day. There's a small fee. A motel at the highway entrance has a restaurant, lounge, and gift shop. Picnicking and camping facilities are nearby.

Hualapai Indian Reservation. Peach Springs, in the juniper hills 50 miles east of Kingman, is the headquarters and trading center for the Hualapai Indians, whose reservation spreads over almost a million acres along some 110 miles of the Colorado River's south bank. The tribe numbers about 1,400; close to half live on the reservation. The Indians welcome hunters but require tribal permits and compliance with state game laws.

Grand Canyon Caverns offers a cool stopping place for summertime travelers.

For a small fee you can visit the reservation; an additional small fee allows you to camp anywhere on it, but there are no improved campsites. You'll find water year-round at Fraziers Well, 25 miles northeast of Peach Springs on a graded road 8,000 feet high in a pine forest. Elsewhere, carry your own water and be prepared for unimproved and unmapped roads.

About 25 miles north of Peach Springs on another gravel road is Diamond Creek, the first access to the Colorado River below Phantom Ranch. River runners touch shore here to pick up supplies. The scenic road is adequate for cars and pickups, except after a heavy rain.

For information on visiting the reservation and for hunting arrangements, write to Hualapai Wildlife and Outdoor Recreation, Box 216, Peach Springs, AZ 86434.

Hualapai Mountain Park. The upland forest of Hualapai Mountain Park near Kingman surrounds one of the highest peaks in western Arizona. It offers a respite from highway driving and a cool place for a picnic or for camping.

The road to the park starts 1½ miles east of the junction of U.S. 93 and State 66. In the half-hour, 14-mile drive, you go from desert to mountain pines.

Set among the trees in the park are picnic tables, grills, campsites, and water faucets. You'll find furnished cabins for rent; bring your own bedding and cooking utensils.

A mile beyond the park, Hualapai Lodge offers meals and overnight accommodations.

Kingman's connections

Kingman, the seat of Mohave County, has become the principal stopover point in this part of Arizona because of its location at the junction of Interstate 40, State 66, and U.S. 93.

Both the Kingman Area Chamber of Commerce (open daily) and the Mohave Museum of History & Arts (open weekdays and weekend afternoons) are located at the junction of the highways. The Chamber of Commerce provides information about points of interest in Mohave County and can help visitors plan area side trips. Among other exhibits, the museum displays a collection of carved turquoise mined in the Kingman area and a life-size Hualapai wickiup. The museum gallery sells local artwork.

South to Verde Valley

Less than an hour south of Flagstaff on U.S. 89A is one of the best-known landmarks in Arizona, much-photographed Oak Creek Canyon. Situated at its southern end — and surrounded by the canyon's red rock walls—is the picture-postcard town of Sedona.

From its source in the back country of north-central Yavapai County, the Verde River winds east and south for almost 130 miles until it joins the Salt River near Phoenix.

In the middle reaches of its course, the river crosses a broad basin of rolling range, roughly 25 by 40 miles, bounded by the metallic Black Hills on the southwest and west, the tinted walls of the Mogollon Rim on the north and east, and Hackberry Mountain and the Mazatzals on the southeast. This irregular basin, south of Sedona, is known as Verde Valley.

The cycles of time have left a graphic record here: pueblos built by pre-historic Indians, barracks that once sheltered frontier cavalries, abandoned sites of modern industry, and an interesting former ghost town, now lively again.

Getting there. Two routes from Interstate 40 approach this most attractive area from the west and east: U.S. 89 south from Ash Fork and Interstate 17 south from Flagstaff. The most scenic route of all, U.S. 89A, originates in Flagstaff and heads diagonally southwestward to meet U.S. 89 north of Prescott.

This route, which passes through Sedona in dramatic Oak Creek Canyon, takes motorists into the bottom of the valley, across the river at Cottonwood, and up the slope of Mingus Mountain through the new bustle of historic, hillside Jerome. Along the way you can visit the prehistoric Indian pueblo of Tuzigoot.

Lodging. You'll find modern accommodations in the larger communities (principally at Cottonwood and Camp Verde) and at outlying resorts. Infor-mation is available from the Verde Valley Chamber of Commerce, 1010 S. Main Street, Cottonwood, AZ 86326.

Oak Creek Canyon

Though U.S. 89A enters the northern end of the canyon just a few miles from Flagstaff, switching down the steep, forested canyon wall below a series of fine overlooks, the recommended approach to Oak Creek Canyon is from the south. It is from there that you experience the full impact of the huge red rock formations that have made this area second only to Grand Canyon as a state scenic attraction. Traveling through the canyon in autumn when the poplar and sycamore trees blaze with color is particularly spectacular.

Getting there. For the most dramatic approach, follow State 179, which turns north toward Sedona from Interstate 17 about 45 miles south of Flagstaff. The sweeping curves of the road cut through sagebrush country brightened with sycamore-lined washes. The earth itself begins to change color, from white to orange to red. Within 6 or 7 miles, you glimpse the erosion-carved buttes ahead. Finally, a curve in the road brings you your first full view of the canyon's brilliant temples and cliffs, always startling when seen for the first time in this spacious setting.

Canyon attractions. The famous multi-spired Cathedral Rock (reproduced on wall calendars all over the world), Bell Rock, and several other eroded, color-fully named giants are situated in the open end of the canyon south of Sedona. Others surround the town itself, forming a vivid backdrop from any angle.

Turn on Chapel Road to view the Chapel of the Holy Cross, an architecturally striking structure perched among the jagged cliffs. It took nearly 20 years to complete the design and construction.

North of town, the canyon rises, narrows, and gradually changes character, becoming cool and densely wooded. Vertical rock walls give way to steep slopes of dark pine forest. Here and there a bare cliff face appears.

In this upper canyon are five improved Forest Service campgrounds (open Memorial Day to Labor Day and almost always fully occupied) and many commercial resorts, lodges, trailer parks, and cabins, many of which are closed in winter. A favorite summer cooling-off place, this section of the canyon offers many swimming holes along the creek, as well as good trout fishing.

Numerous drives and hiking trails wind through the area, particularly in the southern end of the canyon. The popular Schnebley Hill Road (unpaved) climbs eastward from Sedona and ends at Interstate 17, rewarding visitors with excellent views of the big rocks to the southwest. Not recommended for passenger cars, the road is often included on itineraries of four-wheel-drive sightseeing tours.

Pretty, popular Sedona

Sedona reflects an entire community's effort to incorporate and combine the best of frontier styles and contemporary materials while rejecting neon and plastic disfigurations. In this setting of eroded red rock mesas and pillars towering behind every store front and residence, the town does its best not to insult nature even though it plays host annually to some 2 million Arizona residents and out-of-state tourists who flock here year-round.

The town's businesses include art galleries, crafts shops, Indian art stores (look in Garland's for one of the largest collections of Navajo rugs outside the reservation), and antique shops. A number of restaurants, motels, rental cabins, and trailer parks located in and around town cater to tourists. Several large motels at the southern end of town afford excellent views across Oak Creek.

You'll find the largest concentration of shops in the Tlaquepaque Arts and Crafts Village on State 179. Named for a suburb of Guadalajara, Mexico, the collection is housed in a replica of a Mexican village complete with courtyards, fountains, and a belltower that is a Sedona landmark.

For information on accommodations and recreation activities, write to the Sedona-Oak Creek Canyon Chamber of Commerce, P.O. Box 478, Sedona, AZ 86336.

Tuzigoot National Monument

Tuzigoot (Apache for "crooked water") is a major prehistoric Indian ruin on a ridge 2 miles east of Clarkdale. Built during the 12th century, the 110-room pueblo housed Indians who moved here when a severe drought dried up their distant farmlands. Abandoned in the early 15th century, the pueblo fell into ruin and was almost obscured until the 1930s, when it was completely excavated by University of Arizona archeologists.

Exhibits in the monument's museum include a variety of grave offerings — turquoise mosaics, beads, bracelets of shells obtained by barter with Indians near the Gulf of California, and decorated pottery.

A trail walk takes you around this ridge-resting pueblo with its commanding valley views. Tuzigoot is open daily; there's a small admission fee to visit.

The ups & downs of Jerome

The former copper-mining center of Jerome, called by its boosters "America's Largest Ghost City", sits on the slope of Cleopatra Hill just up Woodchute Mountain, in one of the ranges bordering Verde Valley on the west.

From its peak in the 1920s, when its population hit 15,000, the boom town gradually dwindled to a ghost town as high-grade ore deposits dwindled. When the last mines closed in 1953, some of the town's die-hards formed the Jerome Historical Society and began to call attention to the town's history, quaint appearance, and tourist appeal. Today, residents number about 500 and tourists total over a million yearly.

The serpentine streets on the steep slope are lined with a casual mixture of sagging ghost-town hulks and rebuilt or newly built residences; those on the downhill side are supported by stilts. From anywhere in town you'll get an incomparable view across Verde Valley to the cliffs of the Mogollon Rim and the red rock of Oak Creek Canyon.

Artists, of course, love the area, and many have settled here. Beckoning tourists are art galleries, a number of antique and crafts stores, an outlet for one of Arizona's top clothing designers, restaurants, and a bed and breakfast inn.

The Jerome State Historic Park Museum, occupying a former mine owner's mansion, displays mining machinery and a fascinating three-dimensional model of the maze of mine shafts that riddles the ground beneath the town.

Camp Verde

Just 2 miles east of Interstate 17 about 41 miles south of Flagstaff is the town of Camp Verde. Near the center of town is 10-acre Fort Verde State Historic Park, which commemorates the garrison that served as a base of operations against the Apaches until 1885. Four of the original twenty buildings remain; all have been restored and refurnished.

The visitor center displays relics of the post. You can tour the Commanding Officer's house, Bachelor Officers' Quarters, and post doctor's home.

The old fort is open to visitors daily April through October (closed Tuesday and Wednesday the rest of the year); there's a small admission fee. A picnic spot lies nearby.

Montezuma Castle & Well

Not really a castle at all, the famous ruin in Montezuma Castle National Monument is one of the most impressive of all the prehistoric cliff dwellings. To reach the monument, take Montezuma Castle Road north from Camp Verde for 5 miles.

The Castle. Part of the dramatic impact of this apartment house is due to its sudden appearance, high on the cliff, as you walk along a path from the monument's handsome visitor center. The advantage held by the ancient Sinagua defenders is obvious.

Visitors are no longer permitted to enter the well-preserved structure, but signs and exhibits, including a cutaway model, explain the prehistoric settlement. The Sycamore Trail walk takes only a few minutes; a pamphlet at the site describes what you're seeing.

Plan to spend some time in the visitor center, where you'll find excellent archeological and natural history displays.

The Well. Within a detached area of the Montezuma Castle National Monument, 7 miles northeast of the castle, is another surprise — a limestone sink creating a small lake (470 feet across, 55 feet deep), fringed with large trees.

The calm, mysterious surface of Montezuma Well gives no hint that it's contributing 1½ million gallons of water a day to adjacent Beaver Creek and the area's irrigated farms.

The Indians who lived here centuries ago engineered an irrigation system to divert the water to their fields; you can still see sections of the ditches. Ruins of their houses are visible along the trails (be alert for rattlesnakes).

Drive back to Interstate 17 and travel north on the highway for about 2½ miles to reach a roadside rest area marked by an observation tower. Picnic ramadas and rest rooms make this a good picnicking site, and the top of the tower commands a memorable panorama of the Verde country.

Until Jerome's recent rebirth, the figures on this mannequin's shirt accurately reflected the population's rise and fall. Today, residents number around 500.

Three would be a crowd in second-story dining perch at Tlaquepaque shopping center in Sedona. This Mexican village replica houses an array of restaurants and arts and crafts shops.

Light snow dusts old buildings on Cleopatra Hill, site of former copper-mining center of Jerome.

Though their settings differ dramatically, both Prescott and Wickenburg retain much of the state's frontier feeling. Prescott is a mountain town whose site was chosen in 1864 by the men President Lincoln sent west to organize a government for the new Territory of Arizona. Governor John Goodwin picked a spot at the edge of a vast pine forest that has a seasonal climate its residents have considered ideal ever since.

In the lower desert 60 miles to the south, Wickenburg claims almost year-long sunshine, averaging 292 sunny days. Sun-soaked days, clear, crisp evenings, and temperatures ranging from 45° to 85° make this a favorite vacation spot from November to May.

Prescott & vicinity

From its beginnings, Prescott has been a center of mining and cattle ranching. Appropriately, it claims to be the birthplace of the distinctively American sport of rodeo. The community traces its annual Fourth of July Frontier Days celebration back to 1888, but there's evidence of an even earlier rodeo here—a silver buckle engraved "Prescott July 4th 1886, Best Time 59½ Sec."

Prescott lies on U.S. 89 about midway between Ash Fork (Interstate 40) and Wickenburg. From Interstate 17, head west on State 69 or 169. On State 69 you'll pass through the charming old stage stop town of Mayer.

For information on points of interest, contact the Chamber of Commerce (117 W. Goodwin), Box 1147, Prescott, AZ 86302.

The Plaza. Dominating the broad walk on the north side of the Yavapai County Courthouse is a dynamic equestrian statue, a memorial to the Rough Riders. It portrays Captain William (Bucky) O'Neill, former Prescott mayor and sheriff who was killed in action in Cuba in 1898. The bronze sculpture is the work of Solong Borglum, brother of Gutzon of Mount Rushmore fame.

Of the business blocks that face the plaza, one is more famous than the rest — part of Montezuma Street, better known as Whiskey Row. Opposite the southeast corner of the plaza is the modern city hall.

The Chamber of Commerce is opposite the southwest corner of the big courthouse on Goodwin Street, around the corner from U.S. 89 (Montezuma Street).

Sharlot Hall Museum. Several structures typical of Prescott a century ago stand three blocks west on Gurley Street. Buildings in the Sharlot Hall Museum complex include the first Governor's Mansion, containing period furniture and relics of pioneer days; the first boarding house in town, known as Fort Misery; a reconstruction of the first schoolhouse; Bashford House, an 1878 Victorian that today provides gallery space for Prescott's Mountain Artists Guild; and the John C. Fremont House, furnished in period antiques.

A modern, solar-heated museum center houses historical photos and documents, Indian arts and crafts displays, and other mementos of early Prescott. The complex is open weekdays (except Monday) and Sunday afternoons; admission is free.

Smoki Museum. Across town at Willis Street and Arizona Avenue, the Smoki people display a fine collection of Indian objects — prehistoric, historic, and contemporary. The museum is open from June to Labor Day on weekdays (except Monday) and Sunday afternoon. A small donation is requested.

The Smoki are a cross-section of Prescott business and professional people whose organization grew out of a lighthearted parody of Indian Snake Dances at a community celebration in 1921. The society that resulted has studied and perpetuated the songs, legends, and ceremonies of American Indian tribes for more than half a century.

Each year in August, the group presents a unique pageant of Indian songs and dances, culminating in the spectacular Smoki Snake Dance, based on the famous Rain Dance of the Hopis. Some Indians have resented the Smoki reenactment of their religious rituals; others have cooperated and assisted, as have anthropologists and archeologists.

Fort Whipple. Less than a mile east of town on U.S. 89 stands one of Arizona's historic Army posts, now a Veterans Administration hospital. Fort Whipple, originally located a few miles away, was established on this site in May, 1864. From 1869 to 1886, the final years of the Apache campaigns, it was headquarters for the Military Department of Arizona. You are welcome to drive or walk around the tree-shaded grounds.

Granite Dells. Near the junction of U.S. 89 and 89A, about 5 miles north of Prescott, the Granite Dells area is a pleasant stopping place for tourists and a picnic and recreation spot for local residents. Upthrust rocks create a maze of small hideaways and rim two small lakes stocked with warm-water game fish. The size of the lakes fluctuates with the seasons, since they are irrigation reservoirs. Off U.S. 89A, follow a dirt road to a tree-shaded creek and picnic spots. There are camping areas north of Watson Lake.

The evergreen forests ringing Granite Dells on three sides offer many outdoor recreation areas, quiet retreats, and excellent camping. Granite Basin Lake is a warm-water fishing lake 10 miles northwest of Prescott on a year-round dirt road off the Iron Springs road. Lynx Lake, 7 miles east of town on Walker Road off State 69, and Goldwater Lake, 4½ miles from downtown on the Senator Highway, are stocked with bluegill, trout, and crappies. All have improved Forest Service campgrounds nearby. You'll find larger campgrounds among the pines off U.S. 89 about 3 miles south of town.

Out Wickenburg way

Year-round residents of Wickenburg number around 3,800, but the town swells to almost double that size in winter when the "snow birds" arrive. Lying along the Hassayampa River at an altitude of 2,093 feet, this town still retains Old West flavor in the false-fronted buildings, overhanging roofs, and hitching posts of Frontier Street. At the Wickenburg Gallery on the highway, you'll see a fine stable of Western art. In the center of town the old "jail tree," where lawmen chained prisoners, still stands.

The town was named for Henry Wickenburg, who, according to one legend, threw a rock at his burro in 1863. Since the rock was heavy with gold, it fell short of its mark—and thus was the Vulture Mine discovered. During the two decades after its discovery, the mine turned out 30 million dollars in gold.

Accommodations in the Wickenburg area are many and varied. For information, write to the Roundup Club (Wickenburg's version of a Chamber of Commerce), P.O. Drawer CC, Wickenburg, AZ 85358. The Roundup Club also makes available a "Stay-A-Day" packet of information on the points of interest and visitor activities.

A fine Western museum. Don't miss The Desert Caballeros Western Museum at 20 N. Frontier Street, next to the underpass. Two levels of displays depict Wickenburg's history.

On the street level, talking dioramas augmented by historical displays tell the area's story from geological times to the present. Period rooms show what life was like in a thriving mining community. The Western Art Gallery contains fine paintings, sculpture, and bronzes by such nationally known artists as Remington and Russell.

Downstairs, you walk through a re-creation of an early street scene, visit an extensive mineral display, and tour the Indian room where crafts range from prehistoric to contemporary.

The museum is open Tuesday through Saturday from 10 A.M. to 4 P.M. and Sunday afternoon. Admission is charged.

Guest ranch capital. Wickenburg was once the gold capital of Arizona, but now its residents call it the dude ranch capital of the world. Some of the spreads are big, working cattle ranches. Guests might be encouraged to join such activities as roundups and branding, but they'll definitely participate in one of the frequent "dudeos" in season.

Ranch activities include swimming, tennis, trap shooting, golf, and—by far the most popular of all — horseback riding. The riding terrain is wide-open country: cholla-studded mesas; tawny, tumbled hills ornamented with the tall arms of saguaro cactus; and purple-tinted mountains. Guest ranches offer guided breakfast rides, chuck wagon picnics along the lazing Hassayampa River, and overnight pack trips up rocky canyon trails.

Some special events. Once a year, generally the second weekend in February, tourists from far and wide descend on Wickenburg for its rambunctious Gold Rush Days. The Gold Shirt Gang captures the town on Friday and raises its outlaw flag over the city hall, officially starting three days of activity — parades, dances, rodeos, gold panning, gem show, arts and crafts exhibits, carnival, and melodrama.

On the second weekend in November, musicians from far and wide gather for the Four Corner States Bluegrass Festival. Contestants from all over the country vie for cash prizes, delighting onlookers with their music.

The Joshua forest. One of the West's best concentrations of Joshua trees (*Yucca brevifolia*) stands along Joshua Tree Parkway on U.S. 93. You enter the state reserve 22 miles northwest of Wickenburg and continue for 16 miles through a forest of trees.

Beginning as early as the end of February and often continuing through the first weeks of April, you can see the trees in bloom; large clusters of pale greenish white flowers adorn their branch tips. U.S. 93 is apt to be busy with traffic, but a sheltered roadside rest and numerous broad turnouts along the parkway invite you to stop and enjoy the blossom display.

A sampling of ghosts. West of Wickenburg, U.S. 89 heads north 10 miles to the small settlement of Congress, then turns northeast to wind over the mountains into the Prescott National Forest and into the mid-forest city of Prescott.

Although Congress is an active roadside community and not a true ghost town, you'll find some ruined slabs and foundations on a hill to the north. A dirt road turning south from the highway 2 miles northeast of Congress leads to sites of old mining developments.

> In the center of town the old "jail tree," where lawmen chained prisoners, still stands.

Stanton, 6 miles from the highway in a rocky canyon, grew up around the Antelope Station stage stop established there in 1875 and subsequently took the name of a promoter who developed some notoriety. At one time it included a stamp mill.

The Octave Mine on the east side of Rich Hill, reached by another dirt road, was active from 1900 to 1942. Some stone walls and foundations mark the sites of former buildings, and you'll see heaps of mine tailings.

Valley of the Sun

Ultramodern sculpture and bubbling fountains enhance the Phoenix Civic Plaza. In the surrounding high-rise hotels and office buildings are some of the city's best restaurants.

Why here, of all places? What is this vigorous, metropolitan complex, the biggest inland city in the Pacific Southwest and the ninth largest city in the country, doing here in the middle of a desert? It's the water that makes the difference.

Emerging from the Superstition and Mazatzal Mountains east of the city, the Salt River joins the Verde River waters from the Coconino and Mogollon plateaus and winds westward across this desert to join the Gila River a few miles west. Phoenix was born on this river, grew astride it—and is still growing.

Today Phoenix is a commercial and manufacturing center, but it started out as a farm town living on that water. The lower Salt River Valley—more picturesquely named Valley of the Sun—is still one of the richest agricultural sites in the Southwest.

In the terminal building at Sky Harbor Airport, you'll also see a dramatic mural depicting that mythical bird, the phoenix, which rose from its own ashes—as this city of Phoenix has risen on the ruins of the ancient civilization of the vanished Hohokam.

Arizona's top resort

Picture yourself swimming in one of the valley's 50,000 pools, riding one of its 15,000 horses, driving or putting on one of 83 manicured golf courses, or serving on one of the 1,000 tennis courts. Add to this 300 sun-filled days a year and an average temperature of 72°, and you'll discover why the sum of these numbers makes the Phoenix area a top resort destination.

Phoenix and the Valley of the Sun attract visitors from all over the country. Many of them decide to move here; more than 1½ million people now reside in the 400-square-mile valley. To a visitor, no definite distinction exists between Phoenix and its neighboring communities. As with any major city, you can drive into satellite cities — Scottsdale, Paradise Valley, Mesa, Tempe, and others — without being aware you have left the Phoenix city limits. Attractions are sprinkled throughout much of the suburban area.

When to visit

Though fine weather arrives in the Valley of the Sun about October and lasts into May, traditionally the heavy influx of visitors comes after Christmas and stays until Easter. This means that the early and late portions of the season may offer lower rates and less crowded accommodations.

During the summer, Phoenix is hot (though, mercifully, the humidity is low). Yet so universal has air conditioning become in the valley that publicists advertise Phoenix as the "year-round vacation capital" with some justification.

Along the Tonto Rim

In the summer Phoenicians escape to the high country of the Mogollon Rim (see page 76). Here in Zane Grey territory, you'll find forested campgrounds, quiet lakes and gurgling streams, and some old-time festivals.

The Essentials

A wealth of outdoor activities enlivens the Valley of the Sun during the day. After a day of golf, tennis, swimming, or shopping, many visitors enjoy a gourmet meal in one of the valley's famed restaurants and retire early. Others prefer to remain outside when the sun goes down — taking a moonlight trail ride, dining beside a softly lighted pool, or listening to the music at a western barbecue.

Whatever your fancy, Phoenix can provide the setting. Your choices are limited only by your budget.

Getting around

Phoenix is Arizona's hub. Flights from all over the country land at Sky Harbor Airport. From there, commuter service is available to most other Arizona destinations. The region is also served by Amtrak and by Greyhound and Trailways buses.

All major and local car rental agencies can be found at the airport. From Sky Harbor, an airport shuttle service takes passengers to points in the metropolitan area. Limousine and taxi service is also available.

For information on tours of Phoenix and other parts of the state, arriving passengers can check at the Visitor Information Center at terminals 2 and 3.

Where to stay

With a reasonable amount of advance planning, you should not have difficulty getting reservations, even for a visit at the height of the season. Accommodations are plentiful, and more hotels are being built each year.

For information. The Phoenix & Valley of the Sun Convention & Visitors Bureau (4455 E. Camelback Road, Suite D-146, Phoenix, AZ 85018) operates a toll-free Valley Reservation Service for more than 100 hotels, inns, and resorts in the Phoenix-Scottsdale area. Visitors also can use this service to make reservations for car rentals, apartments and condominiums, bus and air tours, and accommodations and mule rides in the Grand Canyon area.

Outside the state, visitors should call (800) 528-0483; from within Arizona, call (800) 221-5596.

You can also pick up brochures on accommodations, restaurants, golf courses, and attractions at bureau offices at Sky Harbor Airport, at the corner of Adams and Second streets in downtown Phoenix, and at Camelback Plaza shopping mall.

Accommodations. According to one recent survey, four of the 10 premier resorts in the United States are located in and around Phoenix: the Arizona Biltmore, Marriott's Camelback Inn, The Pointe, and the Wigwam.

Other accommodations range from luxurious to comfortably affordable. Almost all have at least one pool. Most of the major hotel chains are represented, along with numerous single-hotel properties. The largest number of hotels is found in the Phoenix-Scottsdale region, but you'll discover others throughout the metropolitan area.

Among some of the well-known names are The Boulders (Carefree), The Clarion Inn at McCormick Ranch, Stouffer's Cottonwoods (villas with hot tubs), Doubletree, Hotel Westcourt, Hyatt Regency, Red Lion's La Posada, Loew's Paradise Valley, Phoenix Hilton, Mountain Shadows, Radisson Scottsdale, The Registry, Sheraton Scottsdale, and SunBurst resorts.

What to do

Phoenix and surrounding countryside present countless recreational opportunities. Your best view of the region might come from jeep rides around Scottsdale and Carefree, hot-air ballooning over the city, or flightseeing en route to the Grand Canyon.

The Phoenix Parks and Recreation Department, the Maricopa County Parks and Recreation Department, and various valley communities offer activities for residents and visitors of all ages. Excellent nature walks, for example, are sponsored by the county.

Horseback riding. Regional parks and other open countryside areas provide the best opportunities to confront the desert on horseback. The banks of all 130 miles of the Salt River Project canals (closed to private vehicles and motorcycles) are open to horseback riders. A bridle path, pleasantly shaded by a canopy of arching trees, parallels North Central Avenue for several miles north of Bethany Home Road.

In winter, the Maricopa County Parks and Recreation Department sponsors monthly trail rides in regional parks. For addresses of rental stables, see the Yellow Pages under "Stables." Many resorts maintain their own stables.

Golf and tennis. For those in search of a "dogleg to the right," the Phoenix area abounds in choices. The terrain is marked with the rolling fairways of 83 golf courses.

You'll find tennis courts at resorts, clubs, parks, playgrounds, and schools. John Gardiner's Tennis Ranch (private club and resort) offers tennis clinics on 24 courts.

Boating and water-skiing. Manmade lakes provide many excellent sites for these popular water activities. You can rent boats and motors at Lake Pleasant (lower lake is closed to motors) and at all four Salt River lakes (see page 83). Saguaro Lake, the closest, is reached from State 87.

Fishing. Phoenix lakes yield bass, bluegill, channel catfish, and crappie. The canals, too, often reward the patient angler. Licenses are sold at sporting goods stores.

Hiking and camping. With a good pair of walking shoes, some drinking water, and a hat, you can take advantage of many miles of hiking trails. The banks

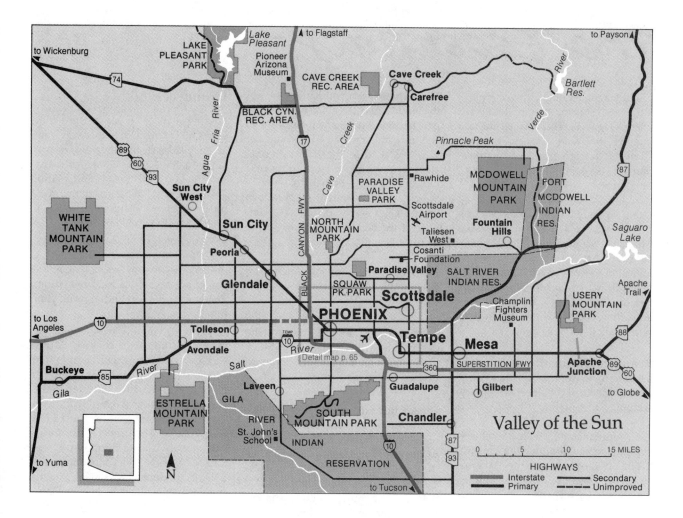

Valley of the Sun

HIGHWAYS
Interstate — Secondary
Primary — Unimproved

of the Salt River Project irrigation canals offer good hiking. Or acquaint yourself with the life of the desert while camping in one of Maricopa County's regional parks or in the Tonto National Forest.

A list of Forest Service recreational facilities is available from the Tonto National Forest, 102 S. 28th Street, Phoenix, AZ 85038.

Bicycle trips. In Phoenix and the adjacent desert, the Arizona Bicycle Club (4838 S. Second Street, Phoenix, AZ 85040) organizes weekend rides. Beginners take relatively short jaunts along the canals; intermediate cyclists might ride out to Taliesin West, and practiced bikers go on expeditions as far as Tucson.

Through the center of residential Scottsdale runs a dip in the landscape that's both a verdant chain of parks and lakes and an innovative project to tame summer flooding. Bikers, joggers,

roller-skaters, and walkers explore the 8-mile, paved, traffic-free path during the day or in cooler evening hours — the path is lighted all night.

The best starting point is the Indian School Park visitor center at 4201 N. Hayden Road, open from 8 A.M. to 5 P.M. Monday through Friday. You'll find bike-path maps and a large model of Indian Bend Wash to help you plan your route. Bikes (and skates) can be rented at several locations in Scottsdale; check the Yellow Pages of the telephone book.

Surfing. At Big Surf, in the middle of the desert, the surf's up — and you don't have to worry about the tides. You ride rolling breakers, up to five feet high, created on a large freshwater lagoon by a hydraulic wave maker. The waves roll onto a palm-dotted, 4-acre, sandy beach.

For hours and admission prices, write Big Surf (open March through

September), P.O. Box 320, 1500 N. Hayden Road, Tempe, AZ 85281, or call (602) 947-2478.

Ice skating. If warm temperatures start to bother you, give your air conditioner a rest and head for one of the area's ice skating rinks: Ice Palace East, 3853 E. Thomas Road; Ice Capades Chalet at Metrocenter, west of Black Canyon Freeway; or Oceanside Ice Arena, 1500 N. Hayden Road, Tempe.

For the spectator

Since the valley is alive with activity from fall to spring, the following is only a sampling of what's available. For a more complete listing and specific dates, contact the Phoenix & Valley of the Sun Convention & Visitors Bureau (address on page 60). For a 2-minute recorded message about current events in the metropolitan area, phone (602) 840-4636.

...The Essentials

Major league baseball. The valley has long been a spring training locale for major league baseball teams, including, in recent years, the San Francisco Giants, Chicago Cubs, Milwaukee Brewers, Oakland Athletics, and Seattle Mariners.

Other sports. Phoenix Giants baseball games take place in the Phoenix Municipal Stadium from May through August. The Phoenix Suns play basketball in the Veterans Memorial Coliseum from October through March. Arizona Wranglers (USFL) and Arizona State football games are held at Sun Devil Stadium in Tempe.

Tennis tournament. The Phoenix Thunderbird Tennis Tournament is held in March at the Phoenix Country Club.

Golf tournaments. You can catch the top pros in action during the Phoenix Open in January and the Arizona Open in November, among 75 tournaments held each year.

Horse racing. Turf Paradise track operates from mid-November to February, Arizona Downs from February to May. The horses run Wednesday through Sunday, starting at 1 P.M.

Greyhound racing. Races are held at Phoenix, Apache, and Black Canyon greyhound parks from January to April and from mid-September to mid-December (closed Monday).

Rodeos. The Phoenix "Rodeo of Rodeos," every March in the Memorial Coliseum at the Arizona State Fairgrounds, helps decide the cowboy world championships. You see top ropers, riders, and bulldoggers pitted against tough, fresh rodeo stock.

Scottsdale's colorful Parada del Sol moves into the Scottsdale Rodeo Grounds in early February.

Small rodeos often take place within easy driving distance of Phoenix in winter and spring.

Horse shows and gymkhanas. Some of the world's finest Arabian horses compete in the All-Arabian Horse Show in February at Paradise Park, Scottsdale. The A-Z (Aid to the Zoo) National Horse Show brings riders from around the country to Memorial Coliseum in March. Also in March, the Western Saddle Club stages its annual Stampede at the club arena, 200 E. Myrtle Avenue.

Livestock show. You can attend the Arizona National Livestock Show in early January at the State Fairgrounds.

Cactus show. Examine the plants of the desert during the annual Cactus Show in February at the Desert Botanical Garden in Papago Park.

Dons Club excursions. Every winter this business and professional men's organization hosts a series of weekend trips to points of interest throughout the state. Travel is by bus, although you can tag along in your own car on 1-day outings. The annual highlight is the Lost Dutchman Gold Mine Trek into the Superstitions in early March. For a complete schedule, write to 201 N. Central Avenue, Phoenix, AZ 85004, or call (602) 258-6016.

Plays and concerts. The valley provides a lively agenda of musical and theatrical events. The Phoenix Symphony Orchestra's hall in the Civic Plaza is one of the most handsome in the country. In addition, the city offers community symphony orchestras, a Chamber Music Society, pops concerts, and choral groups. Around the valley, the musical menu runs from classical guitar to grand opera.

The Phoenix Little Theatre, founded in 1920, is the country's oldest continuously running company. Top-name entertainment, visiting ballet and opera companies, and Broadway shows take to the stage on a regular basis year-round. Arizona's newest showplace for performing arts is the Sundome Center in Sun City West.

Dining & nightlife

Finding a place to eat in the valley poses no problem. Whether you want an enchilada, steak and beans, or caviar, you have your choice of many fine restaurants. Rinky-tink piano, Dixieland jazz, Western guitar, rock music, or a Big Band sound—you'll find them all in the Phoenix area.

Many hotels provide a choice of dining and entertainment. Discovering other spots is as easy as looking in the restaurant section of local magazines and newspapers or checking with your hotel's concierge.

Some of the local favorites include Aunt Chilada's (Mexican), Bobby McGee's, Demetri's, Different Pointe of View (Sunday brunch), El Chorro (long-time favorite), Golden Belle (Rawhide), Golden Eagle (downtown), Hunan, La Champagne (elegant), Lunt Ave. Marble Club (several locations), Orangerie (Arizona Biltmore), Oscar Taylor, Pinnacle Peak Patio (don't wear a tie), Pop's (lunch), Rick's Café Americana, Rustler's Roost, The Other Place.

The shopping experience

You'll find excellent shopping for western wear, Indian and Mexican arts and crafts, desert paintings, and unique gifts. For a fine selection of Indian crafts and books, don't overlook the Heard Museum gift shop.

Most of the tourist shopping centers are situated around north Phoenix and Scottsdale. Free trolleys connect many large malls. Shopping centers include The Borgata (a unique walled mall), Biltmore Fashion Park, Camelback Village, Camelback View Plaza, Colonnade, Metrocenter, Scottsdale Fashion Square, and Town & Country. Chris-Town and Park Central malls are closer to downtown Phoenix.

Most of Scottsdale's specialty stores can be found at Fifth Avenue Shops, Old Scottsdale (Scottsdale and Indian School roads), and along Marshall Way. Spanish Village enlivens the Carefree scene.

It's all in the form. Whether your interest in tennis is casual or intense, bring your racquet. The Valley of the Sun provides a collection of courts ranging from public parks to private tennis ranches.

Early morning breezes carry colorful balloons aloft. Soaring silently above the city and surrounding desert, balloons offer a different look at the landscape. Just counting swimming pools keeps you busy.

In the City

Phoenix is both a modern metropolis dotted with attractive parks and a repository for bits of history taking you back in time hundreds of years. Sights range from the Camelback Mountain landmark northeast of Phoenix (from the city it looks like a camel in repose) to the spectacular flower fields south of the Salt River along Baseline Road, where brightly colored carnations, sweet peas, calendulas, and stock put on an annual show from late January until just before Easter.

Downtown Phoenix

The downtown area suffered the fate of many large metropolitan cities when department stores moved out to suburban malls to better serve the sprawling population. Phoenix fought back with a renovation program that brought a new symphony hall, convention center, and heritage park to the city center. Among the high-rise hotels and banking towers downtown, you'll discover restaurants with good city views.

Civic Plaza. This ultramodern "people place," lighted spectacularly at night, includes a concert hall-theater, a convention center complex, and a landscaped plaza between Central and 7th avenues. Half a million dollars was spent for artwork, mainly the plaza's sculpted ballet dancers and fountains.

Heritage Square. One of Phoenix's most fashionable neighborhoods in the 1890s, the area around Sixth and Monroe streets has been elegantly renovated.

Tours take you through the meticulously restored 10-room Queen Anne Rosson House from 10 A.M. to 4 P.M. Wednesday through Saturday and noon to 4 P.M. Sunday; a small admission fee is charged. At the Silva House, 628 E. Adams Street, exhibits explain how Phoenix gets its water. Rotating exhibits in the Teeter House, 622 E. Adams Street, present highlights of history and culture in the valley. The

huge Lath House shades a third of the block.

History room. Displays on early Arizona history occupy a lower level of the First Interstate Bank, 100 W. Washington Street. The free museum is open during regular banking hours.

A telephone museum. Phoenix's smallest museum, and one of its most interesting, is operated by the Coronado Chapter of the Telephone Pioneers of America. Located in a narrow room of the Mountain States Telephone Company administration building at 16 W. McDowell Road, it displays more than 70 telephones (the oldest made in 1887), eight switchboards, and many other pieces of communication equipment. The museum is open from 8 A.M. to 4 P.M.; for tour reservations, call (602) 235-1871.

Duppa-Montgomery Homestead. At 116 W. Sherman Street, 3 blocks south of the Central Avenue underpass, a two-room adobe built between 1868 and 1872 is a graphic reminder of how primitive life was for pioneers.

A living ocotillo fence surrounds the land once owned by Bryan Philip Duppa, the man credited with naming Phoenix and Tempe. Inside, note the tiny, high windows that offered protection from both Indians and summer heat. The adobe is open Sunday through Tuesday afternoons from November through May.

A look at museums

Fine museums tucked around the city tell much of the story of Phoenix, Arizona, and the whole Southwest. Exhibits testify to the turbulent history of the area, the geologic makeup of the land, and the culture of its people. For a superb overview of Indian art, be sure to visit the Heard Museum (next page).

Arizona Mineral Resource Museum. Residents and visitors alike find this

museum a fascinating storehouse of minerals, rocks, and semiprecious stones. Displays include a fossilized mammoth tooth, a meteorite, and one of the world's largest quartz crystals.

Arizona is the nation's leading copper producer; extensive exhibits trace the state's mining industry from early discoveries to present-day technology.

The free museum, open daily, is in the southwest corner of the Arizona State Fairgrounds at McDowell Road and North 19th Avenue.

Arizona Museum. Relics of the state's pioneer days, Indian art, and historic maps make up some of the displays in this museum at 10th Avenue and W. Van Buren Street. It's open 11 A.M. to 4 P.M. Wednesday through Sunday from November through June. Admission is free, but donations are requested.

Central Arizona Museum of History. Inside this early 20th-century brick mansion at 1242 N. Central Avenue, you'll find an exhibit on Phoenix's fling as the ostrich capital of the United States (1867), re-created drug and grocery stores, and a collection of period costumes. There's also a hands-on "discovery room" for children. Museum hours are 10 A.M. to 4 P.M. Tuesday through Saturday; admission is free.

Hall of Flame Museum. An unusual museum at 6101 E. Van Buren contains firefighting equipment from around the world. You'll see everything from hand and horsedrawn vehicles to today's most modern machines. The museum is open daily except Sunday; there is a charge.

Museum of Science & Technology. It's almost impossible to resist getting caught up in the displays in this science center—everything from watching a baby chick hatch to seeing yourself on video tape against a variety of backgrounds. The museum is temporarily located at Second and Adam streets

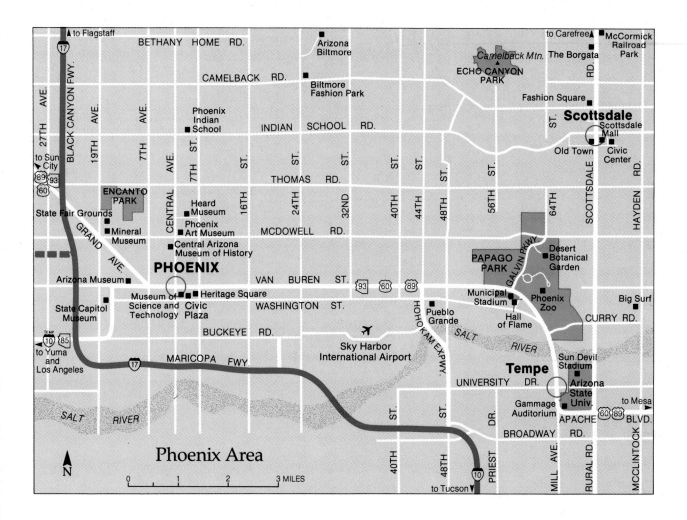

Phoenix Area

0   1   2   3 MILES

N

across from the Civic Center Plaza. Open Monday through Saturday and Sunday afternoon, it charges an admission fee.

Phoenix Art Museum. A part of the Civic Center on N. Central Avenue houses this diverse collection of paintings and sculpture. The museum is open from 10 A.M. to 5 P.M. Tuesday and Thursday through Saturday, 10 A.M. to 9 P.M. Wednesday, and 1 to 5 P.M. Sunday. Admission is free on Wednesday.

State Capitol Museum. The old state capitol, at Washington Street and 17th Avenue, is not a very prepossessing building, but it holds a lot of history. You'll find the flag the Rough Riders carried up San Juan hill during the Spanish-American War, memorabilia of John Wesley Powell's explorations of the Colorado River, and the document that proclaimed Arizona the 48th state.

The free museum is open weekdays; guided tours take place at 10 A.M. and 2 P.M.

An Indian introduction

Much of the character of the Southwest can be attributed to its native Indian inhabitants. Few places afford such a good opportunity to study the development of the Indian tribes from the past to the present. A number of attractions around Phoenix offer insight into Indian history; some reveal facets of tribal life today.

Heard Museum. If you visit no other museum in the Southwest, don't miss this fine showcase of anthropology and primitive art. Exhibits focus on the art of American Indians, with special emphasis on the southwestern tribes. Other major displays include works of contemporary Indian artists and craftspeople.

The permanent displays include one of the most complete collections of Hopi and Zuni kachina dolls in the world. These brightly colored representatives of kachina spirits are imitated for many curio shops, but this gallery gives you a chance to study the real thing.

The liveliest weekend of the year at the Heard Museum is the annual Indian Fair at the end of February. Representatives of a dozen or more tribes gather on the grounds to present their finest artists, craftspeople, musicians, and dancers. You can watch Papago basketmakers coil drab strands of yucca fiber into boldly decorative baskets and plaques, see skilled Pueblo potters transform their clay into exquisite vessels, or sample freshly made *piki* bread. Colorful dance programs offer photographers a chance to record the rituals and costumes of tribes that restrict cameras on their reservations.

(Continued on page 67)

Brilliant Navajo trading blankets from the 1890s capture attention at Phoenix's distinguished Heard Museum. A repository for Indian arts and culture, the museum showcases weavings, kachina dolls, jewelry, pottery, and basketry.

From the fairway at one of the Valley of the Sun's well-manicured courses, golfers get a good look at the famous profiles of Camelback and Mummy mountains.

..In the City

From the first of February until mid-March, the museum features lectures or presentations on regional history or Indian cultures. Newspapers carry the announcements.

In November, the Indian Arts and Crafts Exhibit displays Indian work submitted for competition. All articles are for sale but must remain on exhibit until the close of the show.

The museum, located at 22 E. Monte Vista Road, is open all day Monday through Saturday and Sunday afternoon. There is an admission fee. Don't overlook the large gift shop.

Pueblo Grande. Excavations at this 13th-century village ruin have provided much of our knowledge about the valley's former residents, master farmers who created such an efficient irrigation system that 20th-century engineers followed the same courses for the present-day canals. The Hohokam abandoned this village and the Casa Grande (see page 70) before Europeans came on the scene.

Pueblo Grande is at 4619 E. Washington Street. You can tour the ruin from 1 to 4:45 P.M. Sunday and holidays and from 9 A.M. to 4:45 P.M. Monday through Friday. There is a small admission charge.

Phoenix Indian School. One of the Southwest's oldest and largest Indian boarding schools is located at North Central Avenue and Indian School Road. The majority of students—who number more than 1,000—come from the Hopi, Papago, Navajo, Pima, Apache, and Colorado River reservations; altogether 20 tribes are represented. Run by the Bureau of Indian Affairs, the school welcomes visitors on Friday from 9 to 11 A.M. and 1 to 3 P.M.

City parks

Within its city limits, Phoenix has a gem of a metropolitan park, three rugged near-wilderness preserves, and one area that combines natural terrain with developed facilities.

Squaw Peak Park. The peak itself is a good hike. Ramadas of various sizes accommodate picnickers at this free park north of the downtown area.

To reserve ramadas for picnics at Papago, North Mountain, or Squaw Peak parks, phone (602) 262-6711. For a South Mountain Park picnic reservation, phone (602) 276-2221.

Encanto Park. This downtown park at Encanto Boulevard and 15th Avenue is a favorite sports and recreation area, with free admission. The 200-acre area includes a lagoon (boats for hire) and provides facilities for golf (two courses), tennis, swimming, badminton, shuffleboard, and picnicking. There are also rides and amusements for children, a band shell, wide expanses of lawn, a garden center, and walks through handsome and varied plantings of trees and shrubs.

Papago Park. This combined urban and natural desert park at the eastern city limits offers picnicking, hiking, an 11.3-mile bike trail, horseback riding (rental stables are nearby), an 18-hole golf course, the municipal stadium (home of the Phoenix Giants and spring training park for the San Francisco Giants), seven small lakes where youngsters 15 and under may fish without licenses, the famed Desert Botanical Garden, and the Phoenix Zoo and Children's Zoo. There's no fee to enter the park itself.

Desert Botanical Garden. An enormous array of cactus and succulents provides a good introduction to desert plant life (both native and non-native). Other traditional plants include palo verde, ironwood, mesquite trees, and ocotillo. Stop at the visitors building to buy a booklet explaining what you'll see as you walk through the gardens. The pamphlet's plant-by-plant descriptions cover botanical names, history, kinds of fruit, blooming times, and other bits of informa-tion. The garden is open daily; there's a small entrance fee.

Phoenix Zoo. One of the valley's most appealing attractions for children and adults alike, the zoo has an impressive collection of animals. Here you'll see the first breeding herd of Arabian oryx in captivity. This gazellelike creature's long, straight horns, seen in profile, quite possibly started the myth of the unicorn. Saudi Arabian officials sent 28 of the animals to the zoo in 1963 because of the similar climate; the species, once hunted to near extinction, is making a strong comeback.

A special feature is the Children's Zoo, where youngsters can pet small animals, see a barnyard menagerie including Texas longhorns, and visit the brooder house to observe the development of baby chicks from hatching to five weeks of age. Also of interest is the Arizona Exhibit, an extensive collection of animals native to the Southwest.

The zoo is open daily; if you're inside by 5 P.M., you can stay until sunset. There is a modest fee for admission.

South Mountain Park. For a picnic or a hike, you can't beat the biggest municipal park in the world. Almost 15,000 acres of mostly wilderness, this expanse at the southern end of Central Avenue includes improved picnic sites, 40 miles of hiking and bridle trails (rental stables), and a paved scenic drive to two vantage points for sweeping views of the Salt and Gila river valleys. Pedestrians are admitted free; there's a small charge for vehicles.

North Mountain Park. Far across Phoenix at the north end of Central Avenue (enter from 10600 N. Seventh Street) beckons a small but popular destination for picnickers, hikers, and riders (there's no stable). The grounds include five picnic areas and a children's playground. The ranger's office houses a collection of desert insects and Indian artifacts. Admission to the park is free.

The outlying area contains a potpourri of inviting attractions, all within an easy drive of Phoenix. You can enjoy the rugged and serene beauty of the desert, relax and picnic, or try boating in one of the regional parks.

A fascinating aspect of this region is the constant visibility of history through the remains of the dwellings of early civilizations. You cover a 600-year span in time as you travel from the ancient ruins of Casa Grande to the futuristic studio of Paolo Soleri.

Stylish Scottsdale

A lively resort center just east of Phoenix, Scottsdale is self-styled as "the West's most Western town" and is probably also one of the West's fastest growing towns, among the largest in the state. Western-style outdoor living and the garb of the western rider—levis, boots, and a cowboy hat—set the theme, although the town also boasts 15 golf courses and around 50 tennis courts.

Scottsdale got its start when Army Chaplain Winfield Scott visited the area in 1888 and bought 600 acres just below the Arizona Canal. Soon Scottsdale Road and Main Street became the hub of a small village. When the city was incorporated in 1951, there were fewer than 2,000 residents; today the population approaches 105,000.

Civic Center. The city's handsome Civic Center (city hall and library), designed by architect Bennie Gonzales, suggests the Spanish Morocco style in its clean, monolithic lines. Sunlight streaming through stained-glass windows paints interior walls with color. Dale Wright's welded steel sculpture of Don Quixote rises from the pool fronting the complex; John Waddell's *Mother and Child* and the abstract Children's Fountain stand nearby.

Scottsdale Mall. Between the Civic Center and Brown Avenue, shops, galleries, restaurants, cinemas, and a hotel surround the 20-acre, parklike Scottsdale Mall. Adjacent to the mall, the Center for the Arts features changing art exhibits as well as theatrical, musical, and film productions.

A 45-minute, self-guiding walking tour, laid out by the Scottsdale Historical Society, starts at the Chamber of Commerce, in the Little Red Schoolhouse at 7333 Scottsdale Mall. Pick up descriptive maps at the chamber on weekdays between 9 A.M. and 5 P.M.

A touch of the Old West, downtown Scottsdale looks like a western movie set with its streets of careful replicas of frontier buildings.

Old Town. A touch of the Old West, Old Town (downtown Scottsdale) looks like a western movie set with its streets of careful replicas of frontier buildings. Situated between 68th Street and Bronson Avenue, Second Street and Indian School Road, Old Town is a great place to shop for western attire, an Indian rug, or pottery.

An artist's spot. Scottsdale has long been an artist's center. Galleries are concentrated in two areas west of Scottsdale Road: Main Street, 2 blocks south of Indian School Road; and Marshall Way, between Indian School Road and Fifth Avenue.

"Evenings on Marshall Way" and "Art Walks on Main Street" attract visitors each Thursday night from 7 to 9 P.M. during the season (October through March).

A shopping delight. Many of the area's best shops lie on or near Scottsdale Road. In the Fifth Avenue shopping area, you'll find "Craftsmen's Court" (Kiva Plaza), a landscaped courtyard with benches where tired shoppers can rest in the shade. Perfumed water splashes from a fountain; sheltered doorways lead to intriguing boutiques.

At the Borgata, on Scottsdale Road a block south of Lincoln Drive, you'll discover luxurious shops and restaurants in a walled setting reminiscent of an Old World Italian village.

Motorized trolleys shuttle visitors among shopping centers and hotels.

McCormick Railroad Park. You can ride a five-twelfths-scale steam train at a park devoted to railroads. Situated at the corner of Scottsdale and Indian Bend roads, the 30-acre park displays a full-size steam engine and a Pullman car that once carried the country's presidents. Two turn-of-the century railroad stations serve as shops for memorabilia. Entrance is free; you pay a modest charge to ride the steam train or a smaller model.

Cosanti Foundation. The studio and planning center of architect Paolo Soleri is on Double Tree Road, about a mile west of Scottsdale Road. Models and full-size concrete structures express the unorthodox designer's ideas for future housing.

A small donation admits visitors to the workshops and exhibits, open daily. You can also buy one of Soleri's famous windbells here. For information on Soleri's Arcosanti, see page 75.

Taliesen West. The western campus of the Frank Lloyd Wright School of Architecture east of Scottsdale is a vivid expression of the great architect's building and landscape designs. His concepts are kept alive and in continual evolution by his associates and students. As part of their training, students plan and build additions and maintain the buildings and gardens flowing together in harmony.

The campus is open to visitors year-round, although the faculty and students move to the original Taliesen near Spring Green, Wisconsin, during the summer months.

Hours are 10 A.M. to 4 P.M. daily except when it rains; there is an admission fee. To reach the school, follow the signs off Shea Boulevard north on 108th Street.

To the foothills

North of the city, Scottsdale Road leads to Carefree and Cave Creek, uncrowded and scenic residential communities in the foothills. En route, a turnoff on Pinnacle Peak Road takes you to a spot where you can look out over the valley. Another popular stop along this road is Pinnacle Peak Patio, a huge steakhouse famed for its custom of cutting off the necktie of anyone who defies the "no tie" rule. Thousands of ties cover the ceiling.

Rawhide. A ring of Conestoga wagons beside the road greets visitors to this replica of an 1800s town 14 miles north of Scottsdale. Lining the dusty street are craft shops, a period barber shop, a cavernous saloon and restaurant (Golden Belle) featuring cowboy steaks, a reconstructed "Arizona's first bank," sheriff's office, general store, museum (Geronimo's moccasins, Tom Mix's boots), livery stable, gem display, and, at the end, a mine shaft and ore car. You can pan for gold nearby, ride a stagecoach or burro, and watch a "shootout" or a frontier blacksmith at work.

Rawhide is open from 5 P.M. to midnight weekdays, noon to midnight Saturday and Sunday. Admission is free.

Carefree. A colorful Spanish village with red tile roofs on white stucco shops clusters around a large, flower-filled patio. Like Scottsdale's Craftsmen's Court, the shaded patio invites a pause. This fancy residential community boasts resorts, golf courses designed by the greats, and the "world's largest sundial." Notice the street names — Elbow Bend, Nonchalant Avenue, Never Mind Trail, and the like.

Cave Creek. Over the hill and around the bend to the west of Carefree, another residential settlement has controlled development and preserved the open space and charm of the desert foothills. Stop at Harold's, a bar and steakhouse, for local color. On rare wet days, the rain falls almost as hard under the roof as outside this rambling, ramshackle landmark.

Cave Creek was a mining camp in the 1800s and later became a ranching community when the mines gave out. Today it's a center for dude ranching and a takeoff point for nearby wilderness recreation areas.

From Carefree, a paved road takes you about 14 miles northeast to Camp Creek canyon and campsites. Here the pavement ends, but the gravel road continues a scenic 40-mile swing north through the mountains past Seven Springs, Cedar Mountain, and Brooklyn Mountain to meet Interstate 17 south of Cordes Junction.

Desert foothills scenic drive. This drive reveals the energy and foresight of the concerned citizens of Cave Creek and Carefree. Anxious to preserve the choice desert along the roadside, they decided to make it more meaningful— and thus less prone to damage — to those who passed along the road. So they identified 26 plant species and erected 101 roadside signs to mark them. Some plants are visible from the road; to see others requires a short walk.

A naturalist, aided by students and faculty members of Arizona State University, located and identified the plants. Residents built, carved, and painted the signs, using materials contributed by a lumberyard. Schoolchildren helped clean up the sites and install the signs. Families adopted individual plants and assumed responsibility for their care.

Exhibits are repeated so that either way you approach the loop you may see all the specimens. For a pleasant day's drive out of Phoenix, start at Scottsdale in the morning for browsing and lunch; then make the tour north on Scottsdale Road through Carefree and Cave Creek in the afternoon. Watch the sunset from the Cave Creek Road as you return to Phoenix.

Fountain Hills. Driving east of Scottsdale past the McDowell Mountains on Shea Boulevard, you encounter a strange sight in the desert. Rising from a large lagoon in the plush residential development of Fountain Hills, a tall plume of water claims the record as the world's highest fountain (560 feet) when its three pumps work at full power. A 2,000-pound nozzle constricts water flowing at 7,000 gallons per minute, keeping eight tons of water suspended in the air. There's no waste; the crystal-clear plume is recycled water.

A tall plume of water claims the record as the world's highest fountain (560 feet).

Not surprisingly, Robert McCulloch, the developer who brought the London Bridge to Lake Havasu, also came up with this attraction. The fountain operates for 10 minutes on the hour between 10 A.M. and 9 P.M.

During your visit, you can golf on the development's 18-hole course and shop along the Avenue of the Fountains. The annual Fountain Festival of Arts & Crafts takes place during the first part of November.

...A Look Around Town

A university town

Arizona's fourth largest city, Tempe is best known as the home of Arizona State University, site of the Fiesta Bowl and home field for the Arizona Sun Devils and the Arizona Wranglers.

Tempe also has some interesting museums and a renowned performing arts center. Old Town Tempe, along Mill Avenue next to the university, contains an intriguing collection of small shops.

Arizona State University. The largest university in the Rocky Mountain area, ASU is home for more than 40,000 students. Don't look for ivied halls or ancient courtyards; the beautifully landscaped campus sets off strikingly modern buildings.

Grady Gammage Center for Performing Arts was one of the last major buildings Frank Lloyd Wright designed. Depending on scheduled events, it's open for touring on Tuesday, Thursday, and Saturday afternoons between 1:30 and 3:30 P.M.

At Matthews Center you can view continually rotating art exhibits from the Collection of American Art. The center is open from 8 A.M. to 5 P.M. weekdays and Sunday from 1 to 5 P.M.

Fine Arts Center. A collection of contemporary arts and crafts takes up the second floor of a restored turn-of-the-century building at 520 S. Mill Avenue. The exhibits can be viewed weekdays and Saturday afternoon.

Tempe Historical Museum. In the Tempe Community Center (3500 S. Rural Road), you can take a look at the city's past. Displays in the free museum (open Tuesday through Saturday) feature old-time furniture, clothing, toys, tools, and photographs, plus replicas of period rooms.

Salt River Project History Center. Valley history is on display at the Salt River Project administration building (1521 Project Drive, between Washington and Van Buren). In the free museum (open weekdays) you'll see films, artifacts, and exhibits covering from the days of the Hohokam to the present.

Expanding Mesa

One of the fastest growing communities in the country and Arizona's third largest city, Mesa was founded more than 100 years ago by the Mormons. The bustling city attracts many high-tech employers; as a result, new hotels, shopping centers, and tourist attractions entice valley visitors.

Champlin Fighters Museum. Airplane buffs will enjoy this collection of fighter aircraft from World War I through the Vietnam era. More than 25 planes and memorabilia of fighter pilots are on display. Located at 4636 Fighter Aces Drive (next to Falcon Field Airport), the museum is open daily from 10 A.M to 5 P.M. A fee is charged.

Mesa Museum. Indian and pioneer history is the focus of this free museum at 53 N. MacDonald Street. Displays include Indian dwellings, an adobe schoolhouse, a territorial jail, and a covered wagon. You can visit Tuesday through Saturday and Sunday afternoon.

Mormon Temple. The formally landscaped grounds are open to the public, but the temple itself, one of the largest in the country, welcomes only Mormons. From the visitor center, you can take an hour-long guided tour of the grounds. The center (525 E. Main Street) is open daily from 9 A.M. to 9 P.M.

Some Arizona landmarks

Much of the fascination of the Southwest lies in contrast—the omnipresent signs of the past in proximity to the most modern developments. The area around Phoenix offers a variety of these sights, starting with the silent ruins of Casa Grande and continuing through the blend of early and modern cultures. All provide a chapter in the continuing chronicle of the Southwest; all are short drives from the center of Phoenix.

Casa Grande Ruins National Monument. A strange structure rears up from the desert 40 miles south of Phoenix: a four-story tower built 600 years ago by Pueblo and Hohokam Indian farmers of the Gila Valley.

The tower served as lookout, fort, and possibly astronomical or ceremonial center. Padre Kino named it the Casa Grande when he discovered it in 1694. Today a steel canopy shelters the "large house." Rangers will guide you through the building every day from 7 A.M. to 6 P.M.; a small fee is charged.

You can see other evidence of the Hohokam in the irrigation canals and walled-in ruins on the monument grounds. A museum at monument headquarters displays artifacts excavated from six village compounds. Visitors may picnic in a shaded area provided with water and tables. Signs on Interstate 10 mark the turnoff.

A big celebration called O'Odham Tash (Indian Days) takes place in the nearby town of Casa Grande around the middle of February. More than 700 Indians from Arizona, New Mexico, and beyond participate in a high-quality arts and crafts show and demonstrations, an All-Indian Rodeo, ceremonial dances, and a parade.

Gila Heritage Park. To visit the Pima agency town of Sacaton, headquarters of the Gila River Indian Reservation, take the Casa Blanca off ramp about 25 miles southeast of Phoenix on Interstate 10.

These days the Pimas rarely make the tightly coiled baskets for which they are famous, but you'll find some in the Gila River Indian Arts and Crafts Center along with other traditional crafts, a museum, and a restaurant where you can buy fry bread and other delicacies. At the adjacent Heritage

Gaily striped umbrellas await guests partaking of a day of poolside sunbathing and dining at one of the valley's deluxe resorts.

Designed by Frank Lloyd Wright, Gammage Center for Performing Arts floats on a reflecting pool at Arizona State University. Tours of this architectural gem are offered several days a week.

Park, you'll see re-creations of Hoho-kam dwellings plus more contemporary artifacts. There's no charge to visit, but a donation is requested.

Early rock carvings can be seen at a number of places on the reservation. Hundreds of these petroglyphs are framed in a canyon just outside the old trading post of Oldberg, reached by a road from State 87 east of Sacaton.

St. John's Indian School. Widely known for the colorful ceremonial dancers and drum and bugle corps who represent the school in festivals and parades throughout the Southwest, St. John's is an adjunct of the Franciscan mission at the village of Komatke on the Gila River Indian Reservation.

In addition to Pimas and Maricopas from the local reservation, the school attracts students from as far away as the Pacific Northwest. Visitors are welcome during the school year; telephone (602) 237-2400 in advance for arrangements. To reach the mission, about 16 miles southwest of the city, turn south on 51st Avenue through Laveen and follow the signs.

Guadalupe. Yaqui Indians settled at this small village southeast of Phoenix after fleeing from Mexico. They continue to maintain a somewhat separate culture here. Their celebration of Easter, combining Christian and pre-Columbian elements, attracts interest. The village sits at the northeastern tip of South Mountain Park, an easy drive from downtown Phoenix.

Pioneer Arizona. This Southwestern counterpart of the "living history museum" at Williamsburg, Virginia, has been created on 550 acres north of Phoenix. Costumed guides demonstrate daily activities in authentically restored buildings. A melodrama is staged in the Opera House most Saturdays at 11:30 A.M. and 2 P.M.; phone (602) 993-0212 to verify. On Thanksgiving, a colorful Harvest Festival takes place.

The center is open daily except Monday; admission includes a wagon ride and tour. The museum is located off Interstate 17, about ½ mile north of Bell Road at the Pioneer Road exit.

Regional parks

Though Phoenix is one of the most rapidly growing cities in the West, its planners have taken care to preserve a valuable commodity — open space. Residents of Phoenix and the rest of Maricopa County enjoy one of the largest systems of regional parks in the country, covering some 104,000 acres. Much of the land is in its original wilderness state, unaltered by development.

All of these desert parks can be very pleasant from February through April, when desert flowers bloom. May brings the beginning of hot weather along with cactus blossoms.

For more information, contact the Maricopa County Parks and Recreation Department, 4701 E. Washington Street, Phoenix, AZ 85034, or phone (602) 262-3711.

Lake Pleasant Regional Park. The most developed of the parks, Lake Pleasant, northwest of Phoenix, has paved access roads, shaded picnic areas, swimming beach, launching ramps, docks, fueling dock, and overnight campgrounds. Water sports, fishing, and rock hunting are popular activities.

Black Canyon Recreation Area. If you're interested in perfecting your marksmanship, plan a stop at this recreation area on Interstate 17 north of the city. Shooting ranges include small bore, big bore, skeet, trap, and archery. Non-shooters will enjoy good picnic facilities.

Cave Creek Recreation Area. This undeveloped park north of Phoenix (east of Interstate 17) affords good riding, hiking, and overnight camping.

Bring your own water and camp-stove.

Thunderbird Recreation Area. This close-in park just north of Phoenix offers hiking and picnicking. Drinking water is available.

Paradise Valley Park. A very well-developed urban park to the northeast of the city, Paradise Valley features a large field, riding arena, community building, and racquetball courts.

McDowell Mountain Regional Park. A wildlife refuge east of Scottsdale and next to the Fort McDowell Indian Reservation, this park is popular for riding, hiking, picnicking, and camping. Paved roads provide access; bring water.

The adjacent reservation straddles the Verde River north from where Shea Boulevard meets State 87. Some Apache Indians live and farm here.

Usery Mountain Park. This well-developed park east of Phoenix (north of U.S. 60/89) has picnic tables, an archery range, and a campground with water.

Estrella Mountain Regional Park. Wildlife and people find refuge in this big mountain park adjacent to the Casey Abbott Recreational Area southwest of Phoenix. It offers developed picnic areas (including water), overnight camping units, an archery range, and a nearby 18-hole golf course. Riding and hiking trails lead into the mountains. You'll also find a roping and rodeo arena.

Buckeye Hills Recreation Area. You can ride, hike, and camp at this desert hills sanctuary southwest of the city off State 85. There are picnic sites and a small shooting range, but no water.

White Tank Mountain Regional Park. The largest of the ring of parks, this one west of the city has picnic tables, a campground (no water), and marked hiking trails.

You can become a part of the Old West when you stay at one of Arizona's "dude" ranches, now commonly called guest ranches. Whether you're young or old, tenderfoot or seasoned cowhand, horseback rider or golfer, you'll find a ranch that meets your requirements.

Today's ranches are modern resorts, providing a somewhat romanticized version of life on a ranch. Only the smaller ones give you a chance to "help out." Individual bedrooms and casitas have replaced the community bunkhouse, and the community shower has given way to private baths.

Choosing a ranch

To be most comfortable, you'll want to choose a ranch that matches your preferred lifestyle. Guest ranches range from rustic to posh, usually with prices to match. Every ranch has a distinctive personality. Part of this comes from their setting—cactus-studded desert, rolling rangeland, or pine-clad mountains. The architecture and the owner's personality also contribute to a place's particular appeal.

The ranch itself adds to the ambiance. Take your choice of a working ranch or, more likely, a spread where the cattle are mainly for show. Ranch facilities differ: you may like to eat family style close to the kitchen or prefer a cocktail lounge and large dining room with individual tables. Do you like the children with you during the day and at meals, or would you prefer for them to have supervised activities and a separate table? These are some of the choices you'll want to look for when reading ranch brochures.

No matter which place best matches your interests, informality is the rule at all guest ranches. Shortly after you arrive, you'll be on a first-name basis with the owner and other guests.

Choice of activities

Do you plan to spend your day on horseback enjoying the splendid desert scenery? You'll have a choice of breakfast rides, all-day trail rides, dinner rides with cookouts, and even several-day campouts. You'll also find hayrides, hoedowns, and "dudeos" where guests from several ranches gather at one ranch for a day-long gymkhana.

Instead of riding, you may feel more comfortable with a tennis racquet in your hand; most of the larger ranches offer tennis courts, pros, and clinics. If golf is your game, one ranch has its own 18-hole course. At another you can spend your days counting and banding birds.

Though some ranches encourage guests to participate in activities, it's a very relaxed way of life. And if your idea of a ranch vacation is simply lounging beside the pool, that's possible, too.

What's included in the cost

The price of your ranch vacation includes room and meals and use of the facilities. There may be an extra charge for horseback riding or for riding more than once a day. Tennis instruction and the use of the golf course are added expenses. Most ranches offer free pick-up from major airports.

A ranch listing

The ranches listed below are only examples of what you'll find. For a complete listing, write to the Arizona Office of Tourism, 1480 E. Bethany Home Road, Phoenix, AZ 85014.

Around Wickenburg. Flying E Ranch, P.O. Box EEE, Wickenburg, AZ 85358; Kay El Bar Guest Ranch, P.O. Box 2480, Wickenburg, AZ 85358; Rancho de los Caballeros, P.O. Box 1148, Wickenburg, AZ 85358 (largest of ranches, 18-hole golf course); Wickenburg Inn Tennis & Guest Ranch, P.O. Box P, Wickenburg, AZ 85358 (specializes in tennis, horses available).

Around Tucson. Hacienda del Sol Ranch Resort, 5601 N. Hacienda del Sol Road, Tucson, AZ 85718; Lazy K Bar Ranch, 8401 N. Scenic Drive, Tucson, AZ 85743; Middleton Ranch, P.O. Box 504, Amado, AZ 85645; Rancho de la Osa, P.O. Box 1, Sasabe, AZ 85633 (old Spanish hacienda near Mexican border); Tanque Verde Guest Ranch, Rt. 8, Box 66, Tucson, AZ 85748 (desert orientation classes, plush surroundings); White Stallion Ranch, Rt. 28, Box 567, Tucson, AZ 85743 (working ranch); Wild Horse Ranch Resort, P.O. Box 35743, Tucson, AZ 85740.

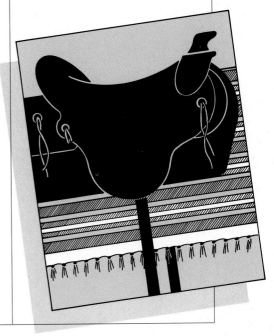

Panoramic views of the entire Salt River

Valley reward hikers atop South Mountain

Park. Containing almost 15,000 acres,

this mountainous expanse is the world's

largest municipal park.

North of Phoenix

The major highway north from Phoenix is Interstate 17, the Black Canyon Freeway, heading straight up toward Flagstaff. Connecting highways turn off to Prescott, the Verde Valley, and Sedona (see "Central Arizona").

A smaller highway, but often considered the most scenic of all the roads out of Phoenix, is State 87, the Beeline Highway, turning northeast from Scottsdale into the Tonto Basin and the spectacular cliffs of the Mogollon Rim country.

Along Interstate 17

The most direct and heavily traveled route between Phoenix and Flagstaff, Interstate 17 is a divided freeway for much of its length.

Rising from the desert floor to the pine-clad Mogollon Plateau, the highway takes you through the transition between two faces of Arizona: the dry, blazing Sonoran Desert and the green, heavily forested highlands where winter snow lies deep.

Along the route you pass historic sites and turnoffs into beautiful and primitive backcountry. About 20 miles north of the city, a turnoff westward takes you to the authentically reconstructed settlement of Pioneer Arizona and to Lake Pleasant Recreation Area (see page 72). About 6 miles beyond, at New River, a gravel road reaches southeast to Cave Creek.

Agua Fria Canyon. You can head out on one-day hikes or longer backpacking trips in this 13-mile-long canyon, undisturbed by roads, along the Agua Fria River. The upper end is the most interesting; here the ruins of the 76-year-old Richinbar Mine buildings sprawl on a hillside, with the mine's hanging flume strung along the canyon.

To reach the top, turn east off Interstate 17 at the Badger Springs exit 3 miles north of Sunset Point and follow the right fork of the road to Badger Creek. From here you can hike in 3 miles to the mine or go all the way down to where the canyon nears the highway.

To reach the bottom end of the canyon, take the Squaw Valley exit near Black Canyon City, follow Squaw Valley Road east for ¼ mile, turn left on Riverbend Road and left again at the fork, and drive 2 miles to the canyon.

Bumble Bee. About 3 miles north of Black Canyon City, a side road turns off westward and then branches. Take the north fork (it's marked) and follow 5 miles of seasonal dirt road to the town of Bumble Bee.

This was the main road from Phoenix to Flagstaff until 1955, when State 79, now the freeway, was built. The old store building at Bumble Bee was first a Wells Fargo stage stop, then a Greyhound bus stop.

Bumble Bee was never a mining center, and it's not a "ghost town," even though prospectors bought supplies here. Behind the store is a "city street" lined with old buildings gathered up in the vicinity and reassembled here. It's picturesque and, though artificial, typical of the real thing.

Horsethief Basin. Nestled high in the mountains of Prescott National Forest west of Bumble Bee, Horsethief Basin is a cool retreat from summer heat. In this fully developed recreation area 6,000 feet high in the Bradshaw Mountains, pine and chaparral-covered slopes attract picnickers and campers from April to October. You can follow hiking trails and hook panfish in the small lake (no swimming). When the ranger is on duty, you can visit the lookout tower for a panoramic view.

The Forest Service maintains improved campgrounds, including some enclosed wooden sleeping shelters as well as tent and trailer spaces. The concession-operated Horsethief Basin Resort (4723 N. 40th Avenue, Phoenix, AZ 85019) offers housekeeping cabins and a small store.

To reach Horsethief Basin from Interstate 17, take the Bumble Bee turn-off. About 5 miles north of Bumble Bee, take the left fork (marked) about 16 miles to the old mining town of Crown King; it's another 7 miles southeast to the basin. Caution: watch out for potholes and rocks on the curvy road.

Sunset Point. This rest area, about 3 miles north of the Bumble Bee turnoff, is the type of roadside pulloff you'd like to find along all major highways. In 1972 it won first prize among 70 entries from 28 states in a Federal Highway Administration competition.

Four large ramadas on the hill west of the highway each shade seven picnic tables, and each table shares the same broad view over the valley to the Bradshaw Mountains. A central ramada contains restrooms, water, and map and photo displays of regional points of interest.

An overlook 100 feet below gives you an unobstructed view of the old stage road, the cluster of buildings at Bumble Bee, and a portion of Horsethief Basin.

East of Interstate 17. From New River north to Cordes Junction, the highway is paralleled on the east at about 5 miles distance by the western borders of first the Tonto, then the Coconino national forests. Few roads penetrate the area, but one gravel road makes a long sweep through it.

The Bloody Basin road turns east about 3 miles south of Cordes Junction and heads south to the Seven Springs and Horseshoe recreation areas. You'll find Forest Service campgrounds, with trailer space, at Seven Springs, on upper Camp Creek, at Horseshoe, and at Bartlett Lake, 15 miles west of the road on the Verde River. It's about 40 miles along this back-road route south to Carefree and Scottsdale Road. Ask about road conditions first, particularly during the rainy season.

Arcosanti. At Cordes Junction, a dirt road leads 2 miles east of Interstate 17 to the town of Arcosanti. When completed, the ecologically sound, energy efficient town will encompass living and working facilities for some 5,000 inhabitants in one structure.

Arcosanti is open from 8 A.M. to 6 P.M. Guided tours are held on the hour. You can get breakfast and lunch at the cafe and bakery.

Mogollon Rim country

For more than 200 miles, the escarpment of the Mogollon Rim angles across the Arizona uplands north and east of Phoenix, marking the edge of the high plateau and tracing a magnificent stretch of scenic vacation land. In a region where dramatic terrain is commonplace, the rim is remarkable for its jutting height and bold cliffs, but most of all for its length.

Seen from the air, the rim (its name is pronounced *Mo*-gee-own or *Mug*-ee-own) can be traced from the juniper-dotted hills near Ash Fork (west of Flagstaff) to the Blue Range of eastern Arizona before it finally disappears into the Mogollon Mountains of New Mexico.

Here and there it has been obscured by encroaching canyons and jumbled mountains, but over most of its length it is distinct, a wall of rock sometimes white, sometimes blue-gray or red or cream. Reaching away in the distance, it is the most abrupt feature of the rugged zone that separates the plateau country from the desert to the south.

Formation. In shaping this wall, the forces of erosion have bared great layers of limestone, sandstone, and shale and bitten deep into the underlying granite. Like the rocks of the Grand Canyon, some of the sedimentary layers were once beneath the ocean; their presence today more than a mile above sea level is evidence that, at some time in the geologic past, the whole area was uplifted from the sea.

Features. Along the line of the rim, above its cliffs and down in its shadow, stretches a quiet forest that beckons the hiker and rider and camper, the angler and hunter, and the auto explorer. Above the rim, aspens gleam against the dark green of Ponderosa pines and Douglas firs; below are broad stands of pine before the land slopes away toward the desert, where bare buttes and stark peaks shape the southern horizon. In fall, bright splotches of color reveal the presence of maple and oak above the rim and in the heads of the canyons at the rim's foot.

Location. The heart of the rim country lies northeast of Phoenix between State 87 and U.S. 60, along that portion called locally the Tonto Rim, from Strawberry down to Punkin Center and eastward into the reservation of the White Mountain Apaches (see maps on pages 45 and 81).

Toward the west end of the rim country is the Oak Creek Canyon area north of Phoenix (see page 53). Far to the east, two principal highways slice through the rim: U.S. 60/State 77, linking central Arizona with Interstate 40, and U.S. 666, the winding, scenic Coronado Trail (see page 89).

Information. Details concerning accommodations, rental of horses, pack trips, and other facilities and services in the rim country can be obtained by writing to the Payson Chamber of Commerce, Drawer A, Payson, AZ 85541.

Tonto Basin. This ancestral hunting ground of several Apache groups was the scene of frequent Indian raids and of skirmishes between Apaches and soldiers from the nearest Army posts—Camp Verde to the west, Camp (later Fort) Apache to the east, Fort McDowell to the south.

When these battles ended (the last one was fought in this area), trouble arose among the settlers themselves. Some of the West's bloodiest feuds between sheepmen and cattlemen erupted in the Pleasant Valley War from 1887 to 1892. Many places in the vicinity of Young are remembered as scenes of ambushes and gunfights during the prolonged series of skirmishes.

Young still lies on a graded dirt road (State 288) running from State 260 east of Christopher Creek southward to the east end of Roosevelt Lake. Inquire locally about road conditions in wet weather.

Zane Grey's cabin. The rim country has become familiar to thousands of readers of Zane Grey's Western novels. *To the Last Man* is based on the Pleasant Valley War, and several of his other books, including *Under the Tonto Rim*, are set in this area.

The author lived for several years in a house just under the rim near the headwaters of Tonto Creek. The building has been restored and is maintained and opened to the public (small donation) by a resident caretaker from March through November. Exhibits include copies of some of the author's original manuscripts and some first editions of his books. The most impressive thing about the house is the setting: the rim looming behind and distant views over the tumbled pine forests of the basin below.

To reach the road to the cabin (and to the Tonto Creek trout hatchery), turn north off State 260 just east of Kohls Ranch resort and follow the gravel road up Tonto Creek. Inquire first at Kohls Ranch for road conditions.

You'll find picnic sites and a campground along boulder-strewn Tonto Creek. This is a popular fishing and recreation area.

Viewing the rim. State 260 from Payson east is one of the most scenic drives you'll find anywhere. Climbing up the rim east of Christopher Creek, the road rewards you with close-ups of the weathered sandstone layers on one hand and panoramic views over the Tonto Basin on the other.

For longer views of the rambling escarpment from below, drive the control road from Kohls Ranch resort west to State 87 just below Pine. You'll go through dense forest and cross the East

Verde River, and through gaps in the pines you'll see the massive wall of rock rearing to the north.

More good views of the rim come into sight in the vicinity of Pine and Strawberry on State 87.

Another great scenic drive is the rim road, running along the top of the escarpment all the way from Camp Verde (north of Phoenix on Interstate 17) into the White Mountains near the eastern edge of the state. This is a seasonal road; ask about conditions before you set out.

Payson. At the junction of State 87 and State 260, Payson serves as the center for adventures into the surrounding rim countryside. The small community retains much of its cowtown flavor, with lumber and resort overtones. In late August, the "World's Oldest Continuous RCA Rodeo" comes to town.

Tonto Natural Bridge. The pleasant road northwest from Payson (State 87) takes you to the dramatic formation of Tonto Natural Bridge. The turnoff is 12 miles from Payson. A 3-mile graded road leads to a guest lodge; the parking lot above the bridge is ¼ mile farther. Privately owned, the bridge area is open daily from 8 A.M. to 5 P.M.; there is an admission fee.

You approach on a level with the top of the bridge, so you are unaware of the remarkable formation until you reach a proper vantage point to look down. An orchard grows on top of the span and Pine Creek flows below. Arching 183 feet above Pine Creek, the great travertine span shades a rocky vault below.

Piles of boulders have dammed the creek to form a quiet pool. You'll find picnic tables under scattered shade trees. A short, steep trail takes you down under the bridge.

Hunting and fishing. The rim country probably has a wider variety of wild game than any other area in the state. Deer (both whitetail and mule), elk, javelina, black bear, and turkeys are all found here.

Big brown and rainbow trout draw more people to the rim country than does any other single attraction. There are at least two dozen well-stocked trout streams in the area and several beautiful lakes, including a string of six artificial lakes in the Sitgreaves and Coconino national forests.

Camping. The Forest Service maintains improved campgrounds near all six lakes, along with others off State 260 at the Canyon Point overlook, at Christopher Creek, and at Ponderosa 14 miles east of Payson; and off State 87 about 5 miles north of Payson at the East Verde crossing, and at Kehl Springs northeast of Strawberry.

Bed & breakfast

Arizona, along with many other states, has embraced the bed and breakfast way of life so popular in other countries. It's a fine alternative to the mundane motel room and offers a chance to meet local people. Many host families enjoy guiding visitors around the countryside, even inviting them to parties or cultural events.

Usually breakfast is included in the price of a room. This may be a continental breakfast of fresh juice, freshly baked rolls, and beverage, but many families prepare a larger offering. At one place, resident hens contribute fresh eggs. Elsewhere, guests may have kitchen privileges and fix their own meals when they choose.

Dinners often are offered as an option at an additional cost.

Four referral companies handle a number of homes throughout the state. Upon receiving your application form and deposit (refundable if your plans change), they match your requirements with those of a host family in the area you wish to visit. When your reservation has been made, you will receive the name and address of your host family and details about their accommodations.

These agencies cover much of Arizona, including guest ranches in the Mogollon Rim country and down near the Mexican border as well as good locations in Phoenix, Tucson, Sedona, and other cities.

Mi Casa Su Casa
P.O. Box 950
Tempe, AZ 85281
(602) 990-0682

Bed and Breakfast in Arizona, Inc.
8433 N. Black Canyon, Suite 160
Phoenix, AZ 85021
(602) 995-2831

Bed and Breakfast of Scottsdale
424 N. Scottsdale Road, Suite 350
Scottsdale, AZ 85251
(602) 990-7212

Barbara's Bed and Breakfast
P.O. Box 13603
Tucson, AZ 85732
(602) 886-5847

Between Phoenix and the New Mexico border stretches a fascinating land that offers travel surprises to the highway driver as well as to the side-road explorer. Here you'll find two Apache Indian reservations, big recreation-oriented lakes, a section of the remarkable Mogollon Rim, the dramatic Salt River Canyon, and the high pine forests and trout waters of the beautiful White Mountains.

Tonto National Forest

East and northeast of Phoenix extends Tonto National Forest, one of the largest national forests in the nation. Much of the "forest" is actually rolling desert, densely covered with creosote bush, palo verde, ironwood, and cactus of many varieties, including magnificent stands of saguaro. Winter rains create a springtime blossom bouquet in the desert.

Land of lakes

Near Phoenix, a series of dams interrupts the flow of the Salt River to create a 60-mile-long chain of lakes. Beginning in the early 1900s, these reservoirs turned the lower Salt River Valley into rich citrus and cotton land. Besides irrigation water and power, they provide recreation: camping, swimming, water-skiing, motorboating, sailing, and fishing for warm-water fish. All four lakes — Saguaro, Canyon, Apache, and Roosevelt — offer Forest Service picnic areas, a few campgrounds, rustic resorts, boats for rent, tackle, and bait.

The dramatic Apache Trail paralleling the Salt River lakes is one of the state's most famous scenic drives; the major highway (U.S. 60) that swings south around the Superstition Wilderness presents quite different rocky landscapes. Together, they make a good day's loop trip from either Phoenix or Globe.

Southeast along U.S. 70 lies another manmade lake, San Carlos Reservoir. Farther to the southeast are the green fields of the upper Gila Valley.

The high country

You'll pass from desert to pines as you follow U.S. 60 to the border, winding through magnificent gorges and rolling across plateaus. Side roads lead to desert lakes and reservoirs, to mountain lakes and streams, to cool forests. Before it reaches New Mexico, the highway climbs to nearly 7,000 feet and runs through deep snow in some winters. This area of east-central Arizona is called "God's Country" by some, simply "the mountain" by others.

Between the two major highways, U.S. 60 and U.S. 70, the beautiful Coronado Trail winds through White Mountain summer and autumn recreation areas close to the Arizona-New Mexico border.

Indian country

Much of the White Mountain region is part of the Apache Indian Reservation —and visitors are subject to tribal law. If you're planning to fish on Indian land, you'll need a permit from the tribe in addition to a valid Arizona fishing license; the same applies to hunting. Ask permission to take any photographs of Indians; you may have to pay for the privilege.

Want to ski? Just south of State 260 is Arizona's newest winter sports complex, the Sunrise Ski Area—developed by the White Mountain Apaches.

Yellow brittlebush adds springtime splash to the bank at Canyon Lake, one of the popular boating and camping sites along the Apache Trail east of Phoenix.

The Apache

The Essentials

East-central Arizona delights—and often surprises—visitors. This is a land of jagged mountain peaks, high desert boating sites, and the cool pine forests and velvet meadows of the White Mountains, interrupted by clear streams and a multitude of sparkling fishing lakes.

You may glimpse some of the animals that roam the mountainsides in summer; after the first snowfall, you're as likely to see parka-clad skiers.

This recreation-filled region is a magnet for valley dwellers when summer temperatures soar. Many city denizens have a second house in the high country.

When should you visit?

Each season brings its own beauty to the land—spring wildflowers brighten desert landscapes and mountain slopes; summer sun sparkles on brooks and ponds; autumn dresses aspens, sumac, and maples with shades of crimson and gold; and winter adds a pristine mantle to mountain shoulders.

Most local festivities take place from spring through early fall—Indian ceremonials, bronco-busting rodeos, and fishing derbies. Winter is reserved for skiers and solitary ice fishers.

Major highways are open year-round; check locally for conditions of secondary roads after rain and snowstorms. Unimproved roads are best traveled in good weather only.

Getting around

You can enter this region from several directions. From Phoenix, you have two choices: State 87 northeast to the intersection with State 260 at Payson, then east along the Tonto Rim to Show Low; or U.S. 60 through Globe, Salt River Canyon, and the White Mountain Apache Reservation.

To reach the lake country along the Apache Trail, take State 88 off U.S. 60 at Apache Junction. Head east on U.S. 70 from Globe to reach the San Carlos Apache Reservation.

To get into the high country from Interstate 40 in the north, turn south on State 77 at Holbrook or U.S. 666 at Sanders. U.S. 666 becomes the Coronado Trail at Alpine.

A series of smaller roads (often unpaved) gives access to lakes and trailheads in the interior.

Tours. Several Phoenix-based tour companies offer 1-day excursions along the Apache Trail. For details, check with your hotel's activity desk.

Where to stay

Because the terrain is so varied, travelers make weekend outings here year-round. It's wise to have reservations for accommodations.

The Lost Dutchman Mine

Somewhere in the Superstition Mountains lies the answer to one of the most tantalizing mysteries of the Southwest—the legendary Lost Dutchman gold mine.

The mine takes its name from one of the few people who claimed to have found it and lived to tell about it. That was the "Dutchman," Jakob Walz, the solitary, immigrant prospector who periodically showed up with bags of nuggets to spend in Phoenix saloons, where he bragged about his fabulous strike but never revealed its whereabouts.

It's said that in the late 1870s, Walz shot two Mexican prospectors and took over their mine. With a deathbed revelation of its location two decades later, he launched a quest that continues today.

Reportedly, the mine is somewhere near Weaver's Needle, the distinctive rock spire that is the most recognizable landmark along the Apache Trail. The Indians called this area the home of the thunder gods (even today, thunderstorms breed in the broiling peaks to rumble and crackle over the countryside). They knew about the mine; it was a sacred place.

Today, the Indian legend is overlaid with new folklore: tales of old-timers, fragmentary reports, rumors, and exhaustive research. The lost gold has been the subject of 53 books and over 800 magazine articles. If it exists, the stash today is worth millions of dollars.

Despite the stories of treasure-seekers who never return and even the discovery of bullet-pierced skulls, thousands of treasure-hunters have ventured into the Superstition Wilderness to look for the mine. Some are unaccounted for; others report hearing shots from nearby rocks. But if the Lost Dutchman exists, it is still keeping its secret.

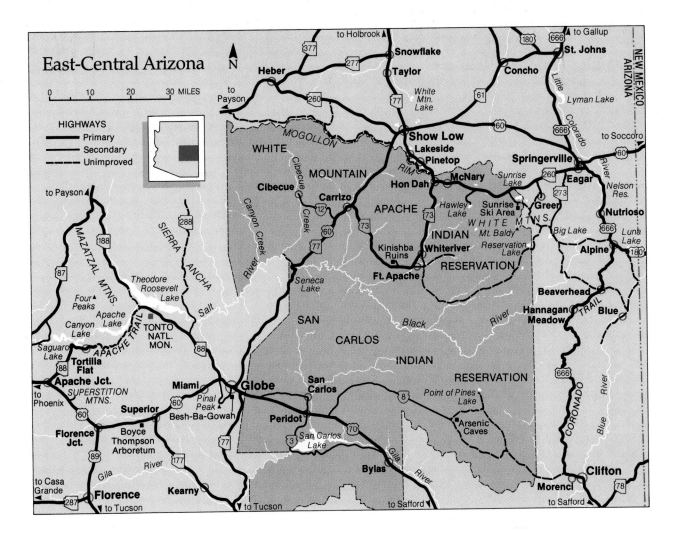

East-Central Arizona

```
0    10    20    30 MILES

HIGHWAYS
━━━━  Primary
──────  Secondary
------  Unimproved
```

Camping. The number of sites available makes camping a popular alternative. At the lower elevations, most campgrounds are open year-round. Up higher, you'll generally find sites accessible from spring into late fall.

Throughout the chapter we mention camping facilities at popular locations, and we include addresses for Apache-Sitgreaves National Forest and the White Mountain and San Carlos Apache reservations. For information on Tonto Rim accommodations, contact the Payson Chamber of Commerce, Drawer A, Payson, AZ 85541.

Accommodations. Major motel centers on the White Mountain Apache Reservation are at Whiteriver, Hon Dah, and Hawley Lake (cabins). At Apache Junction, you'll find The Resort at Gold Canyon Road (golf, tennis, riding) along with other motel rooms. Globe has several motels that make conven-

ient overnight bases for one-day explorations of the Apache Trail, Salt River Canyon, and San Carlos Lake.

The largest concentrations of accommodations in the White Mountains are in the neighboring communities of Show Low (largest town), Lakeside, and Pinetop. Show Low motels include the Paint Pony (conference center, restaurant with entertainment); Lakeside and Pinetop offer modern motels and rustic resorts.

You'll also find accommodations in the towns of Springerville, St. Johns, and Alpine. In the charming little hamlet of Greer, you'll discover some of the area's coziest resorts: Amberian Point, Crozier's Greer Lodge, Molly Butler (state's oldest lodge), White Mountain Lodge, and Elk Trail Lodge (4 miles north). All have restaurants; the Amberian and Elk Trail boast hot tubs. Nighttime activity centers on the town's few saloons.

What to do

This is outdoor country, and most activities revolve around hunting, fishing, hiking, riding, boating, and other water-oriented sports.

Golf. The three best golf courses in the White Mountains lie within miles of each other in Pinetop. Pinetop and White Mountain are private courses but do accept some nonmembers on weekdays, if space is available. You'll find other courses at White Mountain Lakes, Show Low, and Alpine.

Skiing. Most skiing takes place at Sunrise on the White Mountain Apache Reservation (see page 86). Greer Ski Area, owned by the Amberian Point resort, offers beginner and intermediate runs. Greer Ski Tours offers cross-country skiing, and Alpine Ski Tours provides 40 miles of trails.

In a burst of glory, poppies blanket the

hills near Roosevelt Lake. After a few

days, the plants turn to seed to escape

the scorching summer heat.

A Phoenix Loop

The route from Phoenix to Globe forks at Apache Junction, in front of the imposing battlements of the Superstition Mountains. You can choose between the scenic Apache Trail and the more direct U.S. 60 — or combine them for a loop trip.

The left fork, spectacular Apache Trail, leads to Roosevelt, Canyon, and Apache lakes, and to the north side of the Superstition Wilderness. Twenty-five miles of the road are gravel, and this is not a through route for trailers or big vans. Smaller trailers can manage the lake campground roads, but the real obstacle for larger vehicles is a series of sharp turns around the cliffs just before Roosevelt Dam.

The south fork, the major highway (U.S. 60) through Superior and Miami, passes Apacheland Movie Ranch, the turnoff to the north end of the Pinal Pioneer Parkway to Tucson, rocky Queen Creek Canyon, the Boyce Thompson Southwestern Arboretum, and the eroded sandstone pillars of Devil's Canyon.

Though most travelers start a Phoenix-Globe loop tour from Phoenix, starting from Globe will put the sun behind you in the morning going west and again in the evening heading east, a definite advantage. Either way, if you drive this loop as a one-day trip, take the Apache Trail first; explore a canyon, take a cooling splash in a lake, enjoy the scenery, and study the Tonto ruins. The southern route is easier and faster for a return drive.

The Apache Trail

This ancient Indian short-cut through the mountains is now State 88, a dramatic, scenic drive through a wild region of tumbled volcanic debris and massive layered buttes, twisting tortuously through steep-cliffed canyons and skirting sparkling lakes.

Starting at Apache Junction just west of the starkly eroded dacite cones of the Superstition Mountains, the road turns northeast into the foothills.

Goldfield to Tortilla Flat. A roadside curio shop marks the site of the ghost town of Goldfield. Next door is a patched adobe building, once the mining camp's schoolhouse, now a snack bar and the only surviving building. Across the road you'll find the bones of the old town: crumbling foundations and debris from tumbled buildings. Behind the shop, the open shaft of the Bluebird Mine displays minerals and relics of mining days.

Superstition Wilderness. About a mile beyond the mine, at a vista point, a gravel road turns east to First Water Creek and hiking trails into the Superstition Wilderness. Penetrating this rugged wilderness on foot or on horseback can be a challenging adventure in spring or autumn. It's cold in winter, and in summer lack of water and extreme heat create hazardous conditions.

You must carry all the water you will need, since the few permanent waterholes are difficult to find. U.S. Geological Survey maps are recommended equipment for this area. For pack-trip information and lists of packers, write to the Apache Junction Chamber of Commerce, P.O. Box 1747, Apache Junction, AZ 85220.

Canyon Lake. The road to Canyon Lake descends through eroded, folded lava flows to picnic areas, a campground, and boat launching (and rental) facilities. Excursion boats offer sightseeing cruises.

Tortilla Flat. At Canyon Lake, the road swings south, separated from the chain of lakes by intervening buttes and mesas. There's a store, restaurant, and motel at Tortilla Flat, east of the lake (19 miles from Apache Junction). The next store is 29 miles farther on this road at Roosevelt Lake, or you can take a steep side road to the Apache Lake Resort about 16 miles east.

Fish Creek Canyon. East of Tortilla Flat, switchbacks climb through sharp canyons, a natural museum of rocky formations—pink layers of arkose rock cut by dikes of tan lava dusted with glittering specks of quartz and feldspar.

The paved road ends five miles east of Tortilla Flat, just beyond another vista point. The gravel road continues to Roosevelt Lake through the most dramatic part of the drive.

The sharp, winding road descends cliffs into Fish Creek Canyon and takes you to a one-lane bridge across the creek. The canyon's narrow fissure opens south to views of sunlit Geronimo Head — pause here for the scenery, a picnic in the streambed oasis, or a short hike. The terrain is rough; proceed cautiously.

Apache Lake. From the Apache Trail, a gravel road descends sharply to the Apache Lake resort and marina — motel, store, restaurant, boating and fishing supplies. From this saguaro-lined road you can see the Painted Cliffs and Goat Mountain across the lake. Tonto National Forest Service picnic grounds and campsites lie near the lake. A turnoff farther east on the Apache Trail takes you to Burnt Corral campgrounds.

Roosevelt Lake. Wedged into a deep canyon, Roosevelt is the world's largest masonry dam. Begun in 1905 as the first project under the Reclamation Act, the dam was completed in 1911 and dedicated by Teddy Roosevelt. Viewed downstream, where the gravelled Apache Trail loops tightly around almost-vertical ridges, it resembles a smaller Hoover Dam. Behind it, the largest of the interior Arizona reservoirs spreads broadly east and north against the Sierra Ancha Range and the Zane Grey Hills.

A popular boating, water-skiing, and fishing site, Roosevelt Lake offers several Forest Service minimum facility campsites. You'll find a store and gas station about 2 miles southeast of the dam, and a motel, restaurant, gas station, and trailer park are located at Roosevelt Lake Resort about 6 miles southeast of the dam. State 88 beyond the dam is paved.

...A Phoenix Loop

Four Peaks. North of Apache Lake, you can reach the Four Peaks area of the southern Mazatzal Mountains by a jeep road from State 188. This remote area offers summit views of the Tonto Basin to the northeast and the Salt River Valley southwest.

Visitors can camp at a primitive site at Pigeon Spring, 10 miles southwest of State 188 on El Oso Road. If the road is in good shape, you can drive all the way to the camp. You'll find plenty of firewood; bring your own water.

The trail drops from 5,600 feet to 3,800 feet at Big Oak Flat, where a gravel road winds back to State 188.

> *Some scenic hiking trails*
>
> *await you atop timber-clad*
>
> *Pinal Peak.*

Tonto National Monument. Cliff dwellings occupied more than 600 years ago by the Salado Indians are preserved in this canyon about 5 miles southeast of Roosevelt Dam.

The Salado people irrigated and farmed the Salt River Valley. At the visitors' center you can inspect their tools, weapons, jewelry, pottery, and fine weaving. A diorama depicts the reconstructed community.

An hour's walk (through a show of wildflowers in April) takes you to the Lower Ruin—you can wander through its 19 rooms. A 3-hour guided tour to the more distant, 40-room Upper Ruin must be arranged at least two days in advance; write to Tonto National Monument, P.O. Box 707, Roosevelt, AZ 85545, or call (602) 467-2241.

The Lower Ruin is tucked into a cave that is in deep shade by mid-afternoon. Summer temperatures are high; take a hat for protection from the sun, and be sure to wear good walking shoes. The trail closes at 4 P.M.

The southern route

The wide, divided highway on this route to Globe presents a stark contrast to the rugged curves of the Apache Trail. East of Apache Junction, U.S. 60 affords spectacular views of the legendary Superstition Mountains.

Apacheland Movie Ranch. About 7 miles east of the junction, King's Ranch Road leads to this detailed replica of a 19th-century western town complete with about two dozen clapboard and adobe buildings. A permanent movie set, Apacheland is where such TV programs as *Death Valley Days* and *Have Gun, Will Travel* were filmed. An admission fee is charged.

Boyce Thompson Southwestern Arboretum. Established and maintained as a research institution, this Desert Biology Station of the University of Arizona, near Superior, is a popular rest stop and tour attraction. Its remarkable collection includes 6,000 botanical species from around the world, more than 150 kinds of birds, and 40 other species of animals. A small admission fee is charged.

Looming behind the arboretum is 4,400-foot Picket Post Mountain, site of a former Army signaling station.

Superior. At the edge of town visitors can see the entrance to the 3,500-foot shaft and adjacent smelter of one of the few underground copper mines in Arizona. A steep slope topped by a sheer, vertically eroded rock wall known as Apache Leap rims the town on the east. Its name comes from a legend that about 75 Indian warriors flung themselves from the rock's top to escape capture by pursuing soldiers.

Just west of Superior, a sign marks a dirt side road leading to Apache Tears Cave, where you can find the small, gemlike obsidian accretions called Apache Tears embedded in layers of perlite, a mineral mined for use in insulation. The 1-mile drive to the cave is a rough road; after a rain, you need a four-wheel-drive vehicle.

The Globe area

Long hills of mine tailings and slag are scattered between Miami and Globe. The light-colored rubble is waste from the crusher, called tailings. The dark red to black material is slag, burned rock from the smelter.

Once a rip-snorting silver and copper-mining town, the thriving trade center and travelers' stopover of Globe still shows many traces of its frontier beginnings.

Globe today. Still a busy place, Globe is a center for mining supplies, seat of Gila County, gateway to a cattle empire to the east, and a popular residential city for those who like or need its climate, halfway between desert and mountain. One interesting stop might be at the restored Old Gila County Courthouse, where you'll find a fine arts gallery on the first floor.

South of Globe, Jess Hayes Road takes you to the Salado Indian ruins and the campgrounds and trails of Pinal Peak.

Besh-Ba-Gowah. Although not as well preserved as the Tonto National Monument ruins left by the ancient Salado Indians, the Salado site at Besh-Ba-Gowah (meaning "metal camp") is considerably more extensive. Situated a mile south of Globe on Jess Hayes Road, the ruins cover about 2 acres on a bluff above Pinal Creek. Start your trip at the visitor center and museum.

You're free to roam the site; don't remove anything. A small collection of artifacts from the ruins is on display in the Gila County Historical Museum (open Monday through Saturday) in Globe.

Pinal Peak. The highest and coolest campgrounds in the Tonto National Forest, and some scenic hiking trails, await you atop timber-clad Pinal Peak.

The campgrounds usually are open from May to December; exact dates depend on the weather. Check at the Forest Service office in Globe.

Apache Country

Traveling the main highways of east-central Arizona, you can't go far without entering the homeland of the state's Apache Indians. East of Globe, U.S. 70 crosses miles of the San Carlos Indian Reservation; here is big San Carlos Lake, a major fishing and water sports site. Winding northeast on U.S. 60 through the mountains from Globe to Show Low and then across the pine-forested plateau to Springerville, you drive through the White Mountain Apache Indian Reservation. The town of McNary and the western half of the beautiful White Mountain Recreation Area lie within this reservation.

The two reservations, separated by the Black River, cover millions of acres of fine grazing range, farmlands, and forests. Both tribes encourage outdoor recreation on their reservations. The White Mountain Apaches manage the lakes and streams of the White Mountains and also a ski area. Around one of the biggest lakes in Arizona, the San Carlos Apaches are developing thousands of acres of land for public recreational use.

Year-round fishing is popular on both reservations—including ice fishing in White Mountain lakes. Big game hunting is a major attraction. You can obtain permits for reservation hunting and fishing at sporting goods stores throughout the area.

Tribal offices in the reservations' capitals of San Carlos and Whiteriver will provide visitors with information about points of interest. Inquire here about local road conditions.

San Carlos Apache Reservation

You enter the reservation just east of Globe, where a turnoff at Peridot leads you north to the tribal capital of San Carlos. Peridot is a variety of a gemstone, olivine, frequently found in volcanic areas. The San Carlos Reservation is a major source, but prospecting is not permitted. The tribe maintains strict mineral regulations.

The road to San Carlos follows the river through fields and big tamarisk trees. The town clusters around the low buildings of the Indian agency and the tribal council; absence of garish signs and neon gives it the look of another era. If you need information, check with the tribal office.

The San Carlos Apaches hold their annual celebration and rodeo in the fall around the 3-day Veterans Day weekend. The traditional Sunrise Dance, performed during the weekend, honors Apache maidens' "coming out" and is highlighted by the colorful Crown Dancers, also known by the Apaches as the "Mountain Spirit Dancers." These dances are also performed at other times throughout the year, but dates are not publicized. Although visitors are welcome and may take photographs, they should ask permission and keep in mind that the dances are serious religious ceremonies.

For detailed information about the reservation, write the San Carlos Tribe, San Carlos, AZ 85559.

San Carlos Reservation lakes. The reservation offers facilities for campers, boaters, and anglers at three lakes. Passenger cars can reach San Carlos and Seneca lakes year-round. The road to Point of Pines Lake, like most other reservation roads, is best traveled by pickups, especially in winter and the July rainy season.

San Carlos Lake was formed by one of the Southwest's major reclamation structures, Coolidge Dam, completed in 1930 to provide irrigation water and electricity for the upper Gila River. The reservoir covers one of the ancient burial grounds of the Apaches. The Indians turned down a government offer to move the graves, considering this a desecration of the dead; the compromise was a great concrete slab on the lake floor to protect the graves from the water above.

A paved road follows the south shore of the reservoir for about 25 miles, rejoining the main highway near Bylas.

The Apaches call San Carlos Lake (open year-round) the hottest bass lake in the state. It's also a popular site for water-skiing, swimming, skin diving, boating, and waterfowl hunting, but check ahead—these activities may be curtailed when the water level is low.

Facilities at the San Carlos Marina Resort at the west end of the lake include a curio and tackle shop, and a camper-trailer park. This is the only lake on the reservation where gasoline motors are permitted.

Seneca Lake, situated on U.S. 60 just south of the Salt River, offers a store, picnic areas, and campsites. This major resort development is open year-round.

Point of Pines Lake in the eastern part of the reservation is a year-round trout-fishing site, but it's difficult to reach after a rain.

To get to the lake and its campgrounds, turn north from U.S. 70 on the paved road 5 miles east of Peridot (Indian Road 8). After the pavement ends at Juniper, another 35 miles of dirt road take you north to the lake.

Just off the road near the Indian Road 11 intersection lie the Arsenic Caves, where you can puzzle over ancient drawings.

The Salt River Canyon

At the Salt River border between the two reservations, you descend into a small-scale Grand Canyon. U.S. 60 drops more than 2,000 feet in a series of switchbacks, and climbs back out.

On the south side (approaching from Globe), you'll find frequent overlooks and convenient picnic ramadas a short walk from the highway. Concrete steps near the bridge lead down to a large picnic area.

About a half-mile upstream from the bridge, the Salt River tumbles over wide falls. To reach the falls and a view from the bottom of the canyon, turn off the highway immediately north of the bridge and follow the narrow road upstream.

...Apache Country

White Mountain Apache Reservation

Before the organization of the White Mountain Recreation Enterprise, most of the 1½ million acres of this reservation were accessible only by unpaved trail. Then the tribe built access roads, campgrounds, lodging, and other facilities to open up their lands for visitors.

For detailed information, maps, and group arrangements, write to the White Mountain Recreation Enterprise, P.O. Box 220, Whiteriver, AZ 85941. Fishing, hunting, and camping permits can be obtained in advance from this office or in person at sporting goods stores in Phoenix, Tucson, and towns throughout east-central Arizona.

A visit to the primitive settlement of Cibecue, any of the Indian trading posts, and tribal gatherings at which visitors are welcome will introduce you to the Apache people and their way of life.

The town of Show Low (see page 88) is a good point of departure for a visit to Whiteriver and the White Mountain Apache Reservation. Take State 260 southeast from Show Low; the turnoff onto State 73 is at Hon Dah, between Pinetop and McNary. On the corner is the tribe's handsome, modern-rustic motel and cabin complex. Hon Dah, appropriately, means "be my guest."

Whiteriver. Whiteriver looks like many other small Southwest towns — the difference is that the residents are Apaches, among the last of the frontier tribes to accept the authority of the United States Government.

At Whiteriver you'll find the studio, shop, and home of Jack Fowler, whose copper and brass sculptures of western scenes are displayed around the nation, including the White House.

The White Mountain Apaches hold their annual Tribal Fair and Rodeo here in early August. Like their San Carlos neighbors, they conduct Sunrise Maiden ceremonies.

Fort Apache. Three miles south of Whiteriver is historic Fort Apache, established in 1870, a major U.S. Army post during the Apache wars. From here the U.S. Cavalry and the famous Apache Scouts went out after the marauding bands of Geronimo and Natchez.

In 1924 the fort was turned over to the Bureau of Indian Affairs and became the Theodore Roosevelt Indian School. Many of the original buildings still stand, identified by signs. Visitors are welcome.

Kinishba. Seven miles west of Fort Apache are the partially restored remains of Kinishba ("red house" in Apache), a village of the classic Pueblo III period that housed up to 2,000 pre-Apache people near the end of the 13th century.

The two large buildings and several smaller outlying structures have more than 400 rooms. A major archeological site, Kinishba serves as an important training and field research center for the University of Arizona.

McNary. This former lumber-mill town in the pine-forested northeastern uplands of the reservation has an unusual history. Until 1923 it was Cooley, the site of a small mill and lumber company. In that year the corporation was purchased by the Cady Lumber Co. of McNary, Louisiana, whose managers were looking for a new timber supply. They loaded the company's logging and mill machinery and the families and belongings of 500 employees on two long private trains and moved the whole works to the new town built in a Ponderosa pine forest.

On property leased from the Apaches, the Southwest Forest Industries grew until 1979, when the sawmill burned. Subsequently, Southwest rebuilt its lumber operations in Eagar, some 40 miles to the east. Today only a handful of people live in the old company town that once was home to 2,000.

Sunrise ski area. The Apaches' ski resort near Greer in the northeast corner of the reservation is one of Arizona's major ski areas. It's also being developed as a summer resort.

The handsome 100-room lodge, on a hill overlooking Sunrise Lake to the north and the slopes of Sunrise Peak to the south, offers first-class accommodations.

Free buses connect the lodge with the slopes. Six chairlifts (including a triple-chair-opening Cyclone, a newly developed mountain with seven ski runs), two T-bars, and a rope tow can carry 11,000 skiers an hour up the slopes. Midway on the Apache Peak run is a restaurant with patio.

For information on skiing, write to Sunrise, Box 217, McNary, AZ 85930.

Trout hatcheries. The Williams Creek Fish Hatchery near McNary and the Alchesay National Fish Hatchery near Whiteriver both welcome visitors during daylight hours. The first is about 8 miles south of McNary; take the road to Williams Creek and turn east below the rim. The turnoff to Alchesay is marked on State 73, about 5 miles north of Whiteriver; from there it's about 3 miles by dirt road.

Lakes and streams. The reservation's half of the White Mountain Recreation Area, including the Mt. Baldy Wilderness Area, encompasses 26 lakes created by dams built by the Apaches and more than 400 miles of trout streams.

The most accessible and popular big lakes are Hawley Lake, reached by State 473 south of State 260 about 9 miles east of McNary, and Sunrise Lake, on the road south from State 260 to Sunrise ski resort. At Hawley, you'll find a store and boat rentals. Both lakes contain primarily rainbow trout, some brook and brown trout.

Smaller lakes along State 260 between McNary and the Sunrise turnoff — Shush Be Zahze (Little Bear), Shush Be Tou (Big Bear), Bog Creek, Horseshoe, and A-1 (right beside the highway) — are good for trout fishing and offer picnic areas and campsites.

Elaborately garbed, black-hooded
Apaches wait to perform at Devil
Dance ceremonies. Ask for permission
to take photos and expect to pay for
the privilege.

Tonto National Monument preserves
desert ruins left by the Salado
Indians. In the Lower Ruin, you
can explore 19 rooms of ancient
cliff dwellings.

The White Mountains

A cool vacation land of forests, lakes, and streams, the White Mountains are the Arizonans' answer to July and August heat. For anglers, hunters, golfers, and followers of high mountain trails, their appeal is irresistible.

The White Mountains lie within parts of the Apache-Sitgreaves National Forest and the White Mountain Apache Indian Reservation. (For the Apache section of the White Mountains area, see page 86.)

Some of the state's finest forest land awaits you here: Ponderosa pine, spruce, Douglas fir, and aspen fringing blue lakes and emerald meadows.

Show Low

The mountains' "capital" (elevation 6,330 feet) takes its name from an early incident in which one pioneer, gambling with a ranch at stake, challenged another to "show low." His opponent showed a deuce of clubs, won the ranch, and later sold it to the Mormons, who opened it for settlement. In honor of this bet, the town's main street is named after the toss.

Today, the friendly town is the area's major shopping center, with motels, restaurants, conference center, rodeo grounds (Fourth of July is the big one), and many resorts and cabins. Around it are several lakes — Fool's Hollow Lake and White Mountain Lake to the north, Show Low Lake to the south — and both Forest Service and commercial campgrounds.

North of Show Low, State 77 runs through farming and dairy country to meet Interstate 40 at Holbrook. Along the way, it passes through several prim little farming communities — Shumway, Taylor, Snowflake — whose red brick homes, built in down-East style of the 1870s, give them a faintly New England flavor.

South of Show Low, State 260 cuts through the forests to the resort towns of Lakeside and Pinetop and leads into the heart of the great recreational area of the White Mountains.

Along the Rim

In the White Mountains the Mogollon Plateau rises to 11,590 feet at the top of Mt. Baldy. Most of the Mogollon Rim country lies at an altitude of 5,000 to 9,000 feet.

The headwaters of three major rivers flow from the foot of Mt. Baldy; the Little Colorado flows north through the Apache-Sitgreaves National Forest, and the Black and White rivers flow across the White Mountain Apache Reservation. No roads penetrate the 7,400-acre Mt. Baldy Wilderness Area surrounding the peak, but hikers can reach it from Sheep Crossing Campground, about 5 miles south of Greer.

The rim road, a dirt road from the vicinity of Lakeside all the way west to Camp Verde on Interstate 17, offers spectacular views but often is impassable for cars, particularly from Lakeside west to Deer Springs.

Lake country

Thirteen lakes and 250 miles of streams cover the non-reservation lands of the White Mountains between Show Low and Springerville.

The pines beside the highway from Show Low to Pinetop harbor many resorts, lodges, rental cabins, and campgrounds. The towns of Lakeside and Pinetop have modern motels, restaurants, stores, and other services. In Pinetop, attractive commercial buildings harmonize with the rustic setting and the roughhewn look of earlier construction. Several top-rated courses attract golfers.

East of McNary, State 260 climbs to a summit of alpine meadows. You come upon aspen-bordered A-1 Lake before the turnoff to the Apaches' Sunrise ski area.

Greer. At 8,500 feet lies the tiny village of Greer in a secluded mountain valley 5 miles south of State 260. Its winter population of about 120 swells to around 5,000 in the summer as vaca-

tioners move into surrounding lodges, cabins, and campgrounds.

At the small, manmade Greer Lakes, known for their big German brown trout, you can camp at three Forest Service campgrounds or at one campground upstream on the Little Colorado.

Wilderness. From the lakes a gravel road leads south to Sheep Crossing campground on the Little Colorado, and trails head westward into the White Mountain Apache Reservation and the Mt. Baldy Wilderness Area. Farther south, the road continues to Crescent Lake, Big Lake, and the creeks forming headwaters of the Black River.

You'll find detailed maps of the area at local stores and lodges or at the Forest Service in Springerville.

Grazing country

East of the White Mountain Apache boundary, State 260 drops to the grass-covered rolling hills and plains of Arizona's rich cattle country. The bunch-grass grazing lands, studded with dark outcroppings of lava and porous volcanic bombs, extend north past Holbrook.

Eagar. Named for three Mormon pioneer brothers who held out against outlaws and Apaches, the town today is a quiet ranching and farming center of wide, clean streets, tall poplars, and neat houses and yards. The surrounding cattle ranch area is well known for its purebred Herefords.

Springerville. This shopping and service center for lumber and cattle industries was not always so peaceful. During the 1870s and '80s, it was one of the toughest towns in the Southwest, populated by fugitive cattle rustlers, horse thieves, and various other outlaws.

Lyman Lake. For fishing, boating, water-skiing, camping, and picnicking, Lyman Lake State Park makes a pleasant stop between Springerville and St. Johns to the north. The 1,000-acre reservoir lies just off U.S. Highway 666 among rolling grassy hills in a shallow canyon on the Little Colorado River. Fishing for bass and northern pike is good in autumn, winter, and spring. Summer brings boaters and water-skiers.

Facilities at the lake include campsites, showers, trailer pads with hookups, launching ramp, boat rentals, and a store. There's a small fee for fishing.

A little herd of bison is pastured on a hill near the highway entrance. You're likely to see some of the shaggy beasts at feed racks near the highway.

The Coronado Trail

Paralleling the eastern border of Arizona, U.S. 666 links the high plateau country and the desert lowlands. Between Springerville and Clifton you pass through both the Blue and White mountain ranges. The two towns are only 117 miles apart, but the highway twists and winds, stretching the distance to a 3½-hour drive, not counting stops and side trips.

The Coronado Trail takes its name from the Spanish explorer Francisco de Coronado, who passed this way more than four centuries ago. In spite of the scenery, the road was lightly traveled until recent years because portions were unpaved and often closed in winter. Now an all-weather highway, it remains uncrowded.

This region ranks among the best hunting and fishing areas of the Southwest. From your car you might see deer, elk, antelope, and turkeys—perhaps even a bear—as well as countless smaller animals.

Overnight accommodations along this route are limited. You'll find motels in Alpine, cabins at Beaverhead, and a lodge and cabins at Hannagan Meadow. Six unimproved Forest Service campgrounds lie along U.S.

666 between Eagar and Clifton. Another four are on the forks and tributaries of the Black River south of Big Lake, accessible from Beaverhead. On the west side of the ridge, look for the camp at Blue Crossing if you're seeking seclusion. There's another campground north on the river, one near Luna Lake, and one at the 8,500-foot divide north of Alpine.

For specific information on campground locations and hunting and fishing regulations, write to the Forest Supervisor, Apache-Sitgreaves National Forest, Box 640, Springerville, AZ 85938.

Alpine. Passing Nelson Reservoir, a popular lake, you come upon the pleasant crossroads hamlet of Alpine. The scenery in this area is spectacular in autumn, when the white bark and shimmering yellow leaves of the aspens stand out against the deep greens of the conifers. If you have time for some off-highway exploring, consider the following side trips from Alpine.

Escudilla Mountain. The dirt road up 10,955-foot Escudilla Mountain is rough but normally navigable for cars for about 4½ miles. Turn northeast from the highway on Terry Flat Road about 4 miles south of Nutrioso. For a loop trip, turn left from U.S. 180 about 2 miles east of Alpine onto a graded road that takes you to Stone Creek and on around the east and north sides of the mountain. The road eventually swings up to U.S. 666 about 6 miles north of Nutrioso.

Williams Valley — Big Lake. This back road to Big Lake leaves the highway about 2 miles north of Alpine. Grazing cattle create a peaceful scene in Williams Valley, ringed with tall aspens. You can continue on any of several roads to complete a loop drive, but the best way back to the Coronado Trail is the route you just drove.

Blue River. An excursion into the peaceful world of the Blue River starts near Luna Lake, about 3½ miles east of Alpine. You leave U.S. 180 to curve

through pastoral countryside and then drop into a wide canyon elaborately eroded into spires and irregular cliffs.

You can continue for 14 miles beyond the Blue post office to road's end, or you can take the Red Hill Road from Blue out to U.S. 666. The climb to Beaverhead yields splendid views back over the Blue River Valley.

The Mogollon Rim. From Alpine to Hannagan Meadow is one of Arizona's loveliest forest drives, but the really expansive views greet you southward at the Mogollon Rim. When you emerge on the rim, you come to a roadside rest turnout where you can enjoy the view and continue to the left or right onto an unpaved rim road. A short drive in either direction along the rim takes you into handsome groves of aspens.

The Coronado Trail takes its name from the Spanish explorer Francisco de Coronado, who passed this way more than four centuries ago.

Clifton-Morenci. At the southern end of the Coronado Trail, Clifton is part of the historic Clifton-Morenci mining district. A mile north of town is the junction with a 5-mile road to Morenci and its huge open-pit copper mine. More than a billion tons of rock and ore have been moved here, and the pit is so large that it may take you a while to spot the seemingly tiny trains and trucks moving in its depths and over the distant terraces. A sign on a fenced overlook explains the operation.

Tucson & the

Southeast Corner

Known as the "White Dove of the Desert," resplendent Mission San Xavier del Bac, located south of Tucson, is a handsome reminder of the time when the area was a bustling outpost of the Spanish Empire.

A mecca for winter sunseekers, Tucson dominates one of Arizona's most colorful and diverse regions. This fast-growing city (525,000 population) offers cultural sophistication while retaining some of the ambiance of the sleepy pueblo that it once was.

Rich in Indian and Spanish history, Tucson is only a short drive from Mexico. You'll hear Spanish spoken as often as English, along with an occasional Indian dialect.

The city got its name from the Pima Indians, who once had a village at the foot of Sentinel Peak (now known as "A" Mountain) called *Chuk-son*—"foot of the dark mountain." Ultimately, the name became Tucson.

Choose your fun

During a visit to Tucson and its environs, you can explore mountains or desert, afoot or on horseback; dip into history or archeology; or shop for fine Indian and Mexican crafts.

In addition to swimming, tennis, and golf, this area offers a chance to watch working cowboys on a ranch or performing cowboys in a rodeo. In the winter, head for Mt. Lemmon to make a snowman—and take a poolside sunbath an hour later.

Though the 2,390-foot elevation brings some chill winter spells and occasional rainstorms, for the most part Tucson basks in year-round sun.

Land of variety

In Tucson you stand on flat desert surrounded by a protective circle of five mountain ranges. From the high shield of the Catalinas to the close-in Tucson range, they provide a continually changing backdrop — from purple shadows at sunrise to black silhouettes against some of the state's splashiest sunsets.

Tucson is unusual in its lack of satellite communities. Instead, much of the spectacular desert, foothill, and mountain country surrounding the city is protected in public preserves, their extensive trails open to riders and hikers.

To the south, follow the green Santa Cruz River Valley through cotton fields, copper-mining centers, and historic sites to Nogales, gateway to Mexico's West Coast Highway.

Return to Tucson through the even greener San Rafael Valley or continue through the southeastern corner of the state on a loop filled with reminders of the Old West. You can stand where the Earps shot it out with the Clantons and walk Apache trails in the rock-pillared peaks of the Chiricahuas.

Taste of the past

No doubt it was the sheltering mountains around Tucson as well as the water of the Santa Cruz River that attracted prehistoric Indians to this valley. Several sizable Indian communities flourished here by the time the Spanish arrived and established their key Arizona military garrison in Tucson in 1776.

Mexico gained control of the town after her independence from Spain in 1821, followed by the United States with the Gadsden Purchase and, for a brief period during the Civil War, the Confederacy.

The Essentials

A friendly city, the "Old Pueblo" offers visitors a range of accommodations and activities in an atmosphere of relaxation. Easy accessibility to near-by canyons and peaks, rolling grass-lands and green valleys, and saguaro-studded desert makes Tucson a good choice as a base for exploring the state's southeast corner.

Getting around

A number of major and commuter air-lines fly into Tucson International Air-port. The city is also served by Amtrak and by Greyhound and Trailways bus lines. Interstate 10, the major freeway between Los Angeles and El Paso, passes right through the city's down-town area; Interstate 19 connects Tuc-son with Nogales.

If you wish to rent a car, all national rental agencies and a number of local firms are represented at the airport. Arizona Stagecoach Co. provides 24-hour transportation between the airport and most hotels. For public transportation, call Sun Tran, the city's bus system, at (602) 792-9222.

Well-maintained highways reach most destinations mentioned in this chapter. Desert off-road driving can be hazardous; see page 9 for tips.

Southwest Tours, Inc. takes visitors into the desert, canyons, and moun-tain ranges around the city. You'll visit mines, ghost towns, and other historic sites. For more information, phone (602) 795-0038.

Where to stay

The Tucson area provides a wide vari-ety of accommodations, ranging from simple highway motel rooms to lux-urious resorts, guest ranches (see page 73), and spas. We mention a sampling below. You'll also find a number of rec-reational vehicle parks and camping facilities around town.

Tucson. The city's best-known lodg-ings include Arizona Inn (Tucson landmark set in acres of gardens, beau-tifully decorated rooms), Best Western Ghost Ranch, Canyon Ranch Spa (fit-ness resort with exercise program, lo-cal meals, massages), Desert Inn Tucson, Doubletree Hotel (adjacent golf course), Holiday Inns, Howard Johnsons, Lodge On The Desert, Loews Ventana Canyon Resort (new resort with health club and spa, tennis, golf, horseback riding), Quality Inn, Ramada Inn, Rodeway Inns, Ronstadt House (bed and breakfast in historic house), Sheraton Hotels (beautiful set-ting at El Conquistador complex with tennis center, golf, horseback riding), Tucson Hilton, Tucson National Golf Club and Resort (27-hole champion-ship course, tennis center, spa), West-ward Look (tennis clinic), Westin La Paloma (new in 1985, 27-hole Jack Nicklaus golf course).

Around the southeast corner. Farther afield, choices include Tubac Valley Country Club Resort, Tubac (historic setting 30 minutes from Nogales, golf); VisionQuest Wagon Train & Guest Lodge, Elfrida (old lodge offering wagon train adventures in Cochise country, some teepees); Stage Stop Inn, Patagonia (historic hostelry, base for San Rafael Valley exploring); Best Western Lookout Lodge, Tombstone; Copper Queen Hotel, Bisbee (restored elegance, central location, good lunch stop); The Bisbee Inn, Bisbee (bed and breakfast); and Sheraton Rio Rico Resort, Nogales (hilltop setting north of the border, golf and tennis).

Sports & recreation

Whether your favorite activity is swim-ming, golf, tennis, horseback riding, racquetball, biking, or jogging, you'll find plenty of places to enjoy it.

Swimming. Almost anywhere you stay in this area of the state, you'll find a pool. In addition, 15 city pools open for the warmest part of the year.

Two other water-oriented activities invite family fun: Justin's Water World, 3551 San Joaquin Road, a summer-only water theme park; and Breakers, 8555 W. Tangerine, a large wave-action pool open year-round from 5 to 10 P.M. Tues-day through Friday, noon to 10 P.M. weekends.

Golf and tennis. Stop by the visitors bureau for a list of the city's 22 public and municipal golf courses and more than 60 tennis centers, including an exhibition court seating 600 at the Sheraton El Conquistador. Golfers will also find excellent courses in Tubac, Green Valley, and Nogales.

Horseback riding. In addition to the riding programs at guest ranches and resorts around town, several stables rent horses, provide lessons, and offer a variety of trail rides. Look for these facilities in the Yellow Pages under "Stables."

Racquetball. Tucson Racquet Club, 4001 N. Country Club, provides 12 rac-quetball courts in addition to 24 lighted tennis courts and other sports facilities.

Skiing. In season (usually December through March) you can ski at Mt. Lemmon, only 35 miles from Tucson. Two rope tows and a chairlift accom-modate both beginners and advanced skiers; rental equipment is available.

Jogging. Try the parcourse at the Uni-versity of Arizona. The course extends around most of the campus mall area.

Spectator sports. From September through May you'll usually find some sporting event to watch. Fast-paced dog races are held year-round (except in July) at air-conditioned Greyhound Park, S. 4th Avenue at 36th Street. Polo games, horse shows, and rodeos take place throughout the year at Pima County Fairgrounds; La Fiesta de los Vaqueros, one of the world's top 10 rodeos, is in the spring. Several major golf tournaments are scheduled in the winter.

Seasonal activities include Cleveland Indians spring training and exhibition

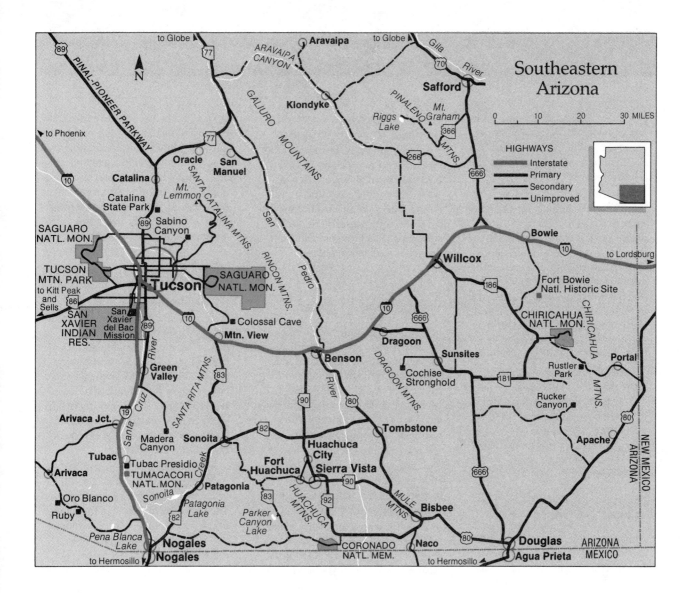

Southeastern Arizona

games, Toros professional baseball, and intercollegiate baseball, basketball, and football.

Dining & nightlife

In addition to some of the finest Mexican food in the country (chimichangas were invented here), Tucson provides dining choices ranging from steak barbecues to haute cuisine. Many restaurants have music and dancing.

You can get a list a restaurants from the visitors bureau, or check at your hotel's activities desk.

Recommendations may include some of the following: Arizona Inn, Charles, El Adobe, El Charro (country's oldest Mexican restaurant), Gold

Room at Westward Look Resort, Hidden Valley Inn (1880s western dining near Sabino Canyon), Janos, Katherine and Company (open for breakfast), Lil Abner's, Palomino (try a Greek dish), Penelope's, Pinnacle Peak Steakhouse (no ties allowed), Saguaro Corners (dining among the cactus), Samaniego House, Scordato's, Solarium, Tack Room at Rancho del Rio (Arizona's only five-star award-winning restaurant), and Triple C Ranch (includes stage show).

Tucson is home to an opera company, a symphony orchestra, a ballet company, and a theater company. Among other performing groups are the Gaslight Theatre (melodrama and vaudeville) and Le Theatre (dinner and show).

Shopping for arts & crafts

Tucson's climate and location certainly have a lot to do with the fact that it's an arts and crafts center. Because the Papago Reservation is close by, the choice of basketry is especially good. You'll also see weaving, silverwork, pottery, painting, carving, and sculpture from the Navajo, Hopi, Zuni, and Apache tribes.

Crafts stores are found in the four large shopping malls around town and in various smaller centers. Of particular interest are the museum shops and Old Town Artisans, downtown in the El Presidio Historic District.

On a weekend in spring and again in December, the 4th Avenue Street Fair encompasses crafts, food, and music.

Don't let the slightly technical name mislead you; the Arizona-Sonora Desert Museum is a "don't miss" destination for any visitor to the Southwest.

Called one of the 10 best zoos in the world, it's certainly the most distinctive—and it's your best introduction to the desert. Outdoors, indoors, and underground, entertaining displays educate you on the area's ecology and explain the terrain you'll see in later desert excursions. In this 110-acre living museum you'll learn about the flora, fauna, and geology of Arizona and adjacent Sonora and Baja California, Mexico.

Just learning the names of the more than 300 native plant species in a 12-acre developed section of the complex is worth the trip. You'll see every type of plant that grows at every elevation of the Sonoran Desert—from giant organ pipe cactus to tiny wildflowers.

A look at wildlife

Almost every kind of desert wildlife can be found in the zoo portion of the museum, from insects to bears, mountain lions, coyotes, foxes, and bighorn sheep. In the walk-in aviary, four different habitats provide natural settings for 80 species of wild birds. Two outdoor "Bird Circles" house such strange and fascinating desert dwellers as the red-tailed hawk, barn owl, and turkey vulture.

Simulated habitats fashioned from rock-sculptured concrete replace fenced enclosures for the larger animals. Small natives such as prairie dogs and rabbits scamper freely across the grounds. Underwater viewing rooms let you watch beavers and otters at work.

A reptilian reception committee greets you at the museum's entrance. Because the rocks are heated to a constant temperature, the usually shy lizards are always on display.

To the right of the entrance is the Orientation Room, a good place to start your tour. Here you'll learn what types of life are found in the desert. This area is also a place to see such intriguing desert "critters" as scorpions, Gila monsters, and rattlesnakes—all behind glass.

Earth Sciences Center

In this trio of galleries, visitors enter the earth's crust and wander through realistic manmade caves complete with stalactites, stalagmites, and bats. Rumbling volcanic sounds beckon you to the circular main gallery for a dramatic journey through the desert's geologic history.

Along a curved wall, a Geologic and Life History Time Line display covers the earth's development from its formation five billion years ago, illustrating the milestone events.

You start with a three-dimensional look at the Milky Way. Photographs suggest how the Sonoran Desert looked in ages past. Along the way you see and touch rocks, minerals, fossils, and artifacts such as meteorites, a mastadon's tusk, and the skull of a saber-toothed cat. A seismograph at the end of the time line is graphic proof of ongoing earth-shaping processes.

A dramatic movie leads to the mineral exhibit—one of the most beautiful displays of its kind in the country. In this mineral wonderland you'll see major pieces from the Sonoran Desert region as well as gemstones, gold, and silver. One entire case is devoted to jewelry and cut and polished gems. Microscopes allow visitors to view the fascinating crystalline formations of microminerals.

Finally, you become an early 20th-century miner, creeping through dimly lit tunnels to stunning vugs (pockets) of malachite, selenite, vanadite, and wulfenite—just as miners might have found them more than 80 years ago. You might find a few mineral treasures to take home around the mine dump outside.

Getting there & around

Situated 14 miles west of the city in Tucson Mountain Park, the museum is open daily from 8:30 A.M. (7 A.M. Memorial Day to Labor Day) until sunset. There is an admission charge. Visitors with motorhomes or large trailers should take Ajo Road west to Kinney Road, turning north on Kinney to reach the museum, instead of coming over scenic but steep Gates Pass Road.

Allow at least two hours for exploring the museum, half a day if you really want to see everything. The best time to visit is in the morning, when it's cooler and the animals are more active. During the hot months, it's advisable to wear a hat.

Late afternoon sun highlights University of Arizona's College of Medicine, north of the main campus. An important economic resource for Tucson, the university has a student population of over 30,000.

Step back to a period of gracious living when you pass through the pink stucco entrance of the charming Arizona Inn. Long a Tucson institution, the hostelry is renowned for its dining facilities and fine accommodations set amidst 14 acres of groomed gardens.

A Look Around Town

Tucson enjoys winter temperatures averaging in the 70s with lows in the 40s. Summer temperatures range from average highs in the 90s to lows in the 50s. Most of the annual 11½ inches of rain falls from July through September and December through March.

You can dress casually for almost every occasion. Even businessmen forego ties in the summer. You might need a light coat or jacket in the winter. For evening dining in one of the finer restaurants, you'll be more comfortable in a dressy outfit.

A look around

Tucson's modern Community Center at 350 S. Church Avenue marks a revival of the aging heart of the city. Broad, landscaped patios separate an arena/exhibition hall, little theater, and large music hall. A shopping village and hotel add to the new look.

Historic portions of the complex include the Samaniego House, built in 1879 and now serving as a restaurant; La Casa de Gobernador, a museum that once was the luxurious residence of Territorial Governor John C. Fremont; and the former home of El Charro, now housing a Greek restaurant. Across Church Avenue, El Adobe Patio (part of the Charles O. Brown house) dates from territorial days.

Around town you'll find a collection of museums (many of them concentrated on the University of Arizona campus), fine arts and crafts shops, and several interesting gardens and parks.

Your first stop

The Metropolitan Tucson Convention and Visitors Bureau at 450 W. Paseo Redondo Street makes a good starting place. You can pick up a historical map of the downtown area here, plus information on events around the city.

Basic guidelines on transportation, accommodations, and recreational opportunities are also given here.

A walk through history

Despite the city's modernization, much of the charm of the old town remains. A walk through the historic districts near the Community Center offers a peek into the past. Browsers will want to explore the specialty stores, art galleries, and craft shops tucked around this downtown area. You can join a Saturday morning walking tour (inquire at the Fremont House Museum, 151 S. Granada Avenue) or set out on your own.

Between 9 A.M. and 3 P.M. on Friday and Saturday an open-air farmers' market takes place in International Alley at Church and Alameda streets. Local musicians frequently entertain here during the noon hour.

Tucson Museum of Art. Created in 1975 through the efforts of Tucson's residents, this museum offers a permanent collection of Spanish-Colonial, Mexican, Pre-Columbian, and Southwestern paintings and sculpture. An excellent Crafts Gallery displaying the work of guild members is a good place to shop for weavings, pottery, jewelry, and glassware.

The ultramodern museum building blends surprisingly well with the four restored adobe houses sharing the 2-acre grounds. Visitors enter at the street level and walk down past the exhibitions on a circular ramp.

Its entrance lies between two of the houses: the Edward Nye Fish house, built in 1868 and now home of the Tucson Museum of Art Library, and the Hiram Sanford Stevens home, now a restaurant.

The other historic adobes are the Romero House, now part of the Tucson Museum of Art School, and La Casa Cordova, home of the Mexican Heritage Museum.

The art museum is located at 140 N. Main Avenue across from El Presidio Park and the city government complex. Hours are 10 A.M. to 5 P.M. Tuesday through Saturday, 1 to 5 P.M. Sunday. Admission is free.

Old Town Artisans. Housed in a group of buildings erected between 1850 and 1870, this intriguing shopping complex combines history and crafts. Though its official address is 186 N. Meyer Avenue, the marketplace fills an entire block. A free brochure provides historical and architectural information.

In the heart of the center a beautifully landscaped, walled courtyard restaurant makes a pleasant luncheon site. For dessert, pick up a pastry from the Old Town Bake Shop.

Old Town Artisans is open Monday through Saturday from 10 A.M. to 5 P.M., Sunday from noon to 5 P.M.

Barrio Historical District. South of the Community Center another pocket of history contains a number of old buildings, among them the Cushing Street Bar and Restaurant at the corner of Meyer and Cushing streets. A block to the west on Main Avenue stand candle-lit El Tiradito, a folk shrine dedicated to the loser in a lovers' triangle, and Carrillo's Gardens, where Teddy Roosevelt once spoke.

Garden of Gethsemane. On Congress Street just west of Interstate 10 and the Santa Cruz River lies Felix Lucero Park, named for the World War I sculptor who created the park's life-sized religious statues.

Across the street stands Tucson's largest tree—a huge *Eucalyptus rostrada* measuring 12½ feet in circumference and 4 feet in diameter.

Reid Park

Largest and greenest oasis in Tucson is Reid Park between Broadway and East 22nd Street west of Alvernon Way. Here are two 18-hole municipal golf courses as well as Hi Corbett Field, spring training base for the Cleveland Indians. Exhibition games bring other major league teams to town. Tennis and racquetball courts and a swimming pool offer additional recreation opportunities.

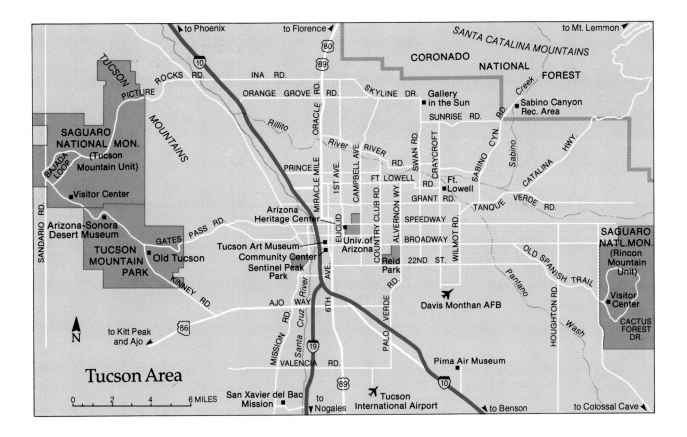

Reid Park Zoo is one of the finest of the country's smaller zoos. Several natural environments represent the African veldt, Asian grassland, Australian outback, and cool polar bear regions. The zoo is open daily; there is an admission charge.

University of Arizona campus

Take time to visit the university a mile northeast of downtown. Self-guiding tour booklets are available at the Arizona State Museum (just inside the main gate at Park Avenue and Third Street) or at the information desk in the Student Union. You can also pick up a calendar of campus events at the Student Union.

The campus plantings themselves make a visit worthwhile. They comprise a subtropical horticultural demonstration—almost 60 kinds of trees, more than 100 kinds of shrubs. Most campus streets are lined with palms or olive trees.

Arizona State Museum. Originally established as a territorial museum in 1893, this anthropological and archeological repository became part of the university when Arizona became a state in 1912. It contains one of the major collections of materials on prehistoric to contemporary southwest Indians. The gift shop sells local Indian crafts. The museum is open during the day Monday through Saturday and on Sunday afternoon. There is no charge.

Center for Creative Photography. In this center are the archives of many famous 20th-century photographers, including Ansel Adams, Edward Weston, and Imogen Cunningham. Two galleries exhibit rotating collections. The center is open weekdays and Sunday afternoons. Admission is free.

Museum of Art. Two large floors of a gallery at the northwest corner of the campus contain one of the country's finest university collections of Renaissance, European, and 20th-century art. In addition to the large permanent collection, special exhibitions are mounted. The museum is open Monday through Saturday and Sunday afternoon. Admission is free.

Mineralogical Museum. A most impressive collection of fossils, minerals, and stones is displayed in the Geology Building on the campus. Exhibits range from fine gemstones to a dinosaur footprint. The museum is open weekdays at no charge.

Flandrau Planetarium. Hands-on public viewing is emphasized in this major planetarium. You can touch a meteorite that dates back as many as 5 billion years, use lenses and mirrors to distort light, and view the Arizona skies at night (weather permitting) with a 16-inch telescope. Impressive hour-long Starshows communicate science to a non-scientific viewer by means of technologically advanced film projection and sound equipment.

Admission to the science halls (1 to 5 P.M. and 7 to 10 P.M. Tuesday through

To the delight of these boys, lizards lounge on heat-controlled rocks at Arizona-Sonora Desert Museum. Named one of the world's 10 best zoos, this living museum contains animals, plants, and fish native to the Sonoran Desert region. You'll need at least several hours to explore.

Another bandit bites the dust at the daily gunfight at Old Tucson. Built in 1939 for the movie Arizona, the re-created western town is still used for movies and television shows. Amusement rides, movie sets, sound stages, and saloons enliven family visits.

Sunday) is free. There is a charge for the theater; for show times, call (602) 621-4556.

Arizona Heritage Center

Operated by the Arizona Historical Society, this cultural museum tells the story of Arizona from the time of the Hohokams to 20th-century mining days. A large mining exhibit includes several walk-in buildings. In the Territorial Mercantile Company, a gift shop recalling the 1870–80s, you'll find Indian baskets, Mexican pottery and glassware, and an extensive collection of books on the Southwest.

The museum (949 E. Second Street) is open Monday through Saturday from 10 A.M. to 4 P.M. and Sunday from noon to 4 P.M. Admission is free.

Fort Lowell

This frontier Army post at Claycroft and Ft. Lowell roads is now a museum and public park offering exhibits of Apache days. A pleasant recreational complex includes softball fields, swimming pool, playground, and ramada-shaded picnic tables.

During the Apache wars, the fort was the base for cavalry and infantry and the social center of the Tucson area, publishing two weekly newspapers and supporting a school, a church, and a theater. Now the authentically restored Commanding Officer's Quarters houses a free museum (open Wednesday through Saturday).

A garden review

Much of the desert landscaping uses cactus and other native plantings; rock gardens seem practical in this type of climate. But here and there around the city you'll see lush, specialized gardens and tropical landscaping.

One such spot is the Tucson Botanical Gardens (2150 N. Alvernon, just south of Grant Road), center for many of Tucson's garden club activities. Southwestern-style buildings are surrounded by gardens of roses, herbs, and iris set among green lawns and fruit and shade trees. Native crops and a tropical greenhouse complete the 5-acre setting.

Open weekdays year-round, from September to May the garden also welcomes visitors Saturday from 10 A.M. to 2 P.M. and Sunday from noon to 4 P.M. Guided tours take place at 11 A.M. and 1 P.M. Saturday and 1 and 3 P.M. Sunday. Admission is free.

Much of the desert landscaping uses cactus and other native plantings ... But here and there you'll see lush, specialized gardens.

At Desert Flora (11360 E. Edison Street) and Tanque Verde Greenhouses (10810 E. Tanque Verde Road) you can view more types of cactus than you can name. Want to take some home? Both places package for travel or shipping. Desert Flora is open Thursday through Sunday; Tanque Verde is open Monday through Saturday.

Tohona Chul Park, a privately owned island in the midst of Tuscon, has 250 species of arid-climate plantings, wild birds, native fish, desert tortoise—and even a weather station.

The park is located at the intersection of Oracle and Ina roads. You might want to bring a picnic lunch to eat under a shady ramada.

DeGrazia's Gallery in the Sun

Ted DeGrazia's art documents the Southwest, both in subject matter and in color. He preserved the area's cultural heritage on canvas — Spanish priests and explorers, Indians, and regional celebrations.

In the gallery DeGrazia built in the Catalina foothills overlooking Tucson he also used materials typical of the area. The unusual modern adobe rests on a slope just up from the Mission in the Sun at 6300 N. Swan Road, a chapel the artist built from desert materials and dedicated to Our Lady of Guadalupe. The grounds are maintained as a botanical garden, featuring southwestern native plants.

The museum, Little Gallery (featuring local artists), and gift shop are open daily from 10 A.M. to 4 P.M.

An aerial look

Airplane buffs will find two aircraft collections side by side in the southeastern part of the city.

Pima Air Museum. More than 130 aircraft are displayed in this collection chronicling America's aviation history. You'll see everything from a Wright Brothers mock-up to the X-15, one of the country's fastest planes. Visit between 9 A.M. and 4 P.M. daily; there is an admission charge. To reach the museum, take Interstate 10 east to the Wilmot exit; turn north and follow the signs.

Davis Monthan Air Force Base. At this active Tactical Air Command base — one of the most diversified Air Force sites—you can see a variety of aircraft, including an unusual collection of historic planes. Look at the display of old planes parked by the perimeter fence, or arrange for a tour through the base. Free tours take place on Monday and Wednesday; call (602) 748-3204 for times.

Short Side Trips

Just beyond the city in any direction, you find the lively Sonoran Desert of saguaro and prickly pear, creosote bush and mesquite, palo verde, riotous spring blossoms, and the small animals that find shelter among these plants.

On three sides of Tucson, some of the most spectacular desert is protected in extensive public preserves. The Saguaro National Monument comes in two parts: the Rincon Mountain Unit and the Tucson Mountain Unit, east and west of town respectively. Also to the west is Pima County's Tucson Mountain Park. This park and the monument contain fine stands of giant saguaro cactus. The desert foothills to the north and northeast, including Sabino Canyon, are part of the Coronado National Forest.

If you find yourself longing for respite from a steady diet of sand, sagebrush, and cactus, the mountains are not far away. The Santa Catalina, Rincon, and Santa Rita mountains rise high enough that their upper reaches are covered with conifer forests, watered by winter snows as well as the summer storms. You can't reach the heights of the Rincons and the Santa Ritas by car, but the Catalinas are easily accessible by paved Hitchcock Highway.

A Phoenix loop

For a leisurely drive north to Phoenix, U.S. 89 takes a bit longer than the interstate but offers a 30-mile stretch of especially handsome desert along the Pinal Pioneer Parkway. Signs are limited to identification markers on desert plants; roadside rests offer shade and barbecue grills.

If you make a loop trip, driving one way on Interstate 10 you pass Picacho Peak, the site of a Union-Confederate skirmish that was the westernmost battle of the Civil War. Picacho Peak State Park's 3,400 acres offer campsites, picnic grounds, and hiking trails.

Catalina State Park

Arizona's newest state park, 9 miles north of the city limits on U.S. 89, provides access to a splendid string of pools. In view of the dramatic southwestern ridges of the Santa Catalina Mountains, the park also offers facilities for horse riders (rentals available), picnickers, and campers. A 1½-mile double loop nature trail introduces Sonoran Desert plants; the longer, more difficult Romero Canyon Trail leads to the pools.

What appears to be a solid rugged wall of the Catalina Mountains east of State 89 is actually slashed by steep canyons.

Best time to visit is from September through spring. If it's hot, head up to Romero Canyon early, spend the day splashing in pools shaded by oak and sycamore woodlands, and hike out as evening nears. Bring a picnic and drinking water (the water in the pools isn't potable).

Sabino Canyon retreat

What appears to be a solid rugged wall of the Catalina Mountains east of State 89 is actually slashed by steep canyons. Sabino, the largest, is a favorite destination of Tucson residents for picnics or day-long retreats. You can fish for trout in the tree-shaded upper creek, hike the trails beside the cascading waters, or swim in deep, boulder-lined pools.

A shuttle bus carries you 7½ miles into the canyon—the road is closed to automobile traffic. Tickets are available at the parking area of the visitor center (open daily). To reach the center, take Tanque Verde Road east to Sabino Canyon Road; the center is about 4½ miles north.

Up to Mt. Lemmon

Reaching skyward 9,157 feet, Mt. Lemmon is the loftiest peak in the Catalinas. On your way to the top (about 40 miles on the Mt. Lemmon and Hitchcock highways), you drive past cactus, through stands of juniper and oak, up to pine-covered slopes. Along the way are camp and picnic sites, spectacular vista points, nature study areas, and a fishing lake. At the top, you'll find a lodge, a restaurant, horseback riding, hiking trails, and a ski area. A ½-mile-long double chairlift (operates year-round) and two rope tows serve the ski area; rental equipment and lessons are available daily in season (generally December through March).

For winter road conditions, call (602) 576-1400.

Saguaro National Monument

Unique preserve of the stately, towering saguaro cactus, this site is divided into two sections on opposite sides of Tucson. Though each part has its own character, both offer an intimate exposure to the fascinating desert ecology.

The Tucson Mountain Unit, northwest of the city, preserves a vigorous forest of young saguaro—the thickest stand in the United States. Stop at the information center to learn about wildlife, wildflowers, and cactus. You have a choice of a 9-mile scenic loop drive or 16 miles of hiking trails. Picnic areas are equipped with tables, shelters, and restrooms; bring your own firewood. Open 24 hours a day, this section is popular for moonlight hikes and barbecues.

In the older Rincon Mountain Unit just east of Tucson, the forest of old giants is in gradual decline because new plants aren't being produced. Nevertheless, a 9-mile loop drive and some good foot trails take you among majestic giant saguaros.

May or early June brings the blooms that earned the saguaro blossom the title of state flower. Best time to view the expanse of blossoms is early morning. The pine-covered heights of nearby Rincon Peak and Mica Mountain are accessible by trail.

Tucson Mountain Park

An 11,000-acre high desert and mountain preserve west of the city, this park includes miles of hiking and riding trails, long views of Avra Valley, picnic sites, day-use areas, and a campground.

It also encompasses the two most popular visitor attractions in the area—Old Tucson and the Arizona-Sonora Desert Museum. The western section of the Saguaro National Monument lies to the north.

To reach the park, take Ajo Road west to Kinney Road (better for motorhomes or large trailers) or drive over Gates Pass Road (an extension of Speedway).

Old Tucson

This year-round amusement park is also the setting for many western movies and television shows, and if you happen along at the right time you can watch a scene in production.

Producers of the movie *Arizona* built the town in 1939 as an almost full-scale replica of Tucson circa 1860. Instead of the usual papier-mâché, painted canvas, and false-fronts of a movie set, they built it solidly of wood and adobe.

Visitors today can see the extensive sets, ride on a replica of the Butterfield Stagecoach, tour dark mine tunnels in a clattering ore wagon, and circle the town in the open-chair cars of the Old

Tucson Railroad. Shops, museums, and other attractions add to the fun, as does the daily gunfight on Front Street.

The park is open daily from 9 A.M. to 5 P.M. Next door, automated scenes in the Old West Wax Museum (separate admission) bring the past to life.

Arizona-Sonora Desert Museum

One of the best introductions you can have to the desert country, the entertaining and educational displays at this desert park will enlighten you about much of what you will see in Arizona and adjacent Sonora and Baja California, Mexico. (For a detailed description of the museum, see page 94).

The botanical section features labeled plants in a 12-acre desert foothills complex and the Desert Museum-Sunset Magazine Demonstration Desert Garden. You'll see almost every kind of desert wildlife in the zoo portion of the museum, where the larger animals live in simulated habitats rather than fenced enclosures.

In the Earth Sciences Center, visitors travel through the desert's history as they follow a geologic time line. A mineral exhibit is one of the best in the country, and a mining display shows you what it was like to search for such mineral treasures as malachite and selenite early in this century.

Located 14 miles west of Tucson on Speedway Boulevard, the museum is open daily from 8:30 A.M. (7 A.M. Memorial Day to Labor Day) until sunset.

Kitt Peak Observatory

About an hour's drive west of Tucson, gleaming white domes dot a crest high above the Papago Indian Reservation. The nation's largest federally supported observatory for research in optical astronomy occupies this site, chosen over all others in the United States for its ideal star-gazing conditions.

Visitors are welcome to view a dozen different telescopes, including the world's most powerful stellar instrument. These, along with a visitor center, museum, and Papago crafts shop are open daily (except Christmas) from 10 A.M. to 4 P.M. Films are shown daily at 10:30 A.M. and 1:30 P.M.; weekend and holiday guided tours take place at the same times.

Bring a lunch and enjoy the picnic grounds about 1½ miles before you reach the top of the mountain. Temperatures on the peak are about 15 to 20 degrees cooler than in Tucson; you might want to bring a sweater.

To reach Kitt Peak, take State 86 (Ajo Way) west toward Gila Bend and the marked turnoff.

Colossal Cave

Reaching far back into the earth beneath the Rincon Mountains southeast of Tucson is Colossal Cave, a colorful product of nature's patience and skill as a sculptor.

The cavern's chain of crystal-walled chambers was formed from solid limestone millions of years ago by seeping water, which eventually created an underground river with an intricate network of tributaries. Today the cave is bone dry, maintaining a constant temperature of 72°.

Once an Indian refuge, the cave has yielded many artifacts now on display. During Wild West days, bandits hid out in the cave.

Visitors can investigate about 1¼ miles of the cavern's far-reaching passageways; steps and walkways make it an easy hour-long walk. There is an admission fee.

The surrounding area is Pima County parkland offering free camping and picnic grounds, along with good views of Tucson and desert sunsets.

To reach the cave, follow Old Spanish Trail 22 miles east of Tucson or take Interstate 10 east to the Vail-Wentworth exit and drive north 5 miles.

South to the Border

The twin cities of Nogales lie 66 miles from Tucson on either side of the Arizona-Mexico border. Driving south on Interstate 19, you'll pass through the lush valley of the Santa Cruz River and arrive at the border in a little over an hour. For a loop trip, take State 82 and 83 through the beautiful ranch country surrounding Patagonia and Sonoita.

Three colonial landmarks

Eusebio Kino, a Jesuit missionary, was the first European to enter the Santa Cruz Valley and to follow it north to the present site of Tucson. You'll pass two of the missions he established and the garrison built to protect them.

San Xavier del Bac. Called "White Dove of the Desert," this twin-towered historic mission stands 9 miles southwest of Tucson on the San Xavier Indian Reservation, home of Papago Indians.

Although the original chapel was destroyed by raiding Apaches, the present church is one of the oldest in the country still in use.

Visitors are welcome at San Xavier any time between 6 A.M. and sunset. Franciscan brothers give 20-minute lecture-tours every hour on the half-hour (except Sunday).

Special religious festivities, celebrations, and processions honoring St. Francis are held in October and December. The annual celebration of the mission's founding in April is a colorful and exciting major event of the month-long Tucson Festival.

Tubac. Established by the Spaniards as a presidio to protect the missions from Indian raids, Tubac was the staging point for the California-bound De Anza expedition that led to the founding of San Francisco. Tubac languished when the garrison moved to Tucson in 1776 but became a center of mining and commerce after the Gadsden Purchase made this territory part of the United States in 1854.

Today the village is a lively center for arts and crafts. You'll find many studios and shops to visit as well as a country club with a golf course and an excellent restaurant. A museum in the Tubac Presidio State Historic Park displays a layout of the original Spanish town plus a good many artifacts from the past two centuries.

Tubac is about 50 miles south of Tucson on Interstate 19.

Tumacacori. The stately ruin of the mission church of San Jose de Tumacacori *(tooma-kah-kori)* stands beside the highway a few miles south of Tubac. Though this was once a magnificent mission, legends of buried riches brought treasure-seekers who pillaged it.

The story begins with the arrival of Father Kino in 1691 to conduct services and teach at a Pima Indian village a few miles away. After the Pima rebellion of 1751, the village was moved here, and in about 1800 the Franciscan fathers, who succeeded the Jesuits, started building this church. Finally, in the mid-1800s Mexican independence, repeated Apache raids, and the ultimate sale of the property led to its abandonment as an active church.

In 1908 the building was made a national monument; partial restoration was begun in 1919. Dioramas and pictorial displays depict life during mission times, and a garden provides a quiet retreat.

The monument is open daily; a small admission is charged per car.

Madera Canyon

In the Santa Rita Mountains section of the Coronado National Forest stands this wildlife haven and cool year-round retreat. More than 200 species of birds visit the tree-shaded canyon, and each year thousands of birders come to see them among the oak, juniper, and sycamore trees along the stony creek. Much of the lumber that built early Tucson came from this canyon—madera means "wood" in Spanish.

Two picnic areas and a campground (fee) provide water. More than 70 miles of hiking trails take off through the countryside, including an 8½-mile trail to the 9,450-foot peak of Mt. Wrightson (highest in the Santa Ritas) and a shorter, steeper trail up Mt. Hopkins.

To reach the canyon, follow Interstate 19 south from Tucson to Green Valley, then take State 93 through Continental to the Madera turnoff, 12 miles southeast of Green Valley.

Nogales—for shopping

Named for identical walnut trees growing on either side of the border, the twin cities of Nogales face each other across the international boundary with Mexico. An important center of commerce and port of entry, Mexico's Nogales retains many of the customs and crafts of Old Mexico. Here you can shop in an international marketplace, feast at good restaurants amid strolling mariachis, and, on certain Sundays, see the top matadors of the Spanish-speaking world in the Nogales bull ring.

Most of the shops lie along either Obregon or Calle Elias, but you'll find several opposite the railroad track on Avenida Ruiz Cortines. Before you start serious buying, visit several stores and markets to compare prices and quality, for they vary considerably.

You'll find rugs, pottery, carved wooden furniture, tinware, glass, and leather from throughout Mexico; perfumes and silk goods from France; cameras, cutlery, and mechanical toys from Germany; cameras and optical products from Japan; and many other imports.

Nogales offers several interesting places to sample Mexican food of a greater variety than is usual north of the border. The oldest and best known is La Caverna (closed at press time due to a recent fire) on Calle Elias, tunneled out of the bluff facing the plaza. A more recent addition is LaRoca, also on Calle Elias. Dining areas overlooking

Weathered remains of San Jose de Tumaca-

cori are now a national monument.

Pictorial displays present life in the

heyday of the mission; the garden provides

a private retreat.

Skirts swirl and mariachi music resounds

in December at Tumacacori mission ruins.

Fiesta time brings together Mexican and

Indian dancers and craftspeople.

a courtyard offer Mexican specialties for lunch and dinner.

Two cool lakes

For fishing, boating, and just cooling off, two lakes north of Nogales attract area residents and visitors. Pena Blanca Lake lies west of Interstate 19; Patagonia Lake State Park can be reached from State 82.

Pena Blanca Lake. Nestled in a mountainous pocket at an elevation over 3,500 feet, mile-long Pena Blanca Lake is well known to local anglers. Stocking of trout monthly from November to March supplements the resident population of bass, bluegills, crappies, and big catfish. Only electric trolling motors are allowed on the lake; you'll find a place to rent both boats and motors. A small campground in the area also accommodates recreational vehicles.

To reach Pena Blanca Lake, turn west off Interstate 19 onto State 289 just north of Nogales. Beyond the lake, a gravel road winds through the Atasco Mountains to the little settlement of Arivaca, passing the ghost towns of Ruby (now fenced and guarded private property) and Oro Blanco. Farther on, a very rough side road turns off to Arivaca Lake, another local fishing spot.

It's about 55 slow miles round trip on this loop back to the highway through rolling grass and mesquite-covered hills studded with buttes, layered slabs of exposed, eroded sandstone, and volcanic palisades. After a rain, the road just beyond Pena Blanca Lake often is flooded in spots.

Patagonia Lake State Park. One of the state's most attractive recreational areas is set in the grassland northeast of Nogales.

At 3,600 feet, the 275-acre lake is high enough to be popular during hot weather. Facilities include a sandy beach, marina with boat rentals, picnic area, and improved campground.

Fishing is for large-mouth bass, bluegill, channel catfish, crappie, and, in the winter, rainbow trout. Motors are allowed on the lake; there's a no-wake speed limit to the north of the marina cove.

Drive northeast from Nogales on State 82 to reach the lake.

San Rafael Valley

The strip of border land from Nogales east to the Huachuca Mountains is known as the most elite cattle country of all the remaining range. The valley itself is a soft sea of grass in a setting of low hills and sharp ridges clothed with pines, junipers, oaks, and mountain mahogany.

Patagonia. The Stage Stop Inn in the community of Patagonia on State 82 makes a good base for exploring the surrounding countryside; from here, guests can take 3-hour, guided motorcoach tours around the area.

The strip of border land from Nogales east to the Huachuca Mountains is known as the most elite cattle country of all the remaining range.

An unpaved road heading southeast from town provides a look at the ghost towns of Harshaw, Mowry, Washington, and Duquesne. Don't try it during rainy weather.

Museum of the Horse. Just across the road from the old railway station in Patagonia (now the town hall) stands an unusual museum—dedicated to the horse. The impressive collection of equine artifacts is not limited to western horsemanship. Objects on display range from an ancient Greek chariot-horse bit to horse brasses from England, hardware collected all across America by the Stradling family for three generations, and western cowboy paraphernalia.

A fine kachina collection fills one of the museum's six rooms. The large carriage room contains surreys, buggies, and broughams. Open daily, the museum charges a small fee to walk through the exhibits.

Sonoita. A center for national horse shows, tiny Sonoita sits at the junction of State 82 and 83. To return to Tucson, follow State 83 north to Interstate 10.

On the gentle slopes of the Sonoita highlands nearby lie the vineyard and winery for Arizona's first estate-bottled wine. There are as yet no facilities for touring the Sonoita Vineyards near Elgin.

Bird Sanctuary. Near Patagonia you pass the Patagonia-Sonoita Creek Bird Sanctuary, a 309-acre strip extending from Patagonia downstream along the creek for more than a mile. Both resident and migratory birds abound, thanks to a year-round water supply, a splendid bordering growth of cottonwoods, willows, oaks, ash, and sycamores—and the location on the flyway to Mexico. More than 300 species have been recorded here.

The sanctuary is bordered on one side by State 82, on the other by a gravel country road (an extension of Patagonia's Pennsylvania Avenue). You enter the fenced area over one of three stiles on the county road side.

Though you can't picnic within the sanctuary, you'll find a shady roadside rest area less than a mile down the highway toward Nogales.

The Cochise Trail

Once the stronghold of the Chiricahua Apaches whose chief, Cochise, gave his name to the county, the southeastern corner of Arizona contains a living museum of the early West. On a loop called the Cochise Trail, you can explore this rugged land.

Start the loop by turning south off Interstate 10 at either Benson or Willcox. You'll find a museum and information about points of interest at the Cochise Visitors Association at Willcox (take the Fort Grant exit).

After completing the loop, you can head north on U.S. 666 to Safford, a convenient base for forays into the Coronado National Forest.

Tombstone territory

The glory—and notoriety—of Tombstone came suddenly and passed quickly. The town achieved its prominent place in western lore in only eight years. But in that brief period one of the West's most remarkable collections of frontier mining town buildings was assembled here.

Tombstone lies about 20 miles southeast of Benson on U.S. 80. The days of the Old West come alive during the town's Helldorado Days, beginning the third Friday of October.

History. The Tombstone hills were still Apache country when Ed Schieffelin first struck silver in September, 1877. "All you'll find will be your tombstone," the doubters had said. The next year the rush was on.

By 1881 mining production was so great and the influx of people so large that Tombstone numbered 10,000 inhabitants. It had its urban problems, chiefly disastrous fires in 1881 and 1882, and lawless strife that culminated in the showdown between Earp and Clanton factions on October 26, 1881.

Booming Tombstone became the seat of a new county named for Cochise, but it paid little attention to a growing problem that was to spell its doom—water in the mines. By the time Tombstone's resplendent $50,000 courthouse was completed in 1882, many buckets of water were being hoisted out of the mines. Pumps were installed the next year, but production was falling, never to rise again. By 1886, Tombstone's heyday was over.

What you'll see. During a stroll around town, you can stand on the site of the bloody shoot-out at the OK Corral in which the Earp brothers, with Doc Holliday, gunned down Billy Clanton and Frank and Tom McLaury (fiberglass figures show the probable

Welcome to Mexico

Although it's easy to visit Mexico's border cities, your trip will be even more enjoyable if you familiarize yourself with some pertinent information before you go.

Tourist cards. You don't need a passport to visit any part of Mexico. In fact, crossing the border at Nogales (or any other border city) for a day's shopping and dining requires no paperwork at all.

If you go more than 75 miles into the interior or stay longer than 72 hours, you will need to obtain a tourist card, free from any Mexican Consulate or Mexican Government Tourist Office. You'll need proof of your United States citizenship.

Driving in Mexico. Most Arizona residents who go to Nogales simply leave their cars in the convenient parking lots on the Arizona side and walk across the border. Shops and restaurants are within walking distance; taxis are also available.

If you are driving farther into Mexico, it's advisable to obtain auto insurance from a Mexican insurance company before you cross the border. American agents are not licensed to do business in Mexico, where an automobile accident is a criminal offense for which you can be detained until claims are adjusted. Short-term Mexican insurance is not expensive.

Currency. All of the border shops are happy to accept U.S. dollars; there's no need to exchange your money. Prices in the stores usually will be shown in U.S. currency.

Customs. United States Customs permits each person to bring back $400 worth of goods without paying duty. Beyond that amount, you must itemize purchases. Visitors may bring back one quart of liquor duty-free.

Plants and produce. These are subject to Department of Agriculture pest and disease controls and rigorous inspection. Some are banned or require written permits.

Saloon visitors get a taste of what life was like in Tombstone, "the town too tough to die."

Pools of Sabino Creek in the Catalina Mountains just outside Tucson offer a refreshing respite from desert heat. Closed to automobiles, the shady canyon is negotiated by tram.

locations of the protagonists). The Wild Bunch re-enacts some of the West's wildest gunfights at 2 P.M. on the first and third Sunday of each month.

At the Historama exhibit Vincent Price retells the city's history on film. Visit the restored Crystal Palace Saloon (its long bar is fitted out with mustache towels); the office of the Tombstone *Epitaph,* in publication since 1880; Schieffelin Hall, a faithful restoration of the city's biggest theater; the Bird Cage Theatre, Tombstone's less proper place of entertainment; the celebrated Rose Tree Inn Museum (a Lady Banksia rose in its courtyard, planted in 1885, spreads over 8,000 square feet); and Gabe's House of Dolls, for a look at children's toys over the years.

Several other museums contain fascinating collections relating to Tombstone's heyday. You can enter the Wells Fargo Museum through the General Store (specializing in old-fashioned candies). The courthouse, in use from 1882 until 1929 during territorial and early statehood days, is now a museum operated by the state.

A tour of Goodenough Mine offers a fascinating glimpse at the processes used to extract every bit of high-grade ore—all by hand. Three tours operate every day; check at the mine for times. The temperature is 53° all year, so take a sweater (a flashlight is also useful).

Some of the area's famed outlaws are buried at Boothill Cemetery (west of town on State 80). The tombstone inscriptions are worth the stop; one reads "George Johnson—hanged by mistake."

Fort Huachuca

Here is a fort that has a special significance in the history of the Southwest; it's the only frontier military post in Arizona that is still active. Location of the U.S. Army Communications Command headquarters here has made it one of the more important Department of Defense installations. In the museum, in addition to the collections of Army weapons and uniforms you

might expect, you'll find a detailed chronicle of the history of the Arizona Territory.

A large collection of old photographs, Indian artifacts, and dioramas of various battles depict the fort's role in the struggle between the Chiricahua Apaches and the U.S. Cavalry. One display tells about the Apache Hohokam and Sobaipuri Indians. A room on the second floor is devoted to the Army's Indian scouts, who last saw active service at the fort in 1947.

Near the museum building, barracks and administrative buildings dating back to 1879 still flank the broad parade ground. Several of the original adobe quarters of the Indian scouts are still standing.

The museum is open daily Monday through Friday and Saturday and Sunday afternoons (closed holidays). Admission is free.

Fort Huachuca is about 5 miles off State 90 southwest of Tombstone; turn southwest at Huachuca City or west through Sierra Vista.

Coronado National Memorial

The first major expedition of Europeans into the American Southwest is commemorated at the point where Francisco Vasquez de Coronado entered what is now the United States in 1540. You can drive up Montezuma Pass for fine views or hike to the top of Coronado Peak for a sweeping vista of the conquistador's route.

Exhibits describe the expedition and natural features of the area. You'll find a picnic area with grills.

Coronado National Memorial is reached by a paved road that turns southwest from State 92 about midway between Sierra Vista and Bisbee. A gravel back road from the monument to State 82 takes you past Parker Canyon Lake, a cool retreat (5,460 feet) for fishing, camping, and picnicking. The lake is stocked by the Arizona Game

and Fish Department; you pay a Forest Service fee. Facilities include a lodge, motel, store, and boat rentals.

Overnight accommodations and restaurants can be found nearby at Sierra Vista and Bisbee.

Photogenic Bisbee

Stacked along the ravines and gullies of the Mule Mountains, Bisbee is a proud turn-of-the-century mining town that's fast becoming a tourist favorite. You reach it 24 miles southeast of Tombstone near the junction of U.S. 80 and State 92.

Soon after copper was discovered here in 1877, Bisbee became a Phelps Dodge Company town. In 1975 mining stopped, ending a productive 98-year, $2-billion era.

A delight to explore, Bisbee is rich in uncontrived nostalgia with open-pit mines and a well-preserved antique town. Explore the narrow streets of the old part of the town on foot. The Mining and Historical Museum on Main Street makes a good starting point. Open daily from 10 A.M. to 4 P.M. (1 to 4 P.M. on Sunday), it displays old mining equipment, photos, and gem and mineral collections. Pick up a free, self-guiding map of the town at the museum or at the Chamber of Commerce on Main Street.

Along Brewery Gulch, O.K. Street, and their cross streets, shops and craft galleries invite browsing. There's still an early-1900s company-town atmosphere to Main Street, west of the mining museum.

The Copper Queen Hotel played host to many colorful characters in the early 1900s. Under a continuing program of restoration and refurbishment, the historic hostelry is a good spot for dining or overnight stays by virtue of its central location.

The Restoration Museum (37 Main Street) displays three floors of antique clothing, furniture, and memorabilia from Bisbee; it's open daily from 10 A.M. to 3 P.M. at no charge.

...The Cochise Trail

Mulheim House, an elegant turn-of-the-century residence on Youngblood Hill overlooking Brewery Gulch, opens its doors for tours Friday through Monday afternoons; there's a small admission fee.

On the Queen Mine tour, visitors are given a rare chance to confront the dark, damp, cold (47°) reality of underground hard-rock mining. Hour-long tours take place at 10:30 A.M., 2, and 3 P.M.; the entrance is across U.S. 80 a half-block east of the police station.

> *Apache Pass was to the early settlers a fiery baptism into the life of Apache country.*

Dramatic in another way is the 11-mile bus tour of enormous Lavender Pit copper mine and the surrounding area. Offered daily at noon, tours take 1½ hours. For reservations, call (602) 432-2071 or sign up at the Queen Mine Building.

Cochise Stronghold

The name leaves no doubt; this was the great Apache chief's stronghold, a natural fortress with thousands of pinnacled lookouts from which any movement below could be seen. Since only a token force of braves was needed from this vantage point to protect the women and children, this was where Cochise led his people after a raid.

You can now camp and picnic where Apache wickiups once circled a clearing. You'll find water here, and the rocks afford a wonderful playground for climbing. To reach Cochise Stronghold, turn west from U.S. 666 just

north of Sunsites, about 18 miles southeast of Interstate 10.

The Chiricahuas

Turning east from State 181 into Bonita Canyon, you come to forested land—the ancestral home of Cochise and the Chiricahua Apaches. Cochise Stronghold, across the valley to the west, was the Chiricahuas' fortress; this was their home.

The road into Chiricahua National Monument winds through the scenic canyon to Massai Point—stop here to look out over the dissected lava beds that have given the area its unique forms. Beside the Bonita Canyon road, you'll come upon a shady campsite.

Several trails take off from the point (6½ miles from monument headquarters) through the Wonderland of Rocks. Choices range from the easy 20-minute Massai Point nature trail to the spectacular 2-hour Echo Canyon Trail. Most rewarding of all is a 6½-hour hike through the Heart of Rocks, a mostly downhill trek ending near park headquarters. Take water and a lunch; arrange for someone to meet you at the other end, or leave your car at monument headquarters and take the shuttle bus (9 A.M. and 2 P.M.) to the point.

A beautiful and varied scenic drive through the mountains starts with Pinery Canyon Road, branching south just before the main road enters the monument. From the Onion Saddle summit of the canyon, a road leads south to intermittent view sites and the Forest Service campgrounds in the flowery meadows of Rustler Park. South from Rustler Park, a skyline trail—about 8,000 feet all the way—traverses forests of pine, fir, spruce, and aspen, skirting grassy parks and occasionally coming out on rocky points with sweeping views.

The road forks north and east at Rustler Park, the main road dropping eastward into the deep, wooded basin of Cave Creek. You'll reach the Southwestern Research Center of the Ameri-

can Museum of Natural History 7 miles below the pass.

The road continues east through the rose and salmon-hued rock towers and cave-pitted cliffs of Cave Creek Canyon, where there are more campgrounds and private cabins, to the little town of Portal. From here you can continue 7 miles southeast to U.S. 80, just across the New Mexico border.

On the west slope of the Chiricahuas, you can turn east off State 181 about 10 miles south of the Chiricahua National Monument road to reach Forest Service campgrounds far up the canyon of Turkey Creek. Still farther south is a second transmountain road giving access to Rucker Canyon and its lake, with more campsites and fair trout fishing. You can also reach Rucker Canyon from south of Apache, turning northwest from U.S. 80.

At Apache a monument commemorates the final surrender of Geronimo, which took place in nearby Skeleton Canyon near the Ross Sloan ranch-house in 1886.

Fort Bowie

Apache Pass was to the early settlers a fiery baptism into the life of Apache country. Everything bound for Tucson passed through here — the mail, settlers' wagons, and the stage.

Until Fort Bowie was built in 1862, it was a gamble whether a wagon or a coach would make it through. Any slow-moving vehicle was a clay pigeon for the Apaches, who knew every rock and shrub in the area. Soldiers stationed here struggled with the Apaches until peace with Cochise came in 1872.

Later, when the Apaches escaped the San Carlos Reservation in 1876, Fort Bowie served as the main base for the Geronimo War. Abandoned shortly after Geronimo's surrender, the few remaining ruins are today a national historic site.

Fort Bowie isn't easy to find. Access is by a 1½-mile foot trail beginning in

Apache Pass, reached by an unpaved road that heads north from State 186 about 9 miles northwest of the Chiricahua monument road. You'll find water and a ranger on duty at the fort's small visitor center.

Amerind Foundation museum

With advance reservations, you can see a remarkable collection of Indian artifacts at this scholarly research center near Dragoon. Because the staff is busy with archeological field work, guided tours (free) are available only on weekends at 10:30 A.M. and 1 P.M. For reservations, write to the Amerind Foundation, Dragoon, AZ 85609, or call (602) 586-3003. Take the Dragoon Road exit from Interstate 10, 12 miles east of Benson.

Around Safford

An excellent take-off spot for excursions into the quiet and beautiful country between Tucson and New Mexico, the pleasant farming town of Safford lies along the Gila River at the junction of U.S. 70 and 666.

Mt. Graham, the highest peak in this part of the state, rises abruptly above the Gila Valley and the arid tablelands to 10,713 feet. Up its eastern flank and along its ridges, a road called the Swift Trail gives access to a popular Coronado National Forest recreation area.

Here you can experience some of Arizona's best camping (5 Forest Service campgrounds), miles of hiking trails, trout fishing in pine-bordered Riggs Lake, and some seasonal hunting for deer, bear, wild turkey, and squirrel.

To drive the Swift Trail, turn west from U.S. 666 onto State 366 about 9 miles south of Safford. The road is paved for 23 miles beyond the turnoff; it swings across a strip of desert to the foothills, then starts its winding climb out of arid, rocky terrain.

You'll come to several vantage points providing fine views of distant mountains and of the desert and grasslands below. One is Heliograph Peak, a 4½-mile detour offering sweeping vistas of the terrain below.

Near the end of the trail is Riggs Flat Lake Recreation Area, a pleasant place to camp, picnic, and fish. You'll also find ample opportunities for fishing in the trout streams near Shannon and Soldier Creek camps.

You can make the drive in a day; allow more time and plan to camp if you want to hike or do much fishing.

Two Apache warriors

The name "Cochise" commanded respect and awe long before the Apache leader's reign of terror gripped the southeastern corner of Arizona. When settlers streamed through Apache Pass between the Chiricahua and Dragoon mountains into Arizona Territory, they passed unmolested, and in 1858 Cochise allowed the building of a Butterfield Stage stop.

All that changed in 1861 when a brash Army lieutenant, wrongly accusing Cochise of stealing stock and kidnapping a boy from a ranch, tried by trickery to arrest him. Cochise escaped, but the Army captured his brother and two nephews. The furious Cochise immediately captured hostages to exchange for them. Negotiations were underway when, by coincidence, two more detachments of soldiers arrived. Thinking that he had been double-crossed, Cochise killed his hostages, and disappeared. The Army hanged the captives—and the war was on.

In the 11 years that followed, thousands were killed, settlements were destroyed or abandoned, and entire areas were depopulated. Finally, in 1872, Cochise agreed that the Chiricahuas would settle on a reservation that included their beloved mountains if his friend, Tom Jeffords, would be appointed their Indian Agent. This was done, and the great chief died on the reservation in 1874.

Though still raiding across the Mexico border, the tribe continued at peace in Arizona. In 1876 the Apaches split into factions; a small band jumped the reservation, and Jeffords asked the Army for help. In response, Jeffords was fired, the reservation was closed, and the Army moved 350 Apaches to a reservation in the Chiricahua Mountains. Another 400 fled to Mexico; among them was Geronimo.

Geronimo was never a tribal chief. Occasionally he was war chief for a specific battle, but more often he was leader of raids, sometimes with only two or three companions. He was stocky, short-tempered, suspicious, tough, courageous, a powerful orator, a heavy drinker—and probably the most effective guerrilla fighter in western history.

Geronimo's guerrilla warfare against Mexicans, Americans, and occasionally other Apaches continued through several captures and escapes. When he finally surrendered in 1886, he became a reformed man, appearing at the St. Louis Exposition and riding in Teddy Roosevelt's inaugural parade. He died in 1909 at Fort Sill, Oklahoma, after dictating an eloquent autobiography.

Born among talus and snow-pack in the Never Summer Mountains northwest of Denver, in most years the Colorado River dies in the salt flats of Baja California, 1,400 miles to the southwest, without ever reaching its natural outlet, the Sea of Cortez.

Between those points, it has over the eons sculpted some of the most superb landscapes on the face of the earth. And, with six national parks and recreation areas stretching along its banks, it has become one of the West's longest, most-used playgrounds.

A river engineered

The Colorado supplies water to millions of people, annually generates billions of kilowatt-hours of electricity, and irrigates a million acres of desert farmlands.

From Hoover Dam south, the Colorado has rightly been compared to a 340-mile-long plumbing system. Peer into a gauge-filled control room deep in the concrete depths of one of its big dams—Hoover, Davis, or Parker—and you'll understand why a Bureau of Reclamation official stated, "The river's flow can be manipulated in the same fashion as the garden hose on the tap outside your home, and is."

Hoover and the other dams on the Colorado and its tributaries store 61.4 million acre-feet of water. Tied to them are more than a dozen diversion projects.

A recreational waterway

Thousands of Las Vegans, Angelenos, and Phoenicians who visit on weekends consider the calm waters of the lower Colorado their back-yard swimming pool. With 822 miles of shoreline, Lake Mead (created by Hoover Dam) is big enough for all the houseboaters, sailors, and striped bass anglers who seek their pleasure here.

The recreation area continues south along the shores of 67-mile-long Lake Mohave — its north end rimmed by Black Canyon, its south end by Davis Dam, north of Bullhead City.

South of Needles, California, lies Topock Marsh, part of the Havasu National Wildlife Refuge. To see its waterfowl, you can explore the marsh by canoe.

Hugging the south shore of Lake Havasu is the state's largest park. Near the southwestern end of the 45-mile-long lake, the huge intake pump lift of the Colorado River Aqueduct climbs the California shore. Nearby is the even bigger intake of the Central Arizona Project, 310 miles of aqueducts and tunnels.

The 14½-mile strip between Parker Dam and the city of Parker has been called "Fort Lauderdale West" for the flocks of bronzed teen-agers and college kids who migrate here seasonally.

The calmer, undammed stretch of river from Blythe, California, to Martinez Lake is popular with canoeists. Then, its flow slowed by Imperial and Laguna dams, the Colorado bends into the desert city of Yuma.

Into the desert

When the old Butterfield Stage crossed the southwestern corner of Arizona, weary passengers looked out at vast stretches of Sonoran Desert punctuated by isolated mountains. Passing the spontaneous spring wildflower show and hidden bighorn sheep, they eventually crossed the Colorado River into California. Travelers who parallel their route today on Interstate 8 see the same arid terrain, with one major change: the taming of the Colorado has transformed much of Yuma's desert into green fields that now yield a variety of crops. Farther east, the large organ pipe cactus is protected in a vast reserve. Visit in the spring to see a carpet of wildflowers.

Mighty Hoover Dam captures the Colorado River, backing it up to form the watery playground of Lake Mead. Below the dam the tamed river cuts through deep canyons en route to Lake Mohave and Parker Dam.

the Colorado

The Essentials

Between Interstate 15 on the northwest and Interstate 8 on the south, the Colorado forms a natural boundary dividing Arizona from the states of Nevada and California to the west.

This section of the river, interrupted by a series of large and small lakes, is carefully controlled by several large dams. Though the dams' primary purpose is to conserve water, they also provide a year-round aquatic playground for residents of the three bordering states and for thousands of visitors.

Getting around

No matter where you fly or drive, you'll need a car to see much of the river. And a boat is even better. Though roads on both sides cut through this area, for much of their distance they lie miles from the river. In some regions, a boat is your only access. Marinas along the river rent everything from houseboats (Lake Mead, Mohave, and Havasu) to canoes (Havasu and Imperial wildlife refuges).

At some public recreation areas (Organ Pipe Cactus National Monument, for example), trailers are welcome in developed campgrounds but prohibited on back roads.

Where to stay

Most hotel and motel accommodations along the lower Colorado River are found in larger cities near the river: Las Vegas, Bullhead City, Kingman, Needles, Lake Havasu City, Parker, Blythe, and Yuma, together with a handful of smaller cities and waterside resorts.

For most people, however, a trip "to the river" means a form of camping, whether in a trailer park, campground, or riverbank area accessible only by boat. The majority of campgrounds lie in the upper stretches (Lake Mead to Parker); much of the lower river accommodations fall into the fishing camp-marina category.

For desert camping, tents with self-supporting frames offer good stability in loose sand or hard caliche and against dusty winds.

Lake Mead. Campgrounds can be found at Temple Bar and, on the Nevada side, around Hemenway Harbor, Las Vegas Bay, Callville Bay, Echo Bay, Overton Beach, and in the Valley of Fire State Park. Most accommodate both tents and recreational vehicles. You'll find supplies, boat fuel, and boat ramps near most campgrounds; some have restaurants.

Lake Mohave. On the California side, Cottonwood Cove has campgrounds for tents and recreational vehicles. There's also a marina with motel, restaurant, grocery store, and laundry.

Katherine Landing, above Davis Dam, and Sportsman's Park, below on the California side, have camping facilities and boat ramps. Katherine Landing provides boat rentals and a restaurant.

Lake Havasu. Cat-Tail Cove in Lake Havasu State Park has tent, recreational vehicle, and boat-only camping, and a boat ramp. Nearby Sandpoint Marina (private) offers additional space plus other facilities, including boat rentals and launching ramp. You'll also find space at Lake Havasu Travel Trailer Park and Crazy Horse Campground on the island, as well as Havasu Landing Resort, London Bridge KOA, and Black Meadow Landing on the lake.

Parker Strip. Public and private campgrounds line both sides of the river in the 14½-mile Parker Strip between the dam and city. Public facilities on the Arizona side include Buckskin Mountain State Park, River Island State Park, Blue Water Marina, and La Paz County Park.

Parker to Yuma. With the exception of a couple of trailer parks around Ehrenberg, most of the northern facilities below Parker are on the California side near Blythe. Here you'll find Mayflower, Palo Verde, and Peter McIntyre county parks; Palo Verde Oxbow (administered by the Bureau of Land Management in Yuma); private trailer parks; and some fishing camps.

Below Cibola Lake are Picacho State Recreation Area (two boat-in campgrounds in addition to tent and recreational vehicle spaces) and recreational sites at Squaw Lake (both sides) and Laguna Dam (Arizona). Private facilities include camps at Fisher's Landing, Imperial Oasis, Laguna Camp, and Martinez Lake Resort (with motel and restaurant).

Visiting the dams

Nowhere is man's control of the river more evident than when you visit the dams along the Colorado. Davis and Parker dams offer free self-guided tours; at Hoover, adults pay a modest fee for a guided tour.

If you explore no other dam, take one of the 30 to 45-minute guided walking tours of Hoover. Tours run continuously from 7:30 A.M. to 7:15 P.M. daily from Memorial Day through Labor Day, 8:30 A.M. to 4:15 P.M. the rest of the year.

In the display building beside the dam, a diorama of the entire Colorado River system is explained by a 10-minute narration. On the tour, visitors descend by elevator into the dam's interior to the enormous generating plant; a guide explains the dam's hydroelectric function and tells the story of its construction.

You can park behind the exhibit building at the west end of the dam. Snacks and soft drinks are available at a nearby stand.

Yuma. The city makes a good base for touring the surrounding desert country. Lodging ranges from economical motels to luxurious hotels; rates drop as much as one-third during the summer. Nearly 7,500 spaces for recreational vehicles and trailers are provided around the city.

Recreation along the river

The Colorado River area is primarily a playground for aquatic sports — fishing, boating, water-skiing — but you'll find everything from casinos (Las Vegas and other cities around Lake Mead, and Laughlin) to frog gigging (on the tule beds of lakes from Topock Marsh to Ferguson).

Boat tours. From Lake Mead Marina near Boulder Beach, boat tours depart on cruises to Hoover Dam. For a strange experience before or after your cruise, buy a bag of popcorn, walk out on the marina dock, and look into the water; throngs of monstrous big-mouthed carp wait for handouts.

Daily three-hour tours of the scenic Black Canyon operate in motorized rafts between Hoover Dam and Willow Beach from March to Thanksgiving. For information, contact Jim Rowland's Black Canyon, Box 96, Boulder City, NV 89005.

Fishing. Anglers need a valid Arizona fishing license and a special use stamp to fish from a boat on the river or from the shoreline of the state across the river. (A Nevada or California license with a special use stamp also enables you to fish on the opposite Arizona shore.) Fishing on Indian reservations requires a special permit, available from the Indian Administration Center in Parker for the Colorado River Indian Reservation, from the Fort Yuma Indian Reservation tribal office in Winterhaven, or from the Fort Mohave Indian Reservation tribal headquarters in Needles. The Chemehuevi Indian Reservation requires a special "trespass" permit.

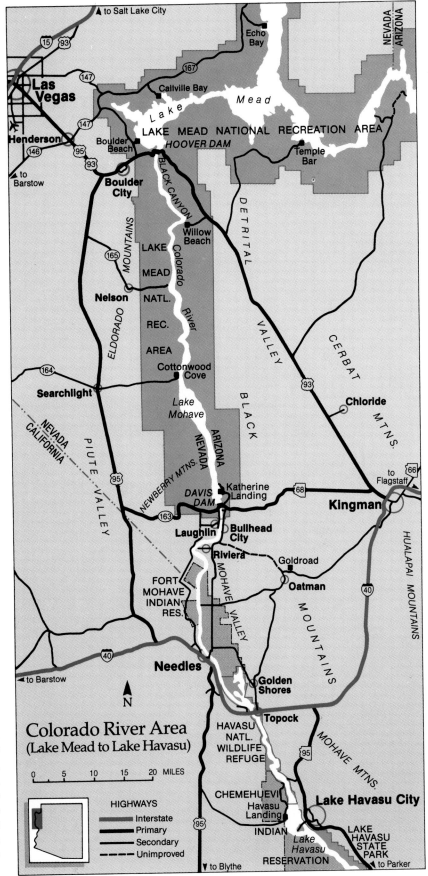

Colorado River Area
(Lake Mead to Lake Havasu)

Conspicuous horsepower is the name of the game along Parker Strip. These speedboat sailors slowed down to extend a friendly wave.

Sundown calm cloaks the river south of Blythe, California. Canoeists will camp ashore before continuing downstream to Martinez Lake.

South to Lake Havasu

From Hoover Dam north and east to the canyons of the Virgin and Colorado rivers, Lake Mead offers vast, rock-walled gorges and endless bays and inlets to be investigated.

To the south, the Colorado River has sliced deep into a thousand feet of volcanic rock to produce the spectacular gorge called Black Canyon at the upper end of Lake Mohave, which is also in the Lake Mead National Recreation Area. Farther south along the river lie scenic Topock Gorge and sparkling blue Lake Havasu.

The backcountry provides an almost limitless field for auto-exploring on the maze of secondary roads that wind through miles of rugged terrain. You'll see forests of Joshua trees and juniper, petroglyphs, and ghost towns and abandoned mines.

U.S. 93 heads northwest from Kingman in a straight line to the heart of Lake Mead National Recreation Area and the start of the Colorado's southward journey. The unsurveyed eastern half of the Lake Mead area, full of exciting finds, can be approached by turning northeast off U.S. 93 on the Pearce Ferry Road, 25½ miles northwest of Kingman.

Lake Mead

Roughly Y-shaped, Lake Mead points one of its arms north to the mouth of the Virgin River in Nevada; the other twists east toward the Grand Canyon. You can stay in a motel or camp on the shore, rent a small boat or launch your own. The National Park Service provides free paved launching ramps at all developed marina areas.

See page 112 for information on accommodations, camping, boating, and fishing. For brochures giving complete information on the whole area, write to the Superintendent, Lake Mead National Recreation Area, 601 Nevada Highway, Boulder City, NV 89005, or stop there or at the Alan Bible Visitor Center at the turnoff to Boulder Beach from U.S. 93 just west of Hoover Dam crossing.

Temple Bar. A paved, two-lane road northeast off U.S. 93 about 18 miles south of Hoover Dam leads to the resort of Temple Bar on the lake's eastern arm. The road crosses the wide valley of Detrital Wash and approaches the often incredibly blue waters of the lake over low, rolling hills peppered with fragments of porous black lava.

As you enter the settlement, the contrast with the harsh desert is immediate and refreshing. The National Park Service campground is shaded by tall palms and eucalyptus, brightened by red and white flowers of glossy oleanders. A trailer village lies in a grove of cottonwoods.

On the north shore

An excursion along Lake Mead's northern and western shores yields insight into the area's history. The following destinations are all on the Nevada side of the lake.

Fish hatchery. At Las Vegas Bay near the western tip of the lake, you can learn about fish production at the hatchery's visitor center, open daily from 8 A.M. to 4 P.M.

Old Vegas. A reproduction of an old fort and town in the city of Henderson contains shops, a restaurant, a museum, and a variety of rides. It's open daily from 10 A.M. to 5 P.M. (6 P.M. April through November).

Southern Nevada Museum. Take a look at Nevada's history from prehistoric times through World War II at this museum in Henderson, open daily.

Lost City Museum. Among the most publicized of tourist attractions along the lake is a collection of relics from the "Lost City," Pueblo Grande de Nevada, a group of pueblo dwellings in the Moapa Valley near Overton that date from A.D. 1.

Most of the villages were covered by water when Lake Mead was created,

but many artifacts were carefully removed and are on exhibit in this museum operated by the state of Nevada at Overton. It's open daily, except major holidays; admission is free.

Valley of Fire State Park. Vivid red sandstone formations and ancient Indian petroglyphs draw visitors to this park. In the 6-mile-long valley you'll find a campground, picnic sites, and a visitor center. Nevada State 169 runs through the park.

Mighty Hoover Dam

Of all the dams built on the Colorado, Hoover is the most suggestive of the demands man has placed on this river. The icy curve of concrete, elegant and austere against a backdrop of burnt rock and blue water, is set in an unbelievably barren landscape. In place of trees and shrubs, a forest of skeletal high-tension power towers leans over the brink of the canyon and seems to stride away over the harsh hills.

Even by today's engineering standards, Hoover is a grand achievement. As many as 5,000 workers labored at once to build it in 1935; 96 of them died in the process. The dam's crest rises 726 feet and spans 1,244 feet across Black Canyon to impound some 28.5 million acre-feet of water. From that water, 17 turbines generate 4 billion kilowatt-hours of electricity each year.

Your only view of the dam is from U.S. 93; there's no way to get below it to glimpse its towering face. The Bureau of Reclamation conducts tours of the dam throughout the day (see page 112).

Lake Mohave

Unlike spreading Lake Mead, Lake Mohave to the south is confined for its whole length between hills or steep canyon walls. It spreads 4 miles at its widest point, but for the most part it is hardly more than a deeper (50 to 150 feet), calmer Colorado River, with a few bays and estuaries.

At an altitude of about 600 feet, with surrounding mountain ranges reaching almost a mile above it, this pleasant stretch of water extends for 67 miles from Hoover Dam to Davis Dam. Though the current is swift below Hoover Dam, it slows as the lake reaches its widest point near Cottonwood Cove (campsites, boat rentals, launching ramps).

The area is ringed by the blacktops of Interstate 40 and U.S. 95 and 93. Lake Mohave itself is accessible by road at several points (Willow Beach and Katherine Landing on the Arizona side, El Dorado Canyon overlook and Cottonwood Cove from Nevada), but Davis Dam is the only place between Hoover Dam and Topock where you can bridge the Colorado. You reach the dam from the east by State 68 and from the west by Nevada State 163.

To circle the lake north of Davis Dam takes about 4 hours. But for the desert explorer, this perimeter swing should be only a preliminary reconnaissance. Away from the main travel routes, you'll find a clean, flint-hard, sparkling kind of desert, sweeping up from the river to crests as high as 5,500 feet.

South of Davis Dam the river meanders through the fast-developing Bullhead City region. Resort subdivisions and mobile parks line the banks.

Bullhead City sprang into being during the construction of Davis Dam. Named for a huge rock that resembled the head of a bull (now under the waters of Lake Mohave), the rapidly growing city swells in population with the seasonal surges of sportsmen.

Across the river in Nevada, Laughlin is a miniature Las Vegas with casinos, hotels, and trailer parking sites. Free ferries convey passengers across the river from parking lots in Bullhead City.

Ghost towns

The paved, two-lane road north of Topock through the old mining towns of Oatman and Goldroad was U.S. 66 before that road (now Interstate 40) was rerouted south through Sacramento Wash. This 54-mile detour adds 9 miles to the trip to Kingman, but you escape the heavy interstate traffic. The road is no longer well maintained; you can expect numerous chuckholes.

If you spend some time exploring the old mining townsites, use particular care while investigating tailing dumps, crumbling walls, and rickety buildings. The slopes surrounding both towns are honeycombed with abandoned mine shafts, often partially concealed by debris.

Oatman. Reviving and very much alive as a winter tourist center, Oatman holds an attraction for artists and their patrons and for collectors of frontier relics. It's named for Olive Oatman, a pioneer girl who survived an Apache massacre near Gila Bend and years of captivity by the Mohave Indians (the Apaches traded her for horses) to return to normal frontier life.

Founded in 1911, the town thrived for two decades on mining operations in the surrounding Ute Mountains. During one 3½-year bonanza period, the United Eastern Mine produced more than $18 million in gold. The town once boasted dozens of businesses, seven hotels, 20 saloons, and a stock exchange; just prior to the Depression, Oatman's population exceeded 12,300. In 1941, after Congress suspended the mining of non-strategic materials, the mines closed.

Nowhere else in the West can you walk down Main Street and in moments be up to your armpits in burros. Offspring of prospectors' burros of long ago, they have come to rely on handouts from camera-toting visitors.

If you arrive on a weekend, you may see a modest flea market at the town's edge — and a shootout by the Oatman Gunfighters. Main Street has the cafes, shops, garages, and other emporia necessary to serve a town of 200 as well as cater to passers-through. At present, there's no place to stay overnight.

Goldroad. Two miles east of Oatman and entirely deserted, the decaying buildings and eroded adobe walls that are the remains of Goldroad sprawl down the steep slopes west of Sitgreaves Pass.

Gold was discovered here in 1902, and the precipitous townsite was not abandoned until World War II. In 1953, all of the remaining buildings were razed or rendered unusable to release them from the tax rolls.

Today the old town looks like an ancient Pueblo Indian ruin, except for the weathered wood window frames. Weeds and lizards flourish among the crumbling walls, and wind flaps rusting sheets of corrugated roofing. Though the town has been picked clean of relics and mining artifacts, it's all very photogenic.

Topock Gorge

A scenic stretch of the Colorado River accessible only by boat lies just below Topock, where Interstate 40 crosses the river. Mohave Canyon, 15 miles in length, leads to 40-mile-long Lake Havasu, a narrow and intensely blue body of water that takes its name from the Indian word for blue water.

Neither roads nor trails approach Mohave Canyon, but boaters can explore bays, sloughs, caves, and side canyons that cut into the steep, colorful walls. Boats and motors can be rented at Topock; those who bring their own boats can use a free launching ramp.

Lake Havasu

Lake Havasu makes a refreshing break in the stark desert, its blue water edged with green tamarisks or tule marsh. This Colorado River reservoir fluctuates so little it has been spared the shoreline band that disfigures most reservoirs.

Lake Havasu State Park, a 13,000-acre preserve, has its headquarters at Pittsburgh Point on the island linked by London Bridge to Lake Havasu City.

Roads penetrate to the shoreline at only a few points, for boat launching. Scattered around the park are 1,290 campsites (water, barbecues, some showers; little shade). Another 250 campsites are accessible only by boat.

From any base on the shore, you can spend a full day just exploring by boat. This sinuous lake is only 3 miles across at its widest point, but it extends nearly 32 miles from its upper end just below Blankenship Bend to the tip of Bill Williams Arm at Parker Dam.

You can combine a lake-length voyage with some good water-skiing. In fact, you can ski for an hour in one direction uninterrupted, if you have the endurance.

Powerful winter winds can turn the lake into a choppy sea. These usually taper off by March, but if one occurs, plenty of sheltered-water refuges are strung along the shore. Havasu is narrow enough that it does not develop waves as big as those, for example, on Lake Mead.

Anglers like Havasu for many reasons; one of the best is the concurrence of the best fishing seasons with the pleasantest weather — in the spring and autumn months. There is no closed season, and you may fish all day and all night.

To reach the lake, turn south off Interstate 40 on State 95 about 10 miles east of Topock. It's about 20 miles to Lake Havasu City on the eastern shore.

Lake Havasu City. Here in the desert is a sun-drenched city carefully planned from the start for a balanced mix of residential and light industrial development. Started in 1963 on the east shore of the blue lake, it now has a population of more than 17,000.

London Bridge. In 1825, the first stone of the New London Bridge was laid on the banks of the Thames; in 1971, the entire bridge stood on the shore of Lake Havasu. The 928-foot span manages to maintain a massive dignity despite its incongruous setting. At one foot sits the English Village, with Tudor-style shops and eateries.

Across London Bridge lies the marina, adjacent to the Nautical Inn. Also on the island is one of the state's busiest airports.

For more information, contact Lake Havasu Visitor and Convention Bureau, 65 N. Lake Havasu Avenue, Lake Havasu City, AZ 86403.

The fall and rise of London Bridge

Everyone seems to have an opinion about the presence in Arizona of this historical British bridge. To some Arizonans, the bridge, its granite scoured clean of London grime and its bright flags snapping in the breeze, is more at home on the desert than it was on the Thames. Others feel that it's a massive anachronism. And visiting Londoners might view the whole phenomenon as an American threat to everything British—wondering, perhaps, if Buckingham Palace may be next to appear at Lake Havasu. You can make your own decision.

Although authentic, this is not the original London Bridge, nor is it the last. The first rude span across the Thames must have been built by Roman legionnaires. A number of wooden London bridges followed, well-suited for burning. The first stone bridge was completed in 1205.

The bridge now in Arizona was the second stone bridge, opened in 1831. In 1902 it was widened by hanging the sidewalks over the sides. But by the late 1960s it was obviously no longer fit for modern traffic, for it was gradually sinking into the riverbed. In 1968 the city of London put it up for sale.

Robert McCulloch, founder of Lake Havasu City, and C.V. Wood, Jr., its master planner, saw the opportunity to make the bridge an important attraction and offered $2.5 million dollars. It took another $5.6 million to dismantle the 130,000 tons of granite, ship them 10,000 miles to Southern California, truck them across the desert, and reassemble them over a structural steel and concrete core.

The project was the epitome of master planning; the bridge was reassembled first on dry land, then the mile-long channel now separating the airport island from the shore was excavated beneath it.

The Lord Mayor of London laid the cornerstone in September, 1968, and a gala celebration marked the bridge's opening in October, 1971. An "English" village sits beside the bridge, complete with village pub, restaurant, and shops. A London doubledecker bus is parked on the waterfront.

The Lower Colorado

Now thoroughly tamed by a succession of dams, the lower reaches of the Colorado River attract lovers of warm-water angling, water-skiing, scenic cruising, and camping from all over the Southwest. The many curves and bends in the river make reference to its east and west banks rather ambiguous; the commonly used distinction is the "Arizona side" or "California side."

You can drive alongside the river from Parker Dam south to Parker or from Yuma upriver as far as Martinez Lake or a few other access points in that region. But the best way to see the large Imperial National Wildlife Refuge that stretches to the north of Yuma is to abandon your car and explore by boat.

You can fish in the Colorado for black bass, bluegills, crappies, and catfish, and tie up along the river at campsites accessible only by water. (No camping is permitted in the wildlife refuge.) Less rugged adventurers can choose rustic cabins, trailer parks, or car camping sites.

Since mid-summer is the peak season on the river for Arizonans seeking refuge from the heat, advance reservations for accommodations and boat rentals are highly recommended. A number of commercial guides and maps covering different stretches of the river are available at marinas.

The Parker Strip

Called the "world's deepest dam," Parker controls the river between Lake Havasu and Headgate Rock Dam, creating the 14½-mile stretch of water known as the Parker Strip. This raucous section of river is a playground for inner-tubers, boaters, and skiers.

Small but scenic Buckskin Mountain State Park provides a refuge in a bend of the river to the north of the strip. This attractive spot for picnicking and camping has semi-enclosed riverbank cabanas facing volcanic cliffs that are mirrored in the water. A small museum displays pioneer relics, tools, and machinery of gold-mining days.

The city of Parker lies near the Colorado River Indian Reservation's northern end. The old Parker jail, on Agency Road, is restored as a historical landmark. A city park in front of the building offers tables under shade trees.

Just south of the city, the Indian Administration Center's museum and library displays crafts from the four river tribes (Mohave, Chemehuevi, Navajo, and Hopi). The center is open daily from Monday through Saturday.

Annual river cruise

A good introduction to the stretch of Colorado River south, between the town of Blythe, on the California side, and Martinez Lake is the annual Colorado River Cruise staged each May by the people of Blythe. On this overnight family campout, each small flotilla of motorboats is accompanied by an experienced pilot.

The well-organized launching begins on Saturday morning at Blythe for the six-hour trip to the night's camp at Martinez Lake; the return cruise the next day, going against the current, takes longer. For more details about the trip and entry requirements, write to the Blythe Chamber of Commerce, 201 S. Broadway, Blythe, CA 92225.

Palo Verde to Picacho

The Palo Verde lagoon and marina south of Blythe are often lively places. Between June and the end of November the lagoon is the scene of nighttime frog hunts. Hunters search the banks from boats equipped with lights, seeking the bullfrogs imported from Louisiana many years ago. The county park of the Palo Verde marina provides picnic, camping, and launching facilities on Oxbow Lake.

Cliffs become more prominent in the Picacho vicinity, which includes a 9-mile shoreline of California state park encompassing the ghost town of Picacho, described by Zane Grey in *Wanderer of the Wasteland*. By land,

the Picacho area can be reached by an unsurfaced road north from Winterhaven.

Across from the park, on the Arizona side of the river, Hoge Rock is worth a climb for the view it affords of the rugged landscape, the tule-ringed lagoon, and backwater lakes.

A chain of lakes

From Martinez Lake (the largest), a chain of lagoons and overflow lakes curves south toward Imperial Dam. Fishing camp-marinas offer boat rentals, cabins, camping sites, restaurants, and stores.

The river spreads into multiple shallow channels, some of them cul-de-sacs, bordered by lush stands of carrizo and tules that often conceal backwater lagoons. Great loads of silt and sand carried along by the currents are deposited when the river is low, blocking access to the smaller lakes.

The Senator Wash Reservoir and Ferguson Lake are popular recreation areas accessible from the California side. Most of the access roads on either side of the river are graded but unpaved and sometimes impassable. Between Picacho and Martinez Lake, you'll find no road to the river.

Imperial Dam

The Colorado River mixes work and play at the Imperial Dam north of Yuma. Here water is diverted to irrigate land in Arizona and Southern California. But the dam also raises the water level of the Colorado 23 feet, widening the river for 30 miles upstream and providing good opportunities for boaters, fishers, and water-skiers. Caution is advisable, though, for the numerous lakes and sloughs formed on the adjacent lowlands can be shallow, often hiding stumps and snags of drowned trees. Water-skiing is confined to the main channel, to deep water above dams, and to other waters known to be clear of hazards.

Iron gates open to notorious Yuma Territorial Prison, built by convicts in 1875. You can pass through to browse in the museum.

Life-giving ribbon of water flows from the Colorado into canals around Yuma to irrigate the area's many citrus groves.

Yuma Territory

Yuma gets more sunshine than any other city in America, declares the U.S. Weather Bureau. In summer, on a low mesa, that's no advantage when the temperatures may reach over a hundred. In other seasons, though, the sun is a prime asset, making the Yuma area a popular vacation site.

Many natives take summer refuge from the scorching sun in Yuma's air-conditioned resorts or by the cool waters of the Colorado. Visitors, however, arrive in autumn or spring to enjoy the pleasures of a cooler desert: a spring garden of white primrose and yellow encelia, the glimpse of a desert tortoise emerging from a brief winter hibernation.

With elevations at or below sea level, you can expect a mild winter and pleasant autumn and spring. Winter nights can be icy, though, and the late spring can bring high winds with accompanying sandstorms.

History. Since the 1500s, the Yuma area has attracted Indians, Spanish explorers, mountain men, and pioneers. The reason? It was here that the mighty Colorado was narrow enough and shallow enough to provide a relatively safe crossing point.

The Quechan Indians were the region's first inhabitants; in 1540, Hernando de Alarcon became the first European to visit. Most of Yuma was part of Mexico until 1854, when the Gadsden Purchase made it a U.S. territorial possession.

It is believed that the name came from the local Indian ritual of making huge fires to induce rain. The billowing smoke from the fires fascinated the Spanish conquistadors. The old Spanish word for smoke was *umo;* over the years the area became "yuma."

Getting around. Though most visitors arrive by car, you can reach Yuma by plane (scheduled and charter), Amtrak, and bus.

You can choose to stay in Yuma's numerous motels and hotels, or try spring or autumn desert camping for a close-up view of desert life. Inquire locally about the condition of unpaved roads, especially if you have a camper or trailer.

Once you leave Yuma for a mountain hike, a search for gems, or a fishing trip on the warm Colorado or the Gulf of California, civilization becomes remarkably sparse. Always take necessary precautions for desert driving and hiking; carry plenty of drinking water, extra food, and good local maps.

Around town

Rich in historical lore, Yuma serves as an anchor for the lower Colorado region. Situated atop a broad mesa, the city dominates the southwestern corner of Arizona. Once a river port when the Colorado was navigable, today this lively community serves as a port of entry, county seat, and capital of an agricultural region of 200,000 irrigated acres with a 12-month growing season.

The Yuma area offers excellent recreational and sightseeing opportunities: water sports on the Colorado, golf and tennis in verdant parks, desert trails for riding or hiking, history museums and art galleries, a historic prison, a rodeo contest (February), and dog and horse racing from late autumn to late spring.

In spring you can visit the county fair or watch the San Diego Padres train and play their exhibition games at the 240-acre Desert Sun Recreation complex.

Downtown. The old Main Street has been transformed into a modern mall, partially closed to automobiles and embellished with landscaping and fountains. An inviting park surrounds a modern library between Third and Fourth streets and Third and Fourth avenues.

Century House Museum, at 240 Madison Avenue, makes a good spot for absorbing local history. Exhibits and a turn-of-the-century gift shop stocked with documents, books, and Mexican crafts are contained in the period rooms of this pioneer house. Surrounding gardens and aviaries add to the 1890s mood. The free museum is open Tuesday through Saturday year-round, plus Sunday afternoons from October through May.

The Yuma Art Center's four galleries of contemporary art are housed in the restored Southern Pacific Railroad Depot at 281 Gila Street. A gift shop features works of local artists. The center is open Tuesday through Saturday and Sunday afternoons from September through June.

The adobe Custom House, one of the state's oldest structures, overlooks the river at Second Avenue behind City Hall. Once part of a major supply center for troops involved in the Indian Wars, it served as a U.S. Customs Service office and residence until 1955. You can tour the building from 10 A.M. to 2 P.M. Wednesday through Sunday.

Yuma Territorial Prison. This notorious old penitentiary, built by convicts in 1875, stands on Prison Hill in a state historic park along the river. Today the rusty iron gates open daily to visitors who wish to browse in a small museum where the mess hall and chapel stood and visit the cell blocks and "hole." Adults pay a small entrance fee; accompanying youngsters under 17 enter free. You can picnic in the park.

Beyond the Yuma mesa

Exploring the territory around the town of Yuma takes you through the green fields and citrus groves of the Yuma Valley; stop at a produce stand for lemons, oranges, grapefruit, limes, and other citrus fruit.

Much of the land that is not farmed belongs to military reservations. Groups can tour portions of the Marine Corps Air Station; contact the Yuma Chamber of Commerce for information.

Old Mexico. Adventurous shoppers can bargain for all sorts of Mexican goods in San Luis, 25 miles south of Yuma. One of the largest cities in the Mexican state of Sonora, San Luis offers a number of shops and restaurants reflecting the colorful Old Mexico ambiance.

Mexicali, the capital of Baja California, is just 55 miles southwest of Yuma. El Golfo Santa Clara, a picturesque fishing village on the Sea of Cortez, lies 75 miles south of San Luis.

Fort Yuma Indian Reservation. The Quechan Indians, or Yumas, were the first to divert the Colorado into irrigation canals to support their crops. Today their reservation lies just north of Yuma, across the river in California.

The reservation includes the site of Fort Yuma, established by the U.S. Army in 1850. The Quechan Indian Museum now occupies the former officers' mess, and a shop there sells Indian crafts. Open weekdays, the museum charges a small admission.

Nearby are tribal headquarters, St. Thomas Mission, and a theater used by Yuma's Gondolfo Players. The Methodist Mission displays Indian dress, pottery, baskets, beaded jewelry, and dolls; some articles are for sale.

Each spring, usually the last week in March, the Quechans host other tribes for the annual Southwest Indian Pow-Wow. You can see traditional ceremonies presented by tribal groups.

Territorial trails. To familiarize visitors with attractions of the area, the Yuma County Chamber of Commerce sponsors a series of guided, drive-yourself tours. Several visit date and citrus operations; others go to military installations. An all-day trip can take you into the desert to a ghost town, to Palm Canyon, or to a tortilla factory.

Tours (small fee) start in November and continue through March. For a schedule, write to the Yuma County Chamber of Commerce, P.O. Box 230, Yuma, AZ 85364. The chamber is located at 377 S. Main Street.

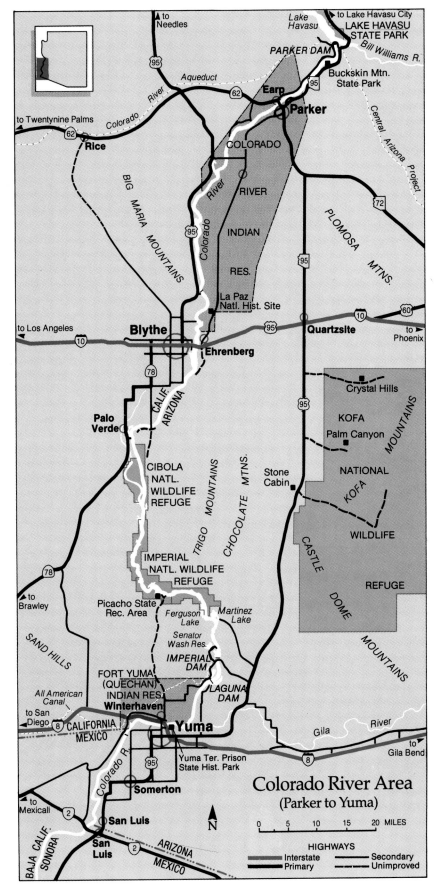

Colorado River Area
(Parker to Yuma)

Multibranched organ pipe cactus stretches tall above a southern Arizona hillside. The organ pipe rewards visitors with its showy blossoms in late May or early June.

The Kofa Mountains

Northward out of Yuma, U.S. 95 takes you past the rocky Castle Dome and Kofa Mountains, refuge of desert bighorn sheep, site of historic gold mines and unique grove of native palm trees, and bonanza country for rockhounds. The Kofa Mountains take their name from the initials for King of Arizona, a gold mine operated here at the turn of the century.

The 83-mile drive to Quartzsite and Interstate 10 or a round-trip excursion from Yuma, with some brief off-the-road sightseeing, can give you a sampling of the country. In-depth exploring or extended hiking requires a longer stay and camping. La Posa Recreation Area (south of Quartzsite) and Alamo Lake are the only campgrounds in the area; elsewhere, take all necessary equipment and supplies with you—even your own campfire fuel or campstove.

Kofa National Wildlife Refuge

One of four refuges for the rare desert bighorn sheep, the Kofas also shelter desert mules, deer, kit foxes, ringtail cats, and coyotes. More than 150 kinds of birds have been sighted in the refuge; the most common are gambel's quail and mourning doves.

The desert bighorn sheep are wary and give humans a wide berth, but with patience and binoculars you may sight some of them.

Palm Canyon. A stand of rare native palm trees is not as elusive as the desert bighorns, but you must be willing to do some rugged hiking to reach it. A small sign on the highway about 9 miles north of Stone Cabin marks the Palm Canyon turnoff. From here a gravel road zigzags 9 miles eastward across the arroyo-cut desert to a turnaround and parking spot.

You leave your car near the mouth of the canyon and hike the rest of the way. Palm Canyon is actually a complex of canyons, and the principal grove of palms—40 to 50 trees—is near the head of the fourth tributary cutting into the north wall of the main gorge.

It's a rugged ½-mile hike between tumbled boulders and a crack just wide enough to wriggle through. Watch your footing and be careful where you grab a handhold—spiny cactus sprouts everywhere, and the canyon is alive with desert creatures.

You can camp at the roadhead, a choice spot for sunset watching and a good base camp for longer hikes. In April and May, many of the desert plants display their blooms—yellow palo verde and scarlet ocotillo, underscored by a carpet of wildflowers.

Rockhounding—an irresistible urge

Collecting specimens of Arizona's beautiful rocks and minerals to cut and polish is hard to resist, particularly in the state's gem-rich southwest corner. Those who have caught gem fever make Quartzsite their headquarters; shops and mineral displays there give a novice an idea of what to look for locally. In other parts of the state you'll find excellent mineral displays at the Arizona Mineral Museum in Phoenix and at the University of Arizona at Tucson.

The Harquahala and Big Horn mountains to the east of Quartzsite and the Crystal Hills area of the Kofa Mountains to the south offer prime rockhounding sites. Between Gila Bend and Ajo, the Sonoran Desert harbors jasper, agate, fire agate, and all the copper minerals, but much of this is within the Luke Air Force Range, and motorists must obtain permission to leave the main road (ask at the gate 5 miles south of Gila Bend).

A rudimentary knowledge of geology is necessary to find and identify rocks and minerals. Fortunately, a number of good reference works are available on the subject. Some collectors are interested purely in adding to their knowledge of geology; others look for beautiful stones to display in jewelry.

You don't have to be an expert, however, to enjoy collecting ore samples from mines, gold "color" from a stream, or a rock that strikes your fancy from along the road.

Collecting mineral specimens is generally permitted on Bureau of Land Management land and in national forests (check with the ranger), but prohibited in national parks and monuments. Always ask permission on private lands and military reservations.

The state Office of Tourism (1480 E. Bethany Home Road, Phoenix, AZ 85014) offers an "Arizona Rockhound Guide." For additional information and suggested reading material, contact the Arizona Department of Mineral Resources, Mineral Building, State Fairgrounds, Phoenix, AZ 85007.

Crystal Hills. A favorite of rockhounds looking for big quartz crystals spewed out by a volcanic fumarole, Crystal Hills is the only site in the Kofas where you can use tools for this activity. A sign 11 miles south of Quartzsite marks the turnoff. However, a campground formerly located here has been closed. You can also hike 2½ miles to an old Indian encampment, but vandals have left little to see there.

Quartzsite

The Tyson's Well Station on the Arizona-California stage line's run to Prescott was established in 1856. The original adobe building still stands just west of the intersection of U.S. 95 and Interstate 10. Around it, mostly to the north and west, the town of Quartzsite has grown.

The name comes from the post office established in 1896 at the Ingersoll Mill, where gold was stamp-milled from white quartz. Thus the town is named Quartzsite (the site of quartz) and not Quartzite, the mineral.

A vintage stamp mill is located on Moon Mountain Road a little more than a mile north of the center of town. Hidden in this desert are some abandoned vertical shafts of placer mining holes. If you find such a hole, keep your distance. The apparently solid surface around it may be only a fragile crust held together by roots; the earth beneath may have collapsed.

The rockhound orientation of the town is clearly evident on the main street west of the highway crossroads. Signs identify a number of mineral and gem shops, and roadside displays include samples of minerals from domestic and foreign sources. Rockhounds from many states gather here for the annual powwow in February; visitors either stay at Blythe, to the west in California, or camp out.

At Quartzsite you can see the grave and monument of Hadju Ali, one of 10 camel drivers imported from the Middle East in 1856 when the Army tested the ill-tempered beasts for transport in the southwestern deserts. After the project was dropped, "Hi Jolly" remained and turned prospector.

The rugged Butterfield Stage

Interstate highways and air-conditioned motels with swimming pools have brought Arizona travel a long way from rugged stagecoach days.

Chartered in 1858 with a $600,000 annual government subsidy, the Butterfield Overland Mail swung a 2,800-mile arc from Tipton, near St. Louis, south through Little Rock, El Paso, Tucson, Fort Yuma, and San Diego to San Francisco. The stage left twice a week, traveling 25 days end-to-end for a fare of $150 (or 10¢ a mile for shorter segments).

The route crossed Arizona from the east near San Simon through the risky Apache Pass to Dragoon Springs, northwest to Tucson and up the Santa Cruz Valley to the Gila River, then along the river and west to Fort Yuma.

On the eastern part of the line, the coaches were the classic, cumbersome Concords, but farther west they often were replaced by wood-framed, canvas wagons—lighter, faster, and less likely to upset.

It was a grueling trip. The nine passengers crowded on three hard benches felt every rattling rock and rut as the coach lurched and swayed. Motion sickness was common, and swirling clouds of dust choked the occupants. Extra passengers on top had it worse.

A weary traveler could stay over at one of the regular stops but might get stuck there, for stage after stage might go through with no empty space.

Between-town stops in the Southwest typically were primitive adobe or native stone shelters, dirt-floored and furnished with packing crates and crude tables. A crowd of 8 to 10 armed men guarded these tiny fortresses against Indians. The menu usually was salt pork or dried beef, beans (probably mesquite), corn bread, and corrosive coffee. This occasionally was varied when some-one bagged a deer or antelope or when the company lost a mule.

Mishaps were frequent. Stages overturned or broke down, rains and floods blocked the trail, or raiding Indians struck. In spite of the rigors, though, the Butterfield line was the main transcontinental public transportation for three years until the Civil War interrupted its eastern service and caused its demise.

Today it is celebrated fondly as a romantic element of the frontier saga—by people who never had to ride it.

Western Sonoran Desert

Coming into Yuma from the west, Interstate 8 parallels the route of the wooden plank road built long ago across the shifting dunes. Although this Sand Hills area has been used as a desert setting in countless movies, such starkness is not all there is in the western Sonoran Desert.

East of Yuma, in marked contrast, the dense vegetation of the Green Belt follows the Gila River and the Butterfield Stage route along Interstate 8. South of this strip, the cactus-studded hills of the Organ Pipe Cactus National Monument are typical of the Sonoran Desert terrain that extends into Mexico.

The Green Belt

Thickets of mesquite and salt cedar crowd around potholes and marshes, sheltering a wide variety of wildlife in this 100-mile-long strip paralleling the Gila River bed from Buckeye (just west of Phoenix) south and west to Dateland. Administered by the Bureau of Land Management, the area is considered by biologists to be one of the finest white-winged dove nesting areas in the country.

A wide variety of other desert birds and wildlife attracts naturalists, wildlife photographers, artists, and hunters in the limited seasons. Camping is permitted more than ¼ mile from any water hole; bring your own water and campstove. High boots are a precaution against rattlesnakes and other desert creatures.

You can reach the Green Belt from a number of roads leading off State 85 or Interstate 8. Many of the dirt roads are unsuitable for passenger cars. For a look at an interpretive display, stop at the overlook just off State 85 about 6 miles south of Buckeye.

Painted Rocks. One of Arizona's richest collections of prehistoric Indian petroglyphs is preserved in Painted Rocks Historic State Park north of Interstate 8 near Gila Bend. Turn off Interstate 8 at exit 102.

Until the advent of the railroad and then the highway, the acre mound of rocks was a landmark on the classic route west along the Gila River. Father Kino, Father Garces, and Kit Carson all mention the site in their journals. General Kearny's army, the Mormon Battalion, and later the Butterfield Stage passed this way.

Present-day Indians have no record explaining the origin of the petroglyphs, though there are several theories. The most popular explanation is that the rocks marked the territorial boundary and defined a permanent peace treaty between the Yuma tribe to the west and the Maricopa Indians to the east. Another theory suggests that this was an Indian gathering place, where Indian travelers left messages on the rocks for subsequent visitors to the area.

To reach Painted Rocks, turn north from Interstate 8 about 15 miles west of Gila Bend, at the sign for Painted Rocks Dam. Follow the paved road for 10 miles to a sign that directs you left onto a ¼-mile dirt road to the site. Picnickers will find several tables with fireplaces adjacent to the parking area; campsites have no running water and no firewood.

Beyond the dirt road turnoff, the paved road continues another 2 miles to dead-end at an earthfill flood control dam on the Gila River. The low hills to the northeast are choice hunting grounds for several of the copper ores and vein agate. The lake offers good boating, swimming, and fishing.

Gila Bend. This agricultural and cattle-ranching center has grown from the Gila Ranch Station established in 1858 on the Butterfield Stage route, which followed the river westward. At Gila Bend, the river makes a sharp turn to the west. The first farms were started here in 1699 by the Jesuit missionary Father Francisco Kino.

Just north of town, the small Gila Bend Indian Reservation is home to Papago Indians. They weave attractive baskets for the tourist trade.

Another way to Tucson

A leisurely trip south and east from Gila Bend along State 85 and 86 doesn't take you to Tucson as fast as Interstate 8 and 10, but the drive offers some fascinating winter or spring desert adventures. In the summer, plan your excursions as the desert tortoise does — in the cool morning or late afternoon.

Ajo. Commonly recognized as the Spanish word for garlic, the name Ajo also comes from the Papago word for red paint, and it is the latter meaning that gave the town its name. Mexican prospectors first explored the area in 1750 in response to Indian stories of a local rock which they ground up for face and body paints. The Mexicans hoped the rock would be silver. Disappointed at finding only copper, they continued their search for the precious metal elsewhere.

The copper boom came later with turn-of-the-century technology, and today the New Cornelia open pit mine on the south side of town is a mile wide and more than 900 feet deep. A visitors' site on the rim offers a complete view of the great pit.

Organ Pipe. Nowhere in the American Southwest will you find a more fascinating sample of the Sonoran Desert environment than in the 516 square miles of the Organ Pipe Cactus National Monument, home of 31 species of cactus and 225 kinds of birds, several unique to this area.

Spring is the time to see the monument's desert country at its sparkling best. In March, wildflowers perk up the scene with bright splashes of desert poppies, magenta owl's clover, blue lupines, yellow encelia, desert marigolds, and apricot mallow.

As a general rule on the desert, the larger the plant, the later it will bloom. Thus you will find the hedgehog cactus opening rose-purple cups as early as March, the ocotillo waiting until April to put on its flame-red trumpets. In most years, late April or early May is the time to find the palo verde decked out in its showiest yellow. But the giant cactus — organ pipe and saguaro — hold off until late May or early June.

Entering the monument from the north on State 85, you drive through 17 miles of park before reaching monument headquarters. The visitor center, open daily, is a good place to begin your tour and get advice on the best way to view the monument's attractions. Throughout the winter and spring, naturalists present guided walks during the day and campfire programs in the evening.

According to Papago legend, the Well of Sacrifice or Children's Well, a short distance beyond the paved road, is where children were once sacrificed to stop a great flood.

The monument has one campground with 208 individual sites and 6 group sites. Water is available, but campers should bring their own fuel. Open campfires are not permitted.

From State 85, which cuts through the monument from north to south, two principal roads penetrate the area. Both are mostly smooth-surfaced gravel with occasional dirt stretches — easy to negotiate in a car.

Ajo Mountain Drive is really a nature trail for auto explorers. The 21-mile, one-way loop east of the highway has numbered stakes identifying principal plant specimens and geologic features keyed to descriptions in the guidebook you obtain at the visitor center. This route offers the best examples of organ pipe cactus. On the two-hour drive there are four picnic spots, but no water. From the Estes Canyon picnic area you can hike about 1½ miles into the canyon.

Puerto Blanco Drive (51 miles) leads you west from the visitor center past the only known stands of the rare "old-man" cactus in the United States. If you enjoy birdwatching, you'll want to stop at Quitobaquito Springs, where more than 180 species have been sighted.

Papago Indian Reservation. A drive through the 3 million acres of the "Desert People" reveals clusters of adobe villages and glimpses of Papago culture. Most of the 8,000 Papagos who live here are involved in cattle-raising and farming, though increasing numbers work off the reservation.

In the middle of the reservation on State 86, the tribal capital of Sells houses Papago offices, police headquarters, and a hospital, mixing modern buildings with sod-roofed adobe houses.

If you need information, go to the Tribal Office or to the government's Papago Agency. An arts and crafts store, open weekdays, offers examples of the handsome basketry for which the Papagos are famous.

Most Papago gatherings and festivals are private affairs, but the public is welcome to attend the annual Feast of St. Francis in Sells in October. Hundreds of Papagos from all over the reservation begin the day with a Mass, followed by the feast, dancing, games, and evening fireworks.

Another event open to the public is the annual Papago All-Indian Rodeo and Fair held in Sells later in the fall. Many spectators come from Tucson for this tribal event, which includes exhibits of basketry and pottery, a parade, singing and dancing, and a beauty pageant. For more information, contact the Papago Rodeo and Fair Commission, Box 837, Sells, AZ 85364.

At the village of Gu Achi (Santa Rosa), northwest of Sells on Indian Road 15, a gravel road turns west to two archeological landmarks. According to Papago legend, the Well of Sacrifice or Children's Well, a short distance beyond the paved road, is where children were once sacrificed to stop a great flood.

The Ventana Cave, 16 miles to the west, saw human habitation at least 10,000 years ago. Many of the artifacts and relics discovered there are exhibited now at the University of Arizona at Tucson. Two of the caverns have been opened for visitors.

You won't find accommodations on the reservation, but camping is permitted for a small fee payable at the Tribal Office in Sells. Visitors should not trespass in seemingly deserted houses. Check road conditions before venturing off main highways; they can be impassable after a storm. Supplies are available at trading posts at Sells, Topawa, Quijotoa, San Simon, and Santa Rosa.

On the eastern border of the reservation stands Kitt Peak Observatory (see page 101).

Topawa Mission. You reach this Franciscan mission by an 8-mile drive south of Sells through a fine stand of giant saguaro cactus. Brown-robed friars show you through the mission church and school. Each day, school buses gather Indian children and bring them to Topawa to be taught in their own language and in English.

East of Topawa, you'll see the great pointed monolith of Baboquivari Peak, 7,864 feet high. Sacred to the Indians, Baboquivari (babbo-*kee*-varee) is Papago for "the narrow apex." To reach a camping site in Baboquivari Canyon from which a trail climbs to the foot of the final 2,000-foot pinnacle, take a graded road east from Topawa for 9 miles and turn off on an ungraded side road. (The water in the canyon is likely to be contaminated — don't drink it.)

Index

Yucca elata

Saguaro

Mesquite